MEDIATED SEX

MEDIATED SEX

Pornography and Postmodern Culture

BRIAN McNAIR

Senior Lecturer in Film and Media Studies,
University of Stirling

A member of the Hodder Headline Group
LONDON • NEW YORK • SYDNEY • AUCKLAND

First published in Great Britain 1996 by
Arnold, a member of the Hodder Headline Group
338 Euston Road, London NW1 3BH
175 Fifth Avenue, New York, NY 10010

Distributed exclusively in the USA by
St Martin's Press Inc.,
175 Fifth Avenue,
New York, NY 10010

British Library Cataloguing in Publication Data
A catalogue record for this book is available from the British Library

Library of Congress Cataloging-in-Publication Data
McNair, Brian. 1959–
    Mediated sex : pornography and postmodern culture / Brian McNair.
    p.   cm.
    Includes bibliographical references and index.
    1. Pornography.   2. Sex in mass media.   3. Mass media and sex.
4. Sexuality in popular culture.   5. Postmodernism.   I. Title.
HQ471.M385   1996
363.4'7—dc20   96–543
                                                                      CIP

ISBN 0 340 61428 5 (Pb)
ISBN 0 340 66293 X (Hb)

Typeset in 10/12 pt Sabon by
Phoenix Photosetting, Lordswood, Chatham, Kent
Printed and bound in Great Britain by
JW Arrowsmith, Bristol

Contents

The central issue is not to determine whether one says yes or not to sex, whether one formulates prohibitions or permissions, whether one asserts its importance or denies its effects, or whether one refines the words one uses to designate it; but to account for the fact that it is spoken about, to discover who does the speaking, the positions and viewpoints from which they speak, the institutions which prompt people to speak about it and which store and distribute the things that are said.

(Michel Foucault, *The History of Sexuality*, Vol. 1)

Preface

The sexualization of mass media is a universally recognized feature of contemporary capitalist culture. Since the 1960s sex in the media – *mediated sex* – has increased quantitatively as, in qualitative terms, it has become more explicit. As this book went to press, Channel Four television in the United Kingdom was broadcasting something called *Dyke TV* – a series of documentaries and feature films by and about lesbians – having not long before transmitted the *Red Light Zone*, a 42 programme series which dealt in hitherto unseen (on British television) depth and frankness with a diverse range of sexual issues. This book is about these programmes, and the many other manifestations of mediated sex which have become so visible a part of western culture, in Britain and the United States in particular, in recent years. It discusses their content, their meaning, and their impact in the context of a social environment characterized by a 'postmodern' sexual politics of communicative play and subversion, in which the media play a central role, and in which the meaning of nothing can be assumed to be quite what it seems, nor quite what it used to be.

My subtitle, *Pornography and Postmodern Culture*, was chosen not just because of its pleasingly alliterative quality, but also because it seems so neatly to encapsulate one of the main themes of what follows. Pornography has emerged in recent years as a cultural category of significance extending beyond the connotations of 'dirty raincoatedness' with which it was traditionally associated, to become a recurring cultural motif found in all manner of media representations, creative contexts, and channels of discourse. Pornography, and the pornographic, has become the focus of the wide-ranging debate about the role of mediated sex in our society, and the direction in which sexual culture is going. The debate has moral, political and sociological dimensions, and has increased in intensity as the conflicting trends of sexual liberalism, feminism, and (reinforced by the discovery of HIV/AIDS) moral conservatism and retrenchment compete for space in the public sphere. It is supported by millions of words of conflicting evidence and oppositional rhetoric presented in polemical tracts, academic books and journals, newspaper articles, lifestyle magazines and television chatshows. It has generated bitter disagreements and intellectual feuds, to an extent matched by few other issues.

Pornography has also been the focus for discussion of that most important of issues in the sociology of communication: effects. Like violence, that other category of representation with which it is frequently (if erroneously) associated, the ongoing societal debate about, and fascination with, pornography is largely the product of concern about what it does: to the people who consume it; to the people who must live with the people who consume it; to those involved in its production; and to the social fabric as a whole. The range of approaches to the effects of mass media in general is present in the pornography debate, finding there a vast quantity of data from which to test hypotheses and draw conclusions.

The cultural and sociological significance of pornography, indeed, could easily justify a title placing it at the structural core of a book such as this one, concerned as it is with examining relationships between sexuality, the media, and society. I have not done so, for two reasons.

First, pornography, as we shall see, is a category for which there is no universally agreed definition or meaning. The term is a political one, signifying very different things to different people and groups, at different times and in different places. The evolution of the term and the struggle for definition of it is one of the central concerns of this book, and using the word 'pornography' in my title might have implied my acceptance at the outset of a particular definition of the term, and my underestimation of its ambiguity as a descriptive category.

Second, while pornography is inevitably at the centre of the debate about mediated sex, it does not exhaust the subject. Much of what follows is concerned with the phenomenon of 'sex talk' in contemporary societies: the public discussion of themes such as safer sex techniques, female sexuality and 's/m chic' in newspapers, magazines and primetime TV broadcasts. While the increasing prevalence of sex talk thus defined may be related to the causes of pornography's explosion into popular culture, the two phenomena are distinct. Sex in the media is more than the pornographic.

Writing a book on this subject has been something of a departure for me, and a considerable challenge. It is difficult to enter a field in which so much excellent work has already been done. Furthermore, writing about sex is not only difficult, it is dangerous, in a way few other topics are. Despite the obvious centrality of sex and sexuality to the human experience, writing and talking about them is uniquely constrained by moral, ethical and political taboos. The gradual erosion of these taboos in recent decades is a recurring theme of this book, but they continue to exert a self-censorial influence on the academic writer, who must weigh up every word and phrase before presenting them to a vigilant and critical public. American journalist Sallie Tisdale put it well when she wrote that 'most sex research [and here we include research on sex in the media] is touched by a slight whiff of eroto-phobia, written dryly and pedantically. ... A surprising amount of intellec-tual material on sex discusses the subject as though it were a form of garbage, interesting in an anthropological way for all it says about the cul-ture that makes it, but unpalatable nonetheless' (1995: p. 8).

I have sought to avoid those pitfalls in this book. The result, I hope, is a text which, while functioning as an introduction to, and critical overview of, a broad range of writings and opinions, is relatively straightforward, non-judgemental and at times enthusiastic about the positive cultural role being played by mass media representations of sex at the end of the twentieth cen-tury. The book contains extensive critical treatment of the continuing impact of patriarchy on contemporary sexual representation, and the ugly head of male sexism is never far away; but, as I hope to have shown at var-ious points, there is no necessary connection between the two. Sex in the media, including the pornographic, is much more than the articulation of patriarchal sexist values.

Acknowledgements

In helping me to confront the challenges associated with writing about sex, sincere thanks must go to David Evans of the Sociology Department at Glasgow University, whose undergraduate teaching first provoked in me what has turned out to be an enduring interest in the media sociology of sex and gender issues. Lesley Riddle, media and cultural studies editor at Arnold, gave me the opportunity to develop the project, and waited patiently for it to be completed. The cities of Berkeley and San Francisco provided an inspirational environment in which to do some valuable research. And thanks to Kay Weaver, for letting me look at her Madonna file.

Acknowledgements are due to the publishers of *On Our Backs* and *Lezzie Smut* magazines for permission to reproduce copyright material. Sincere thanks also to the Jack Tilton and 303 galleries in New York, for permission to reproduce work by Nicole Eisenman and Sue Williams respectively, and to the Collection of Timothy Baum, New York, for the use of Man Ray's, *Erotique Voilée*.

Brian McNair
October 1995

To Kathy,
with love

|1|

Sex, society and the media

W̶e live in a period of unprecedented openness in the public discussion of sex and sexuality. Sex has always been present as a theme in human culture, of course, but usually confined to the margins of respectable discourse: the province of perverts or, in a long tradition stretching back to the Marquis de Sade, libertarian cultural elites with the resources and the philosophically inspired confidence to indulge their interest. Since the 1960s, however, and the 'sexual revolution' of that decade, sex has become a central element of mass, popular culture. Linda Williams has identified 'a contemporary proliferation of discourses of sexuality ... a modern compulsion to speak incessantly about sex' (1990: p. 2). The Attorney General's Commission on Pornography, set up by the Reagan Administration in 1985 to investigate the social impact of porn, reported that 'in virtually every [US] medium, from books to magazines to newspapers to music to radio to network television to cable television, matters relating to sex are discussed, described and depicted with a frankness and an explicitness of detail that has accelerated dramatically within a comparatively short period of time' (Meese, 1986: p. 277). Between 1965 and 1985 pornography became thoroughly commodified in the United States, and widely available in mainstream commercial outlets (Hawkins and Zimring, 1988).

What was true for the United States has been true also of the United Kingdom and other western societies to a greater or lesser degree, as determined by the culturally specific regimes of censorship and moral regulation prevailing in different countries. In Europe, the Scandinavian countries, Germany, the Netherlands and Italy have been in the vanguard of this movement, but even in relatively puritanical countries such as Britain and Ireland the trend towards what one writer calls an 'increasing sexualization of culture' is unmistakeable (Kelly, 1992: p. 121). Through the mass media, western societies have, since the early 1980s in particular, been subjected to 'a blitz of the sexually explicit' (Snitow *et al.*, 1983: p. 1), a 'pronounced

escalation in the already well-established sexualization of developed capitalist societies at all levels'(Evans, 1993: p. 1).

Not just in pornography as narrowly defined, but also in mainstream
Hollywood cinema and primetime television drama, newspapers and magazines, pop music and video, advertising and fashion photography, images of
sexuality and debate about their meaning abound. Key figures in contemporary popular culture – Madonna and (the artist formerly known as) Prince
being notable examples[1] – have focused public discussion around the themes
of gender and sexuality by manipulating symbols of both in their work.
Women's magazines encourage the exposure and exploration of female sexuality in unashamedly graphic terms, while publishers find a ready market
for books which address these themes, both in fiction[2] and nonfiction.[3]

All of this has been taking place in what we may call a 'postmodern' cultural environment. Hal Foster describes postmodern culture as being characterized by 'the effacement of some key boundaries or separations' (1985:
p. 12), such as the longstanding aesthetic distinction between 'art' and
'trash' familiar to students of culture everywhere. Related to this is the
weakening of generic categories in cultural production, and the recycling of
images. In postmodernism 'the past is played and replayed as an amusing
range of styles, genres, signifying practices to be combined and recombined
at will' (Hebdige, 1988: p.171). Postmodernism is also used as shorthand
for a period in the history of ideas when political and philosophical certainties have eroded, and in which the great totalizing worldviews of modernism
and industrial capitalism no longer seem to fit with social realities.

In the context of this book, 'postmodern' is a useful adjective to describe
a climate in which images of sex and gender are being invested with new significance; in which significant dichotomies, such as those between 'low' and
'high' culture, 'pornography' and 'erotica', 'passive feminism' and 'active
masculine', are being challenged; and in which established worldviews and
ways of seeing – feminism in particular – are undergoing internal fragmentation and restructuring. The incorporation of sado-masochistic iconography into the mainstream of popular culture, in such films as *Basic Instinct*
and *Body of Evidence*,[4] or in Madonna's *Sex* book (1992), are clear examples of this trend in the sphere of sexual representation, while the debate
within feminism about the validity of pornography for women illustrates
the contemporary ambiguity of a concept whose political meaning was, not
so long ago, firmly and negatively fixed.

These developments are both the reflection of, and driving force behind,
the compulsion identified by Williams; a compulsion rooted, arguably, in
five main causes. First, and most obvious, is the continuing impact of post-
1960s liberalism in attitudes to sexuality and the traditional nuclear family.
While western governments vary in their ideological and moral leanings,
they administer societies in which the decline of the institutions of religion
and marriage is irreversible; where people live together, and have children,
in altogether more flexible conditions than could have been imagined by

their parents and grandparents; and where sexual experimentation, within and outside of monogamous relationships, is no longer viewed as morally reprehensible.

The second root cause, and as an outgrowth of the 1960s sexual revolution, is the rise of the women's movement and the subsequent success of feminism in shaping the political, social and cultural agendas of western societies. As women have begun to overcome the discriminatory socio-economic effects of age-old patriarchy, so female sexuality has been acknowledged and its complexities recognized with greater frankness than ever before. By far the greatest proportion of the material examined in this book represents women exploring, and debating with other women about, the political implications and significance of the enhanced opportunities for sexual expression which feminism has won.

A third cause of the discursive explosion around sexuality, running parallel with but distinct from feminism, has been the emergence of an organized, politically active gay movement. Since the 1970s gays, male and female, have become increasingly visible and vocal, especially in the art and entertainment industries. As one writer observes, 'lesbians and gay men are achieving ever higher visibility in the media; their lives and loves a focus, it would seem, of unending interest'.[5] Those gays who are 'out' in conditions of celebrity and fame have inevitably engendered debate about homosexuality, bisexuality, and their relationship to the straight world, either through choice or, as was the case with American photographer Robert Mapplethorpe, by unintentionally provoking moral outrage among influential sections of the straight community.

A fourth, tragically unanticipated and unwelcome factor has, of course, been the appearance and spread of HIV and AIDS, a fatal and as yet incurable disease which has forced re-examination by men and women, gay and straight, of much that had, in the course of the 1970s and early 1980s, become newly consensual in the sphere of sexuality. Just as the combined impact of the sexual revolution, feminism and the gay rights movement was winning social legitimacy for an unprecedentedly wide diversity of sexual identities and lifestyles, a dangerous new sexually transmitted disease forced reconsideration of the trend towards liberalization. As a direct consequence of the HIV/AIDS epidemic, promiscuity and sexual adventurism were necessarily replaced in the league of political correctness by the concepts of 'safe' and 'safer' sex, and the need to view much sexual activity as potentially lethal. The distinction between safe and unsafe sex is one which has had to be made in public, and in very explicit terms.

Finally, and related to all of the above factors, has been the resurgence of conservative moral lobbies, whose members have denounced the increasingly public, increasingly explicit discussion and depiction of sexuality as both cause and symptom of the 'permissive society', contributing to family breakdown, moral degeneration, and a host of other social ills associated with contemporary capitalism. These lobbies, in the United States principally, but also in Britain and other countries, have led a succession of campaigns against the 'sexual blitz'.

Each of these factors has contributed to a cultural climate in which sexuality is talked about and depicted more often and more frankly than ever before in the western world, generating a variety of responses.

Some observers view the explosion of sex talk as a 'backlash' to the advances made by feminists and gays in recent decades (Faludi, 1991). From this perspective the sexual blitz is a reactionary trend – the more or less consciously articulated resistance strategy of a hitherto dominant straight patriarchal elite, threatened in the 1980s and 1990s by the real achievements of feminism and the gay movement. The appearance of pornographic iconography in television advertisements,[6] or Hollywood's flirtation with sadomasochism, is deemed to be essentially exploitative, linked directly to the continuing persistence of male sexist attitudes at work and in society generally. An alternative view interprets much, if not all, of this material as the expression of efforts, in an AIDS-afflicted world, to come to terms with new sexual and social realities, while preserving the hard-won gains of feminism and the gay movement. Others still bemoan the moral decay which the expansion of sexual discourse into the mainstream of popular culture allegedly represents. What can be said with certainty of most western cultures is that 'consensus about the meaning of sex and the moral boundaries of legitimate sexual expression has been seriously fractured' (Seidman, 1992: p. 211). This book analyses the background to that breakdown of consensus, and critically assesses the debate which it has produced.

Like many people, I engage with the materials of sexual representation on a deeply personal level, experiencing at one moment desire and another revulsion; at one moment arousal and another guilt. On the one hand, I am angered by the excesses of heterosexist patriarchy; on the other, I am convinced that the rigidity and dogmatism of many of the positions adopted in this debate are oversimplistic and increasingly irrelevant to the sexual politics of the twenty-first century. As the following pages will show, I am hardly unique, among men and women, gay and straight, in these feelings of ambivalence towards images which strike so deeply at our biological and psychological beings. That 'the personal is political' remains as true today as it ever was, and underpins the writing of this book.

As a sociologist, my concern in this book is with the evidence and rhetoric advanced in support of, or opposition to, the competing positions which comprise the debate around sex and the media. The sex-media-society relationship may be seen as a key case in a wider debate about how media images act upon, and interact with the societies in which they circulate. This has always been, and still remains, the most important issue in media sociology, and it is an assumption of this book that the discussion of sexual representation can contribute much of value to its resolution. To achieve this aim, the book includes a detailed review of the communication studies literature on media images of sexuality. That literature can be grouped into four categories.

Since the 1960s the dominant approach, in so far as the largest proportion of work on sexually explicit imagery has been undertaken from this perspective, is the *behaviourist effects* tradition, mainly comprising the empirical, laboratory-based studies of American social psychologists (Donnerstein, 1984; Donnerstein *et al.*, 1987; Donnerstein and Linz, 1990; Goldstein and Kant, 1971). The central concern of this work has been to demonstrate empirically the nature and extent of the effects produced by sexually explicit images in the behaviour and attitudes of those exposed to them. The model typically used in such work is that of stimulus-response, in which pornographic and other sex-related images are hypothesized to stimulate some kind of observable, measurable response (beyond that of mere sexual arousal) in the audience.

A second approach is *historical,* exemplified by the work of Michel Foucault (1980; 1992), Walter Kendrick (1987) and Lynn Hunt (1993). This work seeks to construct historical accounts of the development of key concepts and discourses, and thus more firmly to place contemporary debates about sexuality and the media in their socio-cultural contexts. As Chapter 4 shows, this approach can yield important insights into the socially constructed, culturally specific nature of such concepts as pornography and obscenity.

Third, we may identify a qualitative *ethnographic* tradition, which seeks to analyse the meaning and significance of sexually explicit images by reference to the personal experiences of those involved in producing, distributing or consuming them (Stoller, 1991; Delacoste and Alexander, 1988). Dworkin and MacKinnon have used this approach in their campaigns for the introduction of antipornography legislation. In their case, the personal testimony of women who had been subject to abuse by their male partners was used to link the abuse with the perpetrators' consumption of pornography (MacKinnon, 1994). We can also include in this category the variety of perspectives contained in Catherine Itzin's edited volume of essays (1992).

Finally, there is a growing body of work which applies techniques of *textual analysis* to sexually explicit images. Linda Williams' writings (1992; 1993a; 1993b) have been important and influential in this respect, exemplifying as they do a focus on the generic characteristics of pornography, its codes and conventions, the semiotics of its construction, and its polysemic potential for a variety of audiences. This work is strongly associated with the movement within feminism and cultural studies towards a re-definition of pornography as a form of sexual representation which can have positive 'uses and gratifications', as well as negative effects.

In describing and critiquing these approaches, and the methodological, ideological and political assumptions which underpin them, my aim is to find support for a conceptualization of the relationship between sex, society and the media in terms which go beyond the traditional effects paradigms of cause-stimulus-response. The evidence for and against an effects model will be rigorously explored but, for reasons which will, I hope, become clear, the focus of the discussion will be on the *meaning* of media images of sex, rather than their content taken in isolation; on the *uses* made of those images by those individuals who consume them, rather on what they *do* to people; and on the *context* of their reception, as opposed to their instrumental effects on behaviour, attitudes and values.

Such an emphasis reflects a growing dissatisfaction amongst media scholars generally with the cause-stimulus-response model of how communication works and, as already noted, the establishment of a heuristically unstable, 'postmodern' cultural environment in which the meaning and significance of signs and messages are recognized to vary wildly. It is not merely fashionable postmodernism but empirical fact to observe that we live in an age of pastiche, intertextuality, and breakdown in generic categories and conventions. In the sphere of sexual politics, patriarchy and heterosexism have been fundamentally challenged, if far from overcome. In such an environment it becomes necessary to recognize that, for many men and women, of diverse sexual orientations, images of sexuality no longer mean what they did 10, 20, or 30 years ago. As the political and cultural climates have changed, so has the way we interpret media images, including those which deal with sexuality. This book represents an attempt to plot and analyse those changes.

Chapter 2 lays the foundation for that effort by setting out a brief socio-sexual history of the late twentieth century, focusing on those developments, listed briefly above, which have fuelled the contemporary proliferation of sexual discourse, and politico-discursive responses to it. Chapter 3 examines how this proliferation has been manifested in what Habermas famously called the 'public sphere' (1989) – those (mainly) media institutions, print and broadcasting, from which the majority of citizens in modern capitalism derive the bulk of their knowledge and information about public affairs. How and in what forms have these institutions talked about sex, and depicted sexuality, in recent years?

Chapter 4 presents a history of sexual representation, from Greek and Roman antiquity until the present, intended to illustrate the socially constructed nature of, and hence the difficulty of defining, such terms as 'pornography' and 'erotica'. It then proceeds to review the main definitions of these and related terms currently in use. Chapters 5 and 6 are devoted to a critical review of the effects issue in its many variations, moving from the stimulus-response paradigm to that which stresses the uses and gratifications obtained from sexually explicit media by a range of groups.

Chapters 7 and 8 analyse contemporary sexual representation: first, in the context of the pornography industry proper; then, in the contemporary art of such figures as Jeff Koons, Annie Sprinkle, Robert Mapplethorpe, and mainstream pop performers such as Madonna. This material analyses examples of contemporary cultural production in order to comment on and (it is hoped) illuminate some of the theoretical and methodological issues raised in preceding chapters. Chapter 9 presents the conclusions I draw from what has gone before.

A personal note

Feminist film-makers Bette Gordon and Karyn Kaye welcome the upsurge in interest in all things sexually explicit on the grounds that 'pornographic investigation is a radical act in and of itself' (1993: p. 90). Such investigation, as I have already suggested, is also a risky act. In this field, as perhaps in no other, what one writes is unlikely to be viewed in isolation from what and who one is. While it is my hope and intention that the present book will prove useful for those growing numbers of students and others who are interested in the subject of mediated sexuality, it is also the work of an author formed and socialized in a particular socio-sexual culture. In this sense, my account of the issues is not, and never could be, 'innocent'. On the other hand, few of the protagonists cited in the following pages even pretend to innocence or neutrality in their approach, preferring to state their political agendas from the outset. Much of the existing literature is written from one value-laden perspective or another, adopting a correspondingly dismissive approach to the alternatives. Thus, veteran antipornography campaigner Andrea Dworkin's novel *Mercy* (1990b) has been described as pornographic by at least one feminist writer (Gilbert, 1992),[7] while the same accusation has been made from the opposite end of the spectrum against Gibson and Gibson's edited collection of writings by anti-censorship feminists (1993).[8] Ellis's *Caught Looking* (1986)[9] has also been called pornographic. Mandy Merck wonders whether Dworkin's nonfiction work *Intercourse* (1987), 'despite its critical intentions, is not itself a part of [patriarchal, sexually violent] culture, generating, as its principal product, sexual horror' (1993: p. 214).

I have tried in this book to respect these competing politics, and to give proper voice to all the perspectives and frameworks which drive the debate, from whichever direction they come. While my own views should be evident to anyone who reaches the end of my concluding essay, I trust the reader will judge me to have been fair and honest, in fact and in spirit, in this most contentious and controversial of debates.

Notes

1   Both artists built their careers not only, or even primarily, on the backs of excellent pop music, but on projecting highly, often perversely, sexualized images of themselves, most notoriously in the case of Madonna with her book of sexually explicit photographs and writings, and the promotional campaign which accompanied it (Madonna, 1992).

2   Examples of novels which have been successfully marketed on the basis of their sexual content include, at the popular end of the market Julie Burchill's *Ambition* (1990) and, in the literary market, Nicholson Baker's *Vox* (1992) and *The Fermata* (1994).

3   The phenomenal success of Nancy Friday's books about sexual fantasy, such as *Women On Top* (1991) is perhaps the best example of this.

4   These films, and others examined in Chapter 8, were notable not only for their explicit depiction of sexual activity, but also for having generated intense media debate about the infiltration of pornographic imagery into mainstream culture.

5   Wilson, E., 'Borderlines', *New Statesman and Society*, 2 November 1990.

6   A trend analysed in such articles as: 'And so to embedding', *The Guardian*, 6 June 1988; 'Brylcreem's naked ambition', *Observer*, 14 July 1991; and 'Deviance Sells', *The Guardian,* 11 November 1994.

7   For Gilbert, *Mercy* is pornographic in its narrative structure and content, as pornography is defined by Dworkin herself. What separates it from porn, Gilbert suggests, is its context, i.e. that the sex and violence described in its pages are intended not to arouse a male audience but to make a political statement about incest and sexual abuse. If this is true for *Mercy*, Gilbert concludes, it could also be true for other 'pornographic' texts.

8   Gibson and Gibson's *Dirty Looks* contains, in addition to a number of serious and cerebral essays, some black-and-white stills from the work of artists such as Annie Sprinkle and Grace Lau. These are, undoubtedly, sexually explicit. They are also, from the antipornography viewpoint, part of the problem.

9   *Caught Looking* illustrates essays by such as Gayle Rubin, Kate Ellis and Paula Webster with pornographic images drawn from the nineteenth century onwards.

|2|

A brief socio-sexual history of the late twentieth century

My introduction suggested that the contemporary sexualization of western culture is the product of several factors which together have, on the one hand, had the effect of flooding the media with unprecedentedly explicit sexual representations and, on the other, provoked contentious debates around the meaning and significance of those images. This chapter examines those factors in more detail, beginning with 'the sexual revolution'.

The sexual revolution

The sexual revolution is associated with that period following World War II when capitalist societies abandoned decades of proscriptive attitudes to sexual behaviour and identity, and accepted a new liberalism in such matters. The nineteenth and early twentieth centuries were, in the United States and western Europe, a period of sexual conservatism, founded on Victorian moral values which on the one hand denied female sexuality and on the other compelled men to keep theirs hidden from public view. Male homosexuality, as Oscar Wilde discovered to his cost, was beyond the pale, while for Queen Victoria lesbianism was inconceivable (as a consequence, ironically, it was never subject to the legal sanctions suffered by male homosexuals). In the final decades of the nineteenth century and the first decades of the twentieth, recreational sex was morally unacceptable, while gays were openly persecuted.

Those who sought to make sexuality a matter of public debate, even on the grounds of health and education, were persecuted by moral campaigners and the legal system. Charles Bradlaugh and his associate, Annie Besant, were sentenced to six months' imprisonment in 1877 for publishing an 'obscene' book on methods of birth control. Marie Stopes, whose writings sought to address such pressing health and social problems as excessively large families and general societal ignorance about intercourse, contraception and other aspects of sexual life, found her books attacked and herself ostracized from polite circles. Stopes' books were, in the words of one biographer, 'the most useful guide to sex for the ordinary man and woman, and they created a desire for knowledge among both laity and professionals' (Rose, 1992: p. 160). In the early 1920s, they were sufficiently controversial to be denounced as pornography.

Around the same time, however, male writers such as Havelock Ellis were having more success in publicizing the sexual realm. Ellis was the first 'sexologist' (Jackson, 1987), making respectable the discussion of sexuality, and female sexuality in particular, by turning it into a science. Ellis sought in his writings to rationalize sexual behaviour, making it available to objective analysis and thus to improvement. Immediately after World War II, Alfred Kinsey pursued a similar project, producing a number of influential reports on American sexual attitudes.

The increased involvement of science in the study of sexuality was paralleled, in the immediate postwar period, by developments in the commercial and cultural spheres of capitalism which thrust sexuality into the mainstream for the first time. In October 1953 the first edition of *Playboy* was published (Dines, 1995). In the course of the same decade the iconic figures of Elvis Presley, Marlon Brando, James Dean, Marilyn Monroe and others emerged. These developments signalled the opening of an era of social and sexual tension, amplified by accelerating affluence and consumerism. While Victorian society (in both America and Britain) had suppressed the discussion and depiction of sexual themes, postwar culture legitimized and encouraged a discursive opening-up of the subject. The 'sexual revolution' proper began, leading quickly to increased diversity in the range of sexual lifestyles considered socially acceptable.

Postwar sexual liberalization has been interpreted as a response to the 'crisis' of Victorian sexual culture which had, by mid-century and world war, become stifling and anachronistic (Seidman, 1992). The sexual revolution functioned, from this viewpoint, to reform sexual culture in such a way as to preserve existing sex and gender norms. The sex manuals of Havelock Ellis, the Kinsey reports, and the writings of Masters and Johnson sought to eroticize marriage and monogamy, thus strengthening and reinforcing the institution of the bourgeois nuclear family. Such strengthening became urgent in the context of the invention of the contraceptive pill for women in the 1950s, and its rapid spread in the 1960s, developments which 'liberated women's desires, turning them into sexual beings' (Grant, 1993: p. 61). They also forced the entry of sexual matters into public discourse. Hence, 'a culture of eroticism materialized in America that valued sex as a sphere of pleasure and self-expression' (Seidman, 1992: p. 34).

Such a culture presupposed social liberalization, and a flowering of public discourse about sex. State regulation of sex began to be reduced, and for the first time a 'sex industry' emerged. The process began in the United States, but other countries, including Britain, followed similar cultural paths from Victorian repression to liberalization. Throughout the western world, British critic Bryan Appleyard observes, the 1960s' permissive approach to sexuality 'coincided with, and justified an economic transformation of, the pornography industry from private indulgence to mass medium. Increased affluence, high-quality printing and efficient distribution made simple the mechanics of widely available erotica'.[1]

The 1959 Obscene Publications Act, which removed certain restrictions from texts hitherto banned as obscene or pornographic if they could be 'justified' as art (D.H. Lawrence's *Lady Chatterley's Lover* was the best known beneficiary of the law) was a British reaction to the increasingly obvious outmodedness of Victorian sexual norms (Thompson, 1994). Excessive policing of the sexually explicit had by that time become, in Britain as well as in America, a source of embarrassment to the legal system, threatening to undermine its credibility.

Thereafter in Britain, like America, music, cinema and other forms of popular culture became sexualized to an unprecedented extent, and London became synonymous with 'the swinging sixties'. Media images of sex became more commonplace, and sexual relations liberalized. With the spread of the Pill women's magazines changed to reflect the needs of a generation of newly educated, economically independent, sexually liberated and active women. In both Britain and America, 'between the 1920s and the 1970s, public sexual imagery moved from the margins to the social centre, from a ghettoized, stigmatized sphere of representation to a legitimate multi-billion dollar business' (Seidman, 1992: p. 37). Sexuality was commodified and subsumed within the normal rules of the capitalist marketplace. In the United States the liberal trend was confirmed by the findings of the Commission on Pornography and Obscenity set up by President Lyndon Johnson, which reported in 1970.

Set up in response to fears already being voiced about the pernicious social impact of the sex industry's rapid expansion (and that of pornography in particular), the commission, involving 18 members and a budget of $1 750 000 over a period of two years, concluded that there were no proven negative effects of sexually explicit material. Although the findings of the Johnson Commission (as we shall refer to it hereafter) were officially rejected by the right-wing, morally conservative Nixon Administration, they seemed to endorse (and thus accelerated) the liberalizing trend in sexual attitudes and behaviour, and in the regulation of sexual representation. The Johnson Commission confirmed the gradual withdrawal of the state from sexual regulation, and documented 'the penetration of pornography into mainstream America' (Seidman, 1992: p. 57).

In Britain, similar conclusions were reached by the Home Office Departmental Committee on Obscenity and Film Censorship (the Williams

Committee), which reported in October 1979. While the sexualization of British culture has never approached the degree of explicitness reached in America, a similarly liberal trend was apparent in the 1960s and 1970s.

Feminism and the women's movement

The sexual revolution was from the outset viewed as a progressive movement by an emerging counter-culture which was best placed to enjoy its benefits and could present a political rationale for doing so. This essentially left-wing constellation of individuals and organizations adopted a strategy of sexual experimentation, diversity and transgression as a part of its resistance to the 'repression' of dominant capitalist values. Such a strategy, it was believed, would unite the individual with the group in an erotic and, because of its transgressive nature, politically subversive bond. For the late Linda Singer this was 'the logic which helped to produce the climate of sexual pluralism and tolerance associated with the period of sexual revolution' (1993: p. 64). Seidman, too, observes that in 1960s America sexual rebellion was integral to the growing political critique of society by its younger members, fuelled by the radicalizing experience of the Vietnam war. 'The anti-war protesters and counter-culture frequently connected their social critique with demands for a more sexually open, expressive, eroticized society' (1992: p. 2).

Before long, however, the liberal 'free love' tenets of the (largely male) sexual revolutionaries came into conflict with the aims and objectives of the growing feminist movement. The 'second wave' of feminism (the 'first wave' having been effectively neutralized in the 1920s) has been dated to the publication in 1963 of Betty Friedan's *The Feminine Mystique* (Burstyn, 1985b). Friedan's book was the first of many written by women throughout the 1960s and into the 1970s which articulated a specifically female agenda for sexual, economic and political progress, distinct from and often opposed to that of the male-dominated sexual revolution. That there had been a revolution in sexual attitudes and behaviour was not denied by these early feminists, but to many women it seemed to amount to little more than a convenient rationale for their more efficient sexual exploitation. Many men seemed to be using the ideology of sexual liberation, backed up by the availability of the Pill, to justify a cavalier, predatory approach to sexual relationships which offered few apparent benefits to the young women they selected. Some of the most important counter-cultural figures of the 1960s, such as Eldridge Cleaver and John Lennon, typically 'progressive' on some issues, were vicious sexists in their private lives. The behaviour of many less exalted male participants in the sexual revolution was equally misogynistic, fuelling the development of an alternative feminist view which called for the separation of women from the male-led mainstream. From the late 1960s onwards, feminist writers like Kate Millett began to campaign on a range of 'women's issues' not addressed by the sexual revolution, such as abortion rights, rape, and the socio-economic position of housewives. This movement received confirmation in the 1970s with the discovery of the Pill's harmful side-effects, and the realization that oral contraception was not as liberating for women as men had led them to believe.

Feminism, however, was never a monolithic construct, and as the women's movement gathered strength and pace in the 1970s at least three 'feminisms' could be discerned: *liberal* feminism, advocating a strategy of reform of patriarchal institutions; *marxist* or *materialist* feminism, heavily influenced by Marx' and Engels' writings on the state and the family, which viewed the sexist oppression of women as a product of capitalist social organization and politically subordinated the women's movement to the class struggle; and *radical* or *cultural* feminism, which identified patriarchy as a separate mode of social stratification, requiring political strategies independent of anticapitalist struggle.[2]

From this latter perspective, the key objective of the women's movement was to be 'the development and promotion of a female counter-culture' (Echols, 1984: p. 63). Male oppression of women was not socially but biologically determined, intrinsic to male sexuality. The male sexual drive was viewed from this perspective as instinctively violent and aggressive, and heterosexual intercourse as an act of oppression in itself.

In its most radical variant this subcategory of feminism led to political lesbianism in which, despite the sexual orientation of a woman, *only* sex with other women was viewed as legitimate behaviour.[3] Cultural feminism, of greater or lesser radicalism, had in common a view of female sexuality as 'a semi-mystical bonding, where bodily contact and genital pleasure are secondary and even non-existent' (Weeks, 1987: p. 46).

From the mid-1970s, radical feminists began to articulate a critique of the increasingly liberal sexual cultures of western capitalism, extending the argument about the reactionary character of the sexual revolution as it affected women in relationships to the content of sexual representation in general. Pornography was identified as the symbol and articulation of patriarchal misogyny, since it depicted in explicit detail – and appeared to celebrate – what was predefined within the terms of this strand of feminist ideology as violent, aggressive, abusive behaviour. With the formation in San Francisco in 1976 of Women Against Violence in Pornography, and two years later of Women Against Pornography in New York, the existence and growing public accessibility of pornography became a major campaigning issue for feminists. Shortly thereafter, Women Against Violence Against Women was set up in Britain, to be joined by several other organizations dedicated to the feminist fight against pornography. By the early 1980s, radical feminism and its antipornography agenda had become dominant within the feminist movement as a whole.

The antipornography feminist hegemony was not total, however. Laura Cottingham notes that 'the debates concerning female desire, which have frequently taken place within discussions of pornography, began in the late 70s' (1993: p. 56), at which time 'a general critique of mainstream pornography was an assumed premise of those who considered themselves feminist'. In April 1982, feminists with alternative assessments of the meaning of sexual representation and pornography met at the 'Barnard' conference in the United States, the proceedings of which were published three years later (Burstyn, 1985). Chapters 5 and 6 examine the views expressed at the Barnard conference in some detail. Here we note that Barnard presented the first public challenge, from within the feminist movement itself, to the efforts of one section of that movement to win acceptance for a particular reading of the sexually explicit. While there was no disputing from this direction the overwhelmingly patriarchal character of most pornography this group – described as 'pro-pornography feminists' by their opponents within the movement – argued that 'for the first time in modern history, women [have] access to [the] imagery and language [of] sexuality' (Assiter and Carol, 1993: p. 13), and that this could be, in certain conditions, an empowering as opposed to a degrading experience for women. Sexual representation need not be the monopoly of sexist men, it was argued, nor should some feminists seek to deprive all women of participating in sexual culture, pornographic or otherwise. Antipornography feminists were attacked for imposing on women as a whole 'a sexual code which drastically circumscribes the sorts of sexual expression considered acceptable' (Echols, 1984: p. 64). Cultural feminism was denounced as a form of biological determinism which simply reversed the traditional argument of patriarchy – that women are biologically conditioned into their positions of social and economic subordination by such 'facts of life' as their role in childbirth and nurturing – to assert that women are indeed biologically different, and that this requires a separate cultural and sexual development, apart from the world of men.

More important than the merits of these respective positions, for the purposes of this chapter, is the impact which the intrafeminist dispute had on public discourse. Suddenly, from the mid-1980s onwards, the pornography debate was not principally one between feminists and male defenders of sexism and patriarchy, but between variants of feminism, arguing for and against the right to engage in, and with, mainstream sexual culture. Newspapers and television increasingly acted as the platforms for debate between those such as Catharine MacKinnon and Naomi Wolf and a new wave of 'pro-porn' feminists, of whom Camille Paglia was perhaps the most intellectually ambitious and aggressive (1993). MacKinnon and those of like mind were, by the end of the 1980s, under (very public) challenge from 'a postmodern feminism that explodes the category of 'women' into a multiplicity of desires, identities and lifestyles' (Seidman, 1992: p. 133), undermining the antipornography orthodoxy.

Antipornography feminists, in turn, responded to these attacks by suggesting that they were a manifestation of 'post-feminist backlash' (Faludi, 1991), led (or at least inspired and encouraged) by men whose positions and status successful 1970s and 1980s feminist campaigns had challenged. As Naomi Wolf put it, 'images that turn women into objects or eroticize the degradation of women help to counterbalance women's recent self-assertion' (1990: p. 110). Iris Diamond argued that the increased quantity and (alleged) violence of the pornography in circulation was 'a response to [women's] efforts to alter the sexual status quo' (1980: p. 192). Those women who supported the backlash, or who sought to present it as a positive consequence of women's advancement, rather than a negative reaction to it, were dupes of the patriarchal establishment.

This debate is analysed more closely below. Here we note that the public split which overcame the feminist movement around the meaning of sexual representation gave the issue an added urgency and newsvalue.

Gay rights

Another aspect of the 1960s sexual revolution with special significance for our present discussion was the emergence into public view of a politically assertive, sexually active community of male homosexuals. Until the 1960s, gay subculture (for both men and women) existed largely underground, since 'homosexuals of both genders were potentially subject to psychiatric and medical persecution, not to mention job loss and disgrace' (Valverde and Weir, 1985: p. 103). As the sexual revolution gathered momentum, however, it allowed not only heterosexuals but homosexuals to identify themselves sexually, and to pursue more freely lifestyles in which gay desires and needs could be acknowledged.

For gays, of course, this emergence was a great deal more problematic than for their straight co-revolutionaries. Gay male sexual practices such as anal penetration remained illegal in many countries, while even *being* gay was enough (as it still is) to lead to wholesale discrimination. The sexual revolution early on expanded the possibilities of sex for heterosexuals, but homosexuality still had to overcome deep-rooted, longstanding moral and religious prejudice. While straight people enjoyed the new sexual freedoms of the 1960s, gays continued to be subject to police and other forms of harassment.

The gay liberation movement was 'born' (Shilts, 1988) in June 1969, when New York gays rioted in response to police harassment of a gay bar, the Stonewall Inn. The Stonewall riot was a key moment in the assertion by gay men, first in the United States and thereafter in other western countries, of their right to pursue gay lifestyles openly and without discrimination.

Following Stonewall gay men, in New York and San Francisco principally, forged communities which were at the same time political statements of their right to live freely as gays and structures for facilitating the practice of gay sex.

Institutions emerged, such as the bath-houses of New York and San Francisco, where gay men could seek out and indulge promiscuously in any form of sexual activity which was to their taste. Many 'out' gay men (as opposed to those who kept their sexual orientation secret and lived apparently heterosexual lives) pursued a 'fast-lane' lifestyle, boasting of hundreds of sexual partners per year, touring the bath-houses and clubs for the purpose of uncomplicated, responsibility-free sexual gratification. The gay lifestyles of the 1970s were hedonistic, and unashamedly so. Having been oppressed for so long, the assertive gay subculture of the 1970s viewed sexual promiscuity and indulgence in such exotic sexual practices as 'fisting' (insertion of the fist and arm into a man's anus), 'rimming' (oral-anal contact) and 'pissing' (urinating on one's partner) as *political* acts. Indulging in such behaviour was viewed as an assertion and reinforcement of newly won political rights.

Gay culture was, then, a highly sexual one, and as it gained acceptance (a process always constrained, of course, by lingering homophobia at all levels of straight society) it brought a new sexual dimension to cultural life. While many gay artists and public figures remained 'in the closet' others 'came out', using their gayness as material for their work. Derek Jarman, Robert Mapplethorpe and Keith Haring were among those gay men whose art (cinema, photography, and painting respectively) was both popular and sexual, and which generated controversy when made public. Cultural interventions by gay men in the 1970s and 1980s were frequently the subject of public debate about the meaning of sexual representation. In the field of the sexually explicit the emergence of a gay community was reflected in the rapid expansion of gay pornography. As pornographic materials spread in the 1970s and 1980s, so did that addressed to gay men in particular.

As for gay women, they too found the late 1970s and early 1980s a period of coming out to public view. Their situation was different from that of gay men, in so far as lesbianism was linked from the outset to the politics of feminism (and indeed, as we have seen, political lesbianism was viewed by some feminists as a necessary and radical choice of lifestyle, even for women who did not feel sexually attracted to other women). Gay and straight women had in common the fight against patriarchy (which, of course, gay and straight men did not) so that the fight for lesbian rights was a 'women's issue' in the wider sense too.

That said, many lesbians were not necessarily feminists and lived, like male homosexuals until the late 1960s, in subcultural isolation. As the women's movement gained strength in the 1970s, lesbians benefitted accordingly and were permitted to be more open about their lifestyles, which often turned out, like those of gay men, to involve deviant sexual behaviours like sado-masochism (s/m) and fisting. Associated with these activities was a lesbian pornography of s/m, the existence of which (*see* Chapter 6) was one of the main factors behind the split between pro- and antipornography feminists. As was noted above, the feminist split of the 1980s fuelled much of the sexualization of public discourse which took place in that decade. The fact that some lesbians did not view sexuality and pornography in the same way as their cultural feminist sisters was an important source of that split.

If 's/m dyke' pornography was at the extreme end of this particular cultural spectrum, a softer iconography of lesbianism spread widely in the 1980s and into the 1990s, popularized by pop culture figures such as Madonna and k.d. lang. These representations, particularly those which circulated in the mainstream (*see* Chapter 8) supplied more raw material for the public debate on sexuality.

HIV and AIDS

By the late 1970s the sexual revolution had been consolidated. For feminists and gay rights activists much remained to be achieved in the political, economic and social spheres, but a fundamental change in sexual mores and attitudes had been affected. Women and gays were ascending into positions of political and cultural authority on their own terms. In San Francisco and other big gay centres in the United States homosexuals had become an important electoral constituency, to be ignored at the politicians' peril. Antisexism was becoming consensual; to oppose it gradually coming to be seen as reactionary and old-fashioned.

Then, in early 1981, American skin specialists began to note an extraordinarily high incidence of a rare cancer, Kaposi's Sarcoma, among gay men. Other conditions rarely seen in hitherto healthy young people, such as *pneumocystii carinii pneumonia*, were observed by doctors in Atlanta and Los Angeles. These were the first recognized signs of the disease, present but undiagnosed in the United States since at least the 1970s, which would later be called AIDS (Acquired Immune Deficiency Syndrome).

There are many excellent accounts of how AIDS and the agent which causes it, HIV (Human Immunodeficiency Virus) were discovered and identified (McKie, 1986; Shilts, 1988; Gilmore, 1992). Here we note simply that by the mid-1980s it had become clear that a previously unknown disease of the human immune system was spreading through the United States, western Europe, and indeed the whole world. The disease was transmitted by the exchange of infected bodily fluids, principally blood and semen, in sexual intercourse or by some other means such as blood transfusion or the sharing of infected needles by intravenous drug-users. The disease appeared to be almost universally fatal. There was no vaccine, nor any prospect of finding one before the end of the century, and no curative treatments. Although AIDS first emerged as a disease affecting gay men, by the mid-1980s it was known that the pathways of transmission were by no means exclusive to homosexuals.

That gay men were the first group to develop AIDS in large numbers was a consequence of the fact that their sexual lifestyles (the aforementioned 'fast-lane' of bath-houses, s/m clubs, and all that went on in them) were particularly vulnerable to sexually transmitted disease. Before AIDS, gay men had been severely affected by Hepatitis B and other blood-borne viruses. In the gay male communities of San Francisco, Los Angeles and New York, HIV found an ideal environment in which to multiply and spread. But heterosexuals were just as vulnerable, biologically speaking. Old-age pensioners received the virus in blood transfusions; foetuses from their mother's placenta; young women from penetrative sex with their HIV-positive, intravenous drug-using or prostitute-frequenting boyfriends and husbands.

The discovery of AIDS and the way in which it was reported by the media has been the subject of several books and articles (Watney, 1987; 1988; Greenaway *et al.*, 1992; Miller and Williams, 1993). For the purposes of our discussion the key point is that AIDS forced questioning of many of the 'revolutionary' sexual practices and attitudes that had become by the 1980s, as we have seen, if not mainstream, at least tolerated within the mainstream. Most obviously, because they were the first to acquire the disease in significant numbers, AIDS threw the public spotlight on the sexual lifestyles of gay males. Those for whom the sexual revolution had always been a threatening, socially undermining movement viewed AIDS as evidence of their moral correctness. Religious fundamentalists and the extreme moral conservatives who exerted considerable political influence in the 1980s considered AIDS to be a form of divine retribution for the unnatural acts performed by gay men on each other, and for the permissiveness of the post-1960s population as a whole. AIDS was 'the wages of sin' for societies whose members had forgotten the importance of family values.

More seriously, AIDS eventually (and belatedly, many commentators argued) forced a debate, which had to be conducted in public, about which kinds of sexual activity were 'high risk' in terms of transmitting the disease. Few, apart from the moral conservative lobbies, suggested that sexual culture should return to a pre-1960s puritanism, or that people should give up sex (although some did). Instead, the media became a forum for discussion and education about safer sex: the importance of condom-use, the undesirability of multiple sexual partners, the relative dangers of anal as opposed to vaginal and oral sex. Educational videos were produced showing how gay and straight couples should engage in safer sex.

While all this inevitably required an unprecedentedly explicit discussion of the mechanics of sexual behaviour, it also highlighted such issues as bisexuality, by making visible and urgent the pathways to HIV-infection between gay and straight. Taboo subjects like anal sex (in the straight or gay context) had to be addressed. In all these respects HIV/AIDS required the public scrutinizing of sexuality in a way which had never been possible before, and occasioned a rethinking by those who had been advocates of sexual liberalization.

For the gay community in particular, AIDS challenged the viability of the fast-lane lifestyle, encouraging an end to the aggressive, penetrative, hedonistic maleness of the bath-house and club culture. For straights, likewise, sexual promiscuity could no longer be viewed as a radical progressive choice, but had now to be reassessed as potentially life-threatening behaviour. In Linda Singer's words, AIDS made necessary 'a new sexual politics ... a rethinking of the relationship between bodies, pleasures, and power beyond the call for liberation from repression' (Singer, 1993: p. 113). While HIV/AIDS intensified the moral and legal regulation of sexuality, it also turned 'sexual services and commodities' into 'a real growth area' (Singer, 1993: p. 37). As Singer puts it, 'at a time when uncommodified [interpersonal] sexuality has been constituted as a high-risk zone, the zone of sexual commodification expands as a profit centre' (Singer, 1993). Pornography, she suggests, expanded in the 1980s, alongside the spread of HIV/AIDS, precisely because of its objectifying, dehumanizing qualities. 'In pornography, the commodity is a sexual semiotic ... a phenomenon of sex without bodies. This is part of what makes pornography an appropriate site for erotic investment in the age of sexual epidemic' (Singer, 1993: p. 38). The same is true, she adds, of telephone sex lines, which have also experienced massive growth throughout the western world in recent years.

For Singer, the film *Fatal Attraction*, with its story of a casual sexual encounter gone murderously wrong, was one example among many which emerged from the mainstream of popular culture in the late 1980s of a text which was successful because it 'managed a nexus of contemporary sexual anxieties surrounding changes in the family, alternatives in the cultural theory and practice of feminity, and transformation in the erotic climate induced by the contemporary sexual epidemic' (1993: p. 180). A transformation of sexual culture took place, as the contradictory elements of sexual liberalization on the one hand, and the biological requirements of safer sex on the other, clashed in the mid- to late 1980s.

The moral lobby

A further factor driving the explosion of sexual discourse was the ascendancy in the United States and elsewhere of a loose network of morally conservative, (usually) religious fundamentalist organizations, such as the Moral Majority in the United States, and the National Viewers and Listeners Association in Britain.

Moral lobbies have a long history in western societies, but the 1980s was a particularly fertile period for them to grow and prosper. With the coming of the Reagan administration in America, and the Thatcher government in Britain, conservative moral values were placed at the top of the political agenda in both countries. After decades of sexual liberalism and cultural permissiveness these governments came to power with radically conservative attitudes to the nuclear family and sexual expression. In Reagan's case electoral victories in 1980 and 1984 were attributed not least to the support of organized religious and moral conservative constituencies.

That the Reagan administration's establishment in 1985 of a commission on pornography, headed by the Attorney-General, Edwin Meese, was almost wholly inspired by a conservative agenda was reflected in its composition of well-known moral right and religious figures. The 1980s was a decade in which extreme conservatives like Jesse Helm and Pat Buchanan found ample political support for their assaults on 'obscene' artists like Robert Mapplethorpe and Andres Serrano, and in which artists addressing sexual themes found it increasingly difficult to obtain even modest state support for and endorsement of their work.

Although it is possible to argue that the conservatives have not been especially successful in imposing their agenda on the United States (nor could the likes of Mary Whitehouse in Britain successfully turn back the tide of 'sex and violence' in cinema and television), their activities represented another source from which the public sphere was sexualized. Conservative-orchestrated outrage about Mapplethorpe's homoerotic photographs or Serrano's 'piss paintings' inevitably meant media discussion of such themes, adding another twist to the proliferation of sexual discourse. The publication in June 1986 of the pornography commission's report did not, in the end, lead to significantly increased regulation of the US sex industry, as the moral conservatives had hoped, but *did* lead to intense media coverage of the sex issue. The report was itself, as 'gonzo' journalist Hunter Thompson noted, with typically iconoclastic satisfaction, sufficiently pornographic to be immensely popular when published in paperback.

> The final report by the Meese people will apparently be a voluminous guide to everything ever written or photographed in all aspects of the sex business – hundreds of colour photos, thousands of films and massive lists, discussions and descriptions of every kink, crime and subhuman perversion since Nero and prehistoric Japan. The book, due out sometime in July, is already a guaranteed best-seller (1988: p. 129).

By attempting to make sex a political issue in the 1980s, the powerful moral lobbies increased its media visibility, further encouraging what *Newsweek* called 'the new voyeurism: the middlebrow embrace, in the age of AIDS, of explicit erotic material for its own sake'.[4] Here, at the heart of the American journalistic establishment, we find acknowledgement that 'at a time when *doing* it has become excessively dangerous, looking at it, reading about it, thinking about it has become a necessity. .... From Mapplethorpe to MTV, from the Fox network to the fashion industry, looking at sex is creeping out of the private sphere and into the public.'

For a variety of reasons, therefore, some welcome and others less so, the 1980s were a decade in which sex invaded public consciousness to an unprecedented extent. The next chapter considers how this process was reflected in the content of mass print and broadcast media.

Notes

1 Appleyard, B., 'Way beyond the erogenous zone', *The Times*, 12 September 1992.
2 I use terms such as 'liberal', 'radical', and 'cultural' as they appear in the literature. I am aware, of course, that such terms are never neutral, but carry important connotations for the protagonists in the debate.
3 In the 1980s an organization called the Southern Women's Writing Collective took the cultural feminist position to its logical conclusion by arguing that 'radical celibacy together with desconstructive lesbianism and sex resistance are the only practical choices for women oppressed under male supremacy' (1990: p. 146). For this group, even sex between women was fundamentally an incorporation of patriarchally imposed roles and values.
4 From a collection of articles, not individually bylined, which appeared under the heading 'The Selling of Sex' in *Newsweek*, 2 November 1992.

|3|

'Let's talk about sex, babee...'[1] sex and the public sphere

Channel Four television's eight-week series of sexually oriented pro-gramming, presented under the rubric of the *Red Light Zone*, was broadcast in Britain from March until May 1995. The *Red Light Zone*, and the media coverage accompanying it, was a recent and substantial example of the sexualization of public discourse which so many observers have iden-tified. Not only did the series permit an extended depiction and discussion of sexual themes, in documentary and drama form, but, like comparable series and programmes before it, it also occasioned a debate, conducted in the press and other public fora, about the ethics and appropriateness of such representation, even when compartmentalized, as the *Red Light Zone* was, into the post-watershed, adults-only, late Saturday night slot.[2] It was another example of our compulsion to talk about sex, whether as authors of television programmes, commentators on them, or viewers. To be sure, and despite the self-interested hyping of the series by its commissioning editor and the Channel Four promotional department, the controversy surround-ing the *Red Light Zone* was less intense than that associated with previous examples of ground-breaking television, such as the same broadcasters' 'Red Triangle' series of adult-orientated feature films, transmitted in the 1980s.[3] On that occasion, public outrage was orchestrated by the consider-able figure of Mrs Mary Whitehouse and her National Viewers and Listeners Association.[4] By 1995, Mrs Whitehouse and the moral crusaders whom she led and inspired were in decline. In this sense the *Red Light Zone* may be viewed as marking the end of a period when sex on television could be guaranteed to generate 'Shock! Horror!' headlines in the British press, and to be viewed instead as merely a viewing choice like any other.

The *Red Light Zone* was confirmation of the trend in public, mass-medi-ated discourse, evident since at least the early 1980s, in both Britain and the United States, to talk about sex; to make sex and sexuality the subject of public debate, to an extent unprecedented in the history of the mass media. The trend was both a response to, and part of, cultural phenomena referred to earlier: the expansion of the pornography industry, and the diversification of its market to incorporate not just gays but also 'normal' heterosexual women; the 'pornographication of the mainstream', as reflected in *Basic Instinct* and other Hollywood films; the increasing use of pornographic iconography in artistic activity, including massively popular forms such as Madonna's musical and video performances, or the more restricted works of Mapplethorpe and Koons. It was also a response to HIV/AIDS, and the resulting social necessity to speak openly and accurately about the paths of sexual transmission used by the virus. It was, not least, a reflection of the success of feminism and gay rights in legitimizing sexual politics and forcing sexual issues into the public agenda.

This chapter reviews the process of sexualization of the public sphere, in both print and broadcast media, as it unfolded through the 1980s and into the 1990s. It analyses the forms which this sexualization took, and the content of what was said, against the backdrop of an increasingly 'pornographic' mass culture.

The public sphere: a theoretical note

The concept of the 'public sphere', as articulated most fully by Jurgen Habermas (1989), usually refers in the media studies literature to that sphere of public life in which individuals come together to receive information, have it debated and assessed, and then go on to make rational choices about political and public affairs. In this sense it has a definite political connotation, being viewed as the essential conduit of the information and knowledge on which the citizens of liberal democratic states depend if they are to make correct political choices (in elections, for example). The public sphere comprises those institutions which circulate this information and knowledge, and which provide spaces for it to be discussed: in practice, the mass media which, in their public-sphere role, constitute audiences as *citizens*. Within media sociology there is a lively debate about the contemporary functioning of the public sphere, and the usefulness of the concept in a media environment characterized by (alleged) audience passivity (McNair, 1995). We will not enter that debate here, but take the notion of the public sphere as a useful shorthand to describe those mass-media outlets in which information and knowledge about sexuality (undoubtedly an issue of concern to citizens, if not often a political issue in the electoral sense) is disseminated to society as a whole. What becomes of this knowledge – what is done with it politically – is not my concern here. Rather, I assume that the expanded media discourse about sexuality which characterized the 1980s and 1990s is a significant phenomenon in itself, worthy of description and analysis; that it can be read as an index of how western societies such as

Britain and the United States have become increasingly sexualized; and that the public sphere of contemporary mass-media discourse has become a key site for debate about sexuality.

Sex in the public sphere refers here specifically to newspaper, periodical and television coverage of sexuality – in particular, the content of television programmes, feature articles, columns, and other categories of mediated discourse about sex, pornography and related themes through the 1980s and into the 1990s. This chapter reviews some of what was said over this period. It also considers the extent and significance of the 'sexualization' of mainstream women's magazines – the tendency of *Cosmopolitan*, *Company* and other titles to address sex in unprecedentedly explicit terms over this period.

This discussion, more than any other in the book, focuses on material drawn from the British context, simply because these have been the most easily accessed for a British-based author on a tight schedule and a shoe-string budget. A period of fieldwork in San Francisco did, however, allow for some analysis of the American print media's coverage of sexuality over this period, as contained in over 180 articles drawn from more than 50 periodicals and newspapers. This sample of material has permitted some comparison to be drawn between the content of British and American public discourse on sexuality over the period under discussion.

Sex in print

Although the sexual revolution dates back to the 1960s, the dramatic sexualization of the public sphere noted by many commentators is a 1980s phenomenon. Interest in and depiction of all things sexual has grown steadily since the 1960s, but the most obvious proliferation of sexual discourse occurred after 1985, in both the United States and Britain. Fig. 3.1 shows how the number of articles about sexuality and its representation increased in the British press from only three in 1985 to 31 in 1992.

The data on which the graph is based are far from exhaustive, being compiled from a review of the *British Humanities Index*[5] of press and periodical publications between the years 1984 and 1994 inclusively. The subject categories reviewed were, most obviously, 'pornography' and 'sex', supplemented by subcategories such as 'eroticism', 'gender', 'homosexuality', 'censorship', and 'video recordings, pornographic and violent'. The BHI does not cite straight news reportage, nor do the categories selected for this study include writing about sexual behaviour and sex crimes, unless these had some clear connection with pornography or other sexual representation. They do not, therefore, incorporate the extensive coverage of such issues as the string of 'date rape' cases which passed through the British

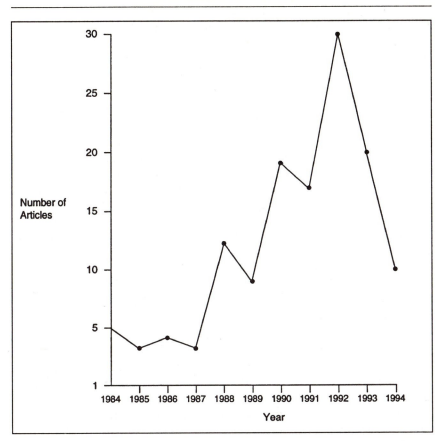

Fig. 3.1 Coverage of pornography and sexuality in the British newspaper and periodical press, 1984–94 (source: British Humanities Index)

courts in the early 1990s, although the latter theme was occasionally mentioned in the context of more general articles about feminism and media sexuality. Moreover, the *British Humanities Index* does not include the popular tabloid newspapers which, it need hardly be pointed out, have always given sexuality in all its guises great prominence. Much of what is routinely said about sex in the print media is omitted from Fig. 3.1, therefore, and no great empirical significance is claimed for the sample represented there.

What Fig. 3.1 *does* show, however, and clearly enough for our purposes, is an expanding role for sexuality in the agendas of the serious print media; a generally rising curve of journalistic interest in sexual themes in the late 1980s and early 1990s, peaking around 1992. They demonstrate, as critic Bryan Appleyard put it in 1993, that 'sex as issue, obsession, public activity and subject of interminable chatter seems to have become an essential element in the public realm'.[6]

Table 3.1 breaks the articles down into content categories. Two articles, for example, reported connections between particular forms of sex crime and pornography. A London *Times'* piece, published in 1987, took the broadcasting of a television documentary about child pornography as an opportunity to report on how paedophile networks were using the then-embryonic information superhighway (Internet) to circulate information and contacts.[7]

Two articles, both by Bernard Levin for *The Times*, addressed what I have categorized as the ethics of sexual representation. Levin, in acknowledging the reality of pornography's spread, and the fact that some women were involved in its production and consumption voluntarily, bemoaned 'the poverty of spirit and imagination that that fact implies'.[8] For Levin, pornography was immoral, not to mention unerotic and anaphrodisiac, signifying as it did, in his view, that 'women are things, objects, receptacles, instruments; that their nature is passive, insensate, usable, empty; that they exist to comply, offer, submit, serve ... a portrait of a woman as nothing but a willing orifice, her world reduced to the filling of it'.[9] Although many of the press articles categorized under the heading 'women's attitudes' debated the meaning of pornography in similar terms (*see* below) it is notable just how few of these moral denunciations there were by prominent male journalists over the sample period.

A number of articles contributed to the debate, examined at length in the next chapter, about how key terms such as 'pornography', 'erotica' and 'obscenity' should be defined. Others addressed what we might describe as the 'mainstreaming' of sexual deviance or perversion -- articles commenting on the growing popularity and respectability of such hitherto hidden behaviours as sado-masochism.

Table 3.1 Breakdown by content of coverage of pornography and sexuality in the British press, 1984–94

Subject	No. of items
Women's attitudes to sexual representation	39
Explicit sex in art and popular culture	28
The sex industry	20
Censorship and regulation	20
Sexual deviation/perversion	7
Sexual attitudes	6
Definitions of pornography	4
Effects of sexual representation	3
Ethics of sexual representation	2
Sexual crime	2
Total	**131**

(source: British Humanities Index)

A significant proportion of the total sample (more than 20 per cent) analysed the use of explicit sexual depictions and pornographic iconography in advertising, mainstream cinema, popular fiction and other media forms not conventionally associated with pornography, reflecting the 'pornographication of the mainstream' identified as a trend above. Throughout the 1980s and into the 1990s, artists working in a variety of media released material into the cultural marketplace which deliberately problematized conventional distinctions between porn and 'not porn' (*see* Chapter 8). These occasions were frequently accompanied by 'think pieces' on the significance of such boundary-breaking.

A large number of articles were concerned with the development of the sex industry. The majority covered established branches such as the production of magazines, videos, and sex shops, while some reported on technology-driven developments, such as the use of computerized information networks and CD-ROM to circulate pornography. These articles frequently touched on the issues of censorship and regulation, although a separate category was assigned to pieces in which these were the main theme. In several articles, interest was focused on the difficulties posed for moral censors by the emergence of new delivery technologies: notably, in the British case, satellite television broadcasts from continental Europe such as those produced by the *Red Hot Dutch* channel.

Women and sex

By far the largest number of articles surveyed concerned women's attitudes to sexuality, pornography and other forms of mediated sex. This category is distinct from the six articles which reported on attitudes to sex shown by the population as a whole, as recorded in various surveys conducted during the sample period. The remaining 39 pieces on women's attitudes reflect the awareness of (mainly) female, almost exclusively feminist commentators of women's apparently growing interest in sex, and a desire to analyse the phenomenon. In their content, moreover, they show how women's attitudes to sex and sexual representation reflected the intensifying split within feminism between 'pro' and 'anti' pornography viewpoints.

Fig. 3.1 covers the period from 1984 until 1994. Although coincidental, this is fortuitous, since 1984 was an important moment in the sex-society-media debate. In the United States at that time the debate was being fuelled by the campaigning activities of Andrea Dworkin and Catharine MacKinnon, and their efforts to restrict the availability of pornography. In 1983 Dworkin and MacKinnon, in co-operation with local moral conservatives, succeeded in persuading the Minneapolis city council to pass an ordinance making the production, distribution, and use of pornography a civil offence.[10] By early 1984, however, the Democratic mayor of the city had vetoed the measure on the grounds that it was excessively 'vague and unworkable',[11] thus generating intense debate within the feminist movement and outside it. In both the United States and Britain in 1984 the Minneapolis Ordinance was a prominent theme of journalistic discourse on sexuality. Efforts to pass the ordinance can indeed be seen as a watershed in the debate, since although the pro- and antipornography split in the feminist movement had already emerged following the 1982 Barnard Conference (*see* Chapter 2) the ordinance issue gave it widespread publicity, linking feminism as it did with the rather surprising bedfellows of the American religious right and other elements not hitherto associated with support for women's equality. The progress of the ordinance revealed for the first time to a mass media public the tensions within feminism which had been created by the attempt to impose an antipornography consensus on the movement, and generated unease about the ethics and tactical wisdom of allying with moral conservatives on the pornography issue. In Britain, where the evolution of the feminist movement followed the pattern of the United States, similar concerns were felt, and reflected in print coverage from 1984 onwards.

A *Guardian* piece in July 1984 reported that the Dworkin-MacKinnon-moral-conservative campaign had moved on from Minneapolis (frustrated by the mayor's veto) to Indianapolis, which city had now become 'the front line of the war against pornography'.[12] The article linked the feminist antipornography campaign to a more general 'backlash' in which the Reagan administration, the Catholic Church, and other moral conservative groups in the United States were attacking the growth of pornography and sexual liberalism in general. The backlash was also a response, it was suggested, to the discovery of HIV/AIDS.

In these early British articles, and many more on similar themes in the American media we see a recognition that the convergence of a number of social, political and (in the case of HIV/AIDS) biological phenomena was making sexuality and its representation a particularly important issue of the 1980s. At this stage of the issue's development the antipornography perspectives identified in Chapter 2 remained 'consensual' in most British media discourse. In a piece published by *New Society* magazine in early 1984, reporting the proceedings of a women's study day on pornography, the 'shame' and 'depression' caused to the participants by looking at and discussing pornography was presented as requiring no further explanation.[13] Already in 1984, however, some objections to the presumption that all women should react to all pornography in the same shamed manner were being voiced.

In the *New Statesmen* of February that year, Annette Kuhn questioned the readiness of some feminists, both in the United States and Britain, to support and campaign for laws against pornography of the Minneapolis Ordinance type. At this time (driven by motivations very different from those of the Dworkin-MacKinnon camp) the British parliament was in the process of passing the Video Recordings Bill, intended to increase restrictions on the violent and sexually explicit content of videos for rent.[14] Kuhn used this conjuncture to urge caution on those feminists who supported such laws, on the grounds that: a) the patriarchal state and its judiciary could never be expected to be pro-women in its functioning (and thus any law restricting sexual representation would backfire against women); and b) that such laws erected an artificial distinction between public and private spheres of sexual behaviour, a distinction rejected by feminists for whom the personal was always political. Such laws, and the campaigns which they generated, were mere diversions. As Kuhn put it, 'images of women in some advertisements, in fashion magazines or in pin-up photos, for example, all recirculate ideas about women, femininity and female sexuality which are basically no different from those offered in pornography, and all offer similar gratifications to the spectator. Why single out pornography for censure?'[15]

This argument, between feminists who justified the censorship and banning of pornography by characterizing it as an especially – uniquely – misogynistic form of sexual representation, and those such as Kuhn who preferred to view pornography in the context of an overall cultural environment dominated by patriarchal norms and stereotypes, drove the development of the sex-society-media issue in the academic literature and was a frequent theme of press coverage during our 10-year sample period.

Rosalind Coward returned to the subject of (feminist) women's appropriate response to the spread of pornography in a 1986 piece, the title of which reflects the unease by then affecting the women's movement on the issue. Asking 'What's in it for women?', Coward began from the premise that, since *some* women had for some time been producing and using sexually explicit materials, often of a sado-masochistic character, 'the hostility of radical feminists to all porn, and their call for the suppression of all porn-derived images inside and outside of feminism, was misguided'.[16] The undoubted offensiveness of much male-orientated pornography was not a reason, she suggested, for opposing all sexually explicit representations. By 1986, also, Coward could note that 'the debate about lesbian sado-masochism is shorthand for a much wider debate about whether [feminists have] been deluding ourselves with the idea of a 'wholesome' feminist sexuality which would bear no relation to its 'nasty' male counterpart'. Coward developed this defence of women's use of pornography in later articles which acknowledged the possibility that 'dirty', or even sado-masochistic, sex (and the pornography associated with it) could be opportunities for women 'to experience the flow between action and passivity, domination and submission, which seems to be integral to the experience of sex but often polarizes around gender'.[17] In a 1989 piece Elizabeth Wilson denounced the antipornography feminists as 'middle-class Victorian philanthropists and Fabian do-gooders'.[18]

Among the few articles identified which straightforwardly defended the antipornography line was a piece by Scottish novelist Janice Galloway, who in 1990 dismissed 'the phoney search for women's erotica'[19] and condemned women's confusion of pornography with sexual intimacy. For Galloway, the boom in sales of pornography amongst women was not 'a sign of increased female freedom' but rather evidence that 'women are getting as confused as men about intimacy and sexuality'. Women users of pornography, like men, were guilty of personal inadequacy, self-hatred and voyeurism. 'Feminist porn? Women being in charge of sexual exploitation is hardly the same as getting rid of the notion of exploitation altogether. It's still sex as commodity.'

In the early 1990s such views were to be found only rarely in the print media. Much more common were pieces similar to that by Chrissy Iley in the *Sunday Times*, which argued that pornography could be, and was, both made and used by women. In evidence Iley cited the case of Dominique Aury, the Frenchwoman who wrote *The Story of O*, a heavily sadomasochistic, 'misogynistic' work of sexual fantasy, and the marketing phenomenon of female 'literary porn', i.e. sexually explicit novels penned, and read, by women (*see* Chapter 8).[20]

Sex on TV

The year 1995, when this book was completed, was a particularly busy year for sex on British television. Programmes about sex and sexuality were prominent on the schedules of all the main terrestrial channels, organized under such rubrics as the *Red Light Zone* and *Dyke TV* (Channel 4), *Forbidden Weekend* (BBC) and the *Good Sex Guide* (ITV). Some of these programmes were about how to have good sex; others reported on the phenomenon of women's increased interest in sexual behaviour and issues related to sexuality; others debated the regulation of sexual representation on television.

While the oft-noted 'explosion' of sex on television was, as for the print media discussed above, a late 1980s and 1990s phenomenon, the process began with the sexual revolution of the 1960s, and its inevitable reflection in the content of television drama and current affairs. In 1964 Mary Whitehouse launched the 'Clean Up TV' campaign, bemoaning the 'sub-Christian' depths of suggestiveness and eroticism to which British broadcasting had allegedly sunk.[21] Thereafter, the broadcast of plays by Dennis Potter and others regularly generated public controversy and debate about the ethics of treating and depicting sex on television.

In September 1986 Channel Four fulfilled its remit to be, and reputation as, ground-breaking in the explicitness of its sexual content by broadcasting a series of adult-orientated feature films. In a pattern which was to be repeated nearly 10 years later with the *Red Light Zone* these hitherto-unseen-on-TV films were broadcast with a moral health warning – a red triangle signifying 'special discretion required', adorning the screen at the beginning of each transmission, alerting viewers to the potentially offensive nature of the material, and at the same time attracting those for whom a little controversy and raunch was something entirely to be welcomed. Not all the films shown in the 'Red Triangle' were selected because of their sexual content (in some, the degree of violence depicted was the main reason for 'special discretion'), but those which generated the most controversy, such as Derek Jarman's *Sebastiane*, usually had a strong sexual theme.

The Red Light Zone

Despite, and indeed partly because of, the outraged response of Mary Whitehouse and her National Viewers and Listeners Association (NVLA), the 'Red Triangle' season was a success for Channel Four, attracting audiences and contributing to its desired image as an innovative, challenging broadcaster. Nine years later, the same channel presented the most ambitious treatment of sexuality ever transmitted on British public service television, in the form of the *Red Light Zone*. Broadcast over eight (late) Saturday nights, the *Red Light Zone* contained 42 items, including documentaries, filmed lectures, short and full-length feature films, and a closing studio debate in which the issues raised by the programmes, and by the very existence of the series, were discussed. Like the 'Red Triangle', the *Red Light Zone* rubric, as Mark Edwards of the *Sunday Times* put it in his preview of the series, was a form of 'heavy branding ... [which] ... works both as a warning and a come-on'.[22] In the flurry of media publicity which accompanied the start of the series, however, the Channel Four commissioning editor responsible for it, Stuart Cosgrove, strenuously denied that the programmes were prurient or pornographic. While the *Red Light Zone* was certainly *about* pornography, and the wider sex industry as a whole, it used this subject-matter as a 'prism' through which 'to view social tensions'.[23] It would also explore 'the public's fascination with red-light zone culture, a magnetism and a voyeurism by no means confined to men'. In doing so, of course, the *Red Light Zone* was bound to be attractive to an audience already used to such programmes as *Sex Talk*, *Eurotrash* and *The Word*, all of which addressed sexuality in relatively explicit and irreverent terms. The series was, for Cosgrove, 'the first substantial attempt to create a zone of underground factual programming that meets the needs of Channel Four's late-night cosmopolitan audience'.

While the commissioning of the series is in itself indicative of the degree of sexualization of the public sphere evident by the mid-1990s, the *Red*

Light Zone also encapsulated many of the debates, ambiguities and tensions around the issues of sexuality and culture outlined in Chapter 2. As the final studio debate revealed, for some viewers the series was part of 'the blokeish backlash against women' and 'just another opportunity to present women as sex objects. ... On the pretext of examining the world of porn, we were subjected to repetitive and gratuitous imagery'.[24] For this viewer, and others of a similar disposition, the *Red Light Zone*'s treatment of sexuality was in fact another example of media sex*ism*. Religious and moral conservative objections to the series were voiced by Brian Mallalieu of the 'Horsham King's Cross Social Concerns Group', who protested that the images portrayed in the programmes were 'a travesty of what the Creator intended for the honour and the beauty of sex and nudity and relationships between men and women'. Speaking in favour of the *Red Light Zone*, on the other hand, were Nikki Wolf, editor of *Fetish Times* magazine and a participant in one of the programmes,[25] for whom 'the series has certainly opened up a lot of things. It's allowed a lot of voices to be heard that weren't being heard before.' For Cherie Matrix of Feminists Against Censorship, 'the best thing about the *Red Light Zone* is that it was not judgmental [about sexuality]'.

I do not have the space to provide a detailed review of the content of all the *Red Light Zone* programmes. What can be said with certainty, nevertheless, is that while many addressed 'red-light-zone culture' in terms which allowed for regular displays of naked female flesh – the ethics of a female New York cop posing in *Playboy* and then being subject to disciplinary action for being photographed in situations where her uniform, and thus her status as one of New York's finest, were clearly displayed;[26] a profile of French pornography film star Tabatha Cash;[27] the work of a Japanese porno video producer[28] – the majority, including the examples listed here, were directed and produced by women, often addressing deviant, marginalized sexualities (fetishism and s/m, transsexualism and transvestism, homosexuality). Even the most titillating material (from the male, heterosexist perspective) was usually concerned with the relations of production governing the sex industry, or such themes as the personal lives of strippers and prostitutes and the motivations of pornographic film performers.[29]

Whatever else it was guilty of, then, the *Red Light Zone* gave most of its prime television time to women making films about women, and about the sexualities of women. As already stated, deviant sexualities were also well represented in the series. It did not present, by any standards, a predominantly male-orientated, heterosexist view of sexuality.

Forbidden Weekend

Shortly after the *Red Light Zone* concluded its run, the BBC presented on its minority-audience channel what was entitled a 'forbidden weekend' of documentaries and feature films dealing with or containing explicit sex and violence, notably Ken Russell's *The Devils*, shown uncut for the first time on British television. More selfconsciously serious and academic in tone than the *Red Light Zone*, the BBC's *Forbidden Weekend* highlighted the extent to which sexuality had become, by 1995, the legitimate preserve of British public service television. In *Doing Rude Things*, for example, the history of the UK softcore pornography industry was considered, with fulsome illustrations, and hardly a single reference to sexism or patriarchy. For the sober denizens of the BBC, as well as the young Turks of Channel Four, talking about sex had become respectable, indeed commercially desirable in terms of addressing an audience increasingly comfortable with such public airings of hitherto taboo subjects.

Interestingly, the transmission of the *Forbidden Weekend* programmes was barely noted by media-watchers in the press and elsewhere. Even the *Red Light Zone*, whose commissioning editor and publicity department understandably appeared to seek out media attention as a way of attracting audiences, was met with little in the way of orchestrated moral outrage. By comparison with the heights of panic unleashed during the heyday of the NVLA, the *Red Light Zone* and the *Forbidden Weekend* came and went with relatively little fuss. The pornographic and the sexually explicit had, as one viewer complained in the *Red Light Zone's* studio debate, become part of 'mainstream television'.

And sex for all

Programmes like those presented in the *Red Light Zone* and *Forbidden Weekend* reflect the newly acquired legitimacy of sexual discourse amongst the 'cosmopolitan' and relatively intellectual (as they would perceive themselves) audiences of Channel Four and BBC2. Here, one could watch documentaries and films about striptease and pornography, fetishism and prostitution, without the guilt traditionally associated with viewing mediated sex. Talking about (and watching others talk about) sex had become respectable. Most of the films were made by women, after all: many by gay men and women, with correspondingly transgressive subject-matter. They were sanctioned as serious discourses and meta-discourses about culture, rather than gratuitous opportunities for voyeuristic pleasure.

The sexualization of television has not only been a phenomenon of minority-audience programming, however. The mass-audience ITV also reflected the trend in such series as the *Good Sex Guide*, which instructs its audience in the techniques of, as its title hints, good sex. Presented by a woman, and largely directed towards women, the *Good Sex Guide* acknowledged by its existence that sexual pleasure is a legitimate aspiration for women, and that it is the proper function of public service television to educate in how to achieve it. It signalled the *public* emergence of women as a sexual community. Presenter Margi Clarke, in her bearing and script, might be argued to epitomize the type of confident, assertive woman, at ease with her sexuality, which the series unambiguously endorsed and encouraged.

Playing a different role within the public sphere, but equally reflective in its way of the arrival of sex, and particularly female sex, in the mass audience television agenda, was *Scottish Women*. This programme, which has been running since 1987 in the Scottish television region, brings together in the studio 100 representative women to debate a topic presumed to be of particular interest to the female audience. Between 1987 and 1993, 14 issues of the programme were devoted to the theme of 'love and sex' (Terribas, 1995). Sex featured again in the edition of *Scottish Women* broadcast on 24 May, 1995 when, in her introduction, presenter Kay Adams acknowledged that now, 'more than we used to', women were talking and reading about sex. The ensuing discussion of female sexuality was led by Kathryn Hoyle, representing 'Sh!' – an 'erotic emporium for women' – who demonstrated a range of dildos, vibrators, 'love balls' and other sex toys. Writer Avedon Carol reinforced Hoyle's assertion of women's right to desire and practise active sexuality, before the audience of mixed class, ethnicity and sexual orientation joined in the debate. Both the content of the discussion (how to use love balls to achieve orgasm while running for the bus, for example) and the fact that it could be chosen as the appropriate subject-matter of mainstream women's television, are indicative of the cultural sexualization which had occurred by the mid-1990s in Britain. This programme, and the many others like it which have been broadcast on mass audience television, are clear evidence, as one observer puts it, that 'something new is happening. The novelty is not that women enjoy sex, and can be sexually greedy, or that they talk dirty when left alone together. ... What is new, and subversive of received opinion across the spectrum from radical feminist theory to cosy women's-mag sentimentality, is the way women's sexual appetites are being acknowledged and exploited'.[30]

Sex in magazines

Nowhere are these appetites acknowledged and exploited more transparently than in women's magazines which, if they once embodied a 'cosy sentimentality' about sex, now address in explicit terms everything from oral sex techniques to the making of pornographic videos. Not only do a new generation of women's magazines like *Marie Claire*, *Cosmopolitan*, *Company* and *New Woman* discuss these subjects, but they are also sold with considerable success largely on the strength of their sexual content.[31] Table 3.2 shows average circulation figures for the top six 'new generation' titles over the five years from 1989 to 1994. All increased their sales, with *Company* and *Marie Claire* – the most strongly associated with explicit sexual content – recording rises of 65 per cent and 175 per cent respectively.

Table 3.2 Average monthly circulations of six UK women's magazines, 1989–94

Title	July–December 1989	July–December 1994
Marie Claire	156 450	430 622
Company	185 364	305 592
She	207 507	281 109
Cosmopolitan	400 135	460 582
New Woman	230 551	257 024
Elle	209 034	230 996

(source: Adult Bureau of Circulation)

Typical of the trend was a four-page piece published by *Company* magazine in January 1995 entitled 'Suburban sex scandal'.[32] The article eavesdropped on the shooting of a film by the 'Shocking Pink' company, which specializes in pornography involving amateurs, giving it a gritty, 'readers' wives' quality, popular with the UK market. Written descriptions of the action were accompanied by photographic illustrations sufficiently explicit to have the magazine 'banned' by some newsagents. The article had a serious intent, however, exploring the workings of this marginal and hidden sector of the UK porn industry, and analysing the motivation of the mainly working-class women who are employed in it. In keeping with many of the articles and television programmes reviewed in this chapter, the piece was nonjudgemental in its approach.

> The anti-porn lobby would say the very presence of porn films is a catalyst for frustration, showing people in a degrading light. But for the girls at Shocking Pink they're in the business to relieve frustration – either to give substance to their meagre incomes and relieve the frustrations of being hard-up, or to fulfil their own fantasies.

The United States

Between 1984 and 1994, according to the *Index of Periodical Literature*, US periodicals printed some 180 articles about sexuality and the media (Fig. 3.2). Coverage was at its height, by this limited measure, in 1984–85 (20

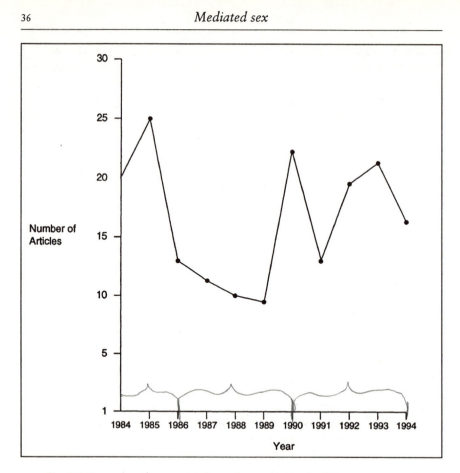

Fig. 3.2 Coverage of pornography and sexuality in the US newspaper and periodical press, 1984–94 (source: Index of Periodical Publications)

and 25 articles were indexed in these years respectively), 1990 (22 articles) and 1992–93 (19 in 1992 and 21 articles in 1993). The increase in coverage evident in 1984–85 is attributable, firstly, to the impact of the Minneapolis Ordinance on the public sphere. To a greater extent than in Britain, where the passage of the ordinance had no direct legal implications, in the United States it raised fundamental constitutional issues: in particular, the extent to which pornographers could expect constitutional protection under the terms of the First Amendment guaranteeing freedom of speech to all American citizens. The perceived threat to this right posed by the ordinance was the subject of many articles in 1984 and 1985. Many feminists wrote on the contradictions and dangers inherent in Dworkin and MacKinnon's tactical alliance with the religious right, adding the issue of 'feminist split' to the agenda. As one writer put it in the feminist *Ms*, the campaign in support of the ordinance had been 'transformed from a feminist case against violence to a Moral Majority protection of family values'.[33]

Much media discussion in this period, and since, was prompted by concerns about the morally disruptive and antisocial effects of new distribution technologies on the consumption of pornography in America. In the early to mid-1980s, telephone sex lines were proliferating, the number of cable television adult channels increasing, and domestic video-cassette players becoming an essential household item. As a consequence, pornography (particularly of the moving image) was becoming more available, not only to adults but also to children and adolescents. Fears about the societal implications of this, and the responses of legal and moral watchdogs, inspired much of the material indexed under 'pornography', 'sexuality' and related categories by the *Readers' Guide* in 1984–85, a pattern repeated a decade later when the rapid expansion of the information superhighway produced similar concerns about the corrupting effects of 'cyberporn'.[34]

A third exploration for the 1984–85 peak in coverage, and itself part of the political response to the above-mentioned concerns, was the announcement in early 1985 of the setting-up of the attorney-general's commission on pornography, which dovetailed with the feminist antipornography campaign to produce a kind of left-right consensus on the urgency of the pornography issue.

For the next four years coverage remained at a rate of around half the rate of 1984–85, peaking again in 1990. By this time journalistic interest had moved away from the 'problem' of pornography, whether defined in feminist or moral conservative terms, to the phenomenon of the growing prevalence of sexually explicit images in American culture, both high and low (*see* Chapter 8). Articles about the familiar evils of pornography and the sexually explicit were outnumbered by analyses of sex in mainstream film and television drama,[35] or by censorship issues raised by the work of such artists as Andres Serrano.[36] In December 1990 pop superstar Madonna released her 'Justify My Love' single and video, their frankly sexual content prompting much coverage.[37]

The emergence of sexuality as an artistic theme in American popular culture – the pornographication of the mainstream – remained prominent in periodical coverage of the early 1990s as novelists, film-makers and musicians flooded the market with artifacts of a sexually explicit nature. Catharine MacKinnon and others periodically appeared with books and articles presenting the antipornography feminist viewpoint[38] but, as in Britain, the tone of most coverage had by the early 1990s become, if not necessarily pro-pornography, considerably less critical of the sexually explicit. In ten years the American media had moved from a fiercely (with some exceptions) antipornography stance which united feminist and moral conservative campaigners, to a commonplace and relatively nonjudgemental acknowledgement of the public fascination (manifested in art and culture) with, and demand for, mediated sex in all its forms, including pornography. As already noted, the *Readers' Guide* does not tell us how straight news journalism covered these issues, and I have been unable to include television in this brief review, but the change in tone between 1984 and 1994, across the range of American periodicals from *Time* and *Newsweek* to *Ms* and *Mother Jones*, is unmistakeable. The explicit representation of sexuality in pornography, and in culture generally, not only increased in public visibility over this period but was, as *Newsweek* put it in 1992, being 'gentrified by artsy pretension and destigmatized out of viral necessity'.[39]

Notes

1 From the hit song of the same name by American female rap group Salt 'n' Pepa.

2 The 'watershed' is that time of day in the United Kingdom (9 pm, it is commonly accepted) after which television programmes with content not suitable for children may be broadcast on network services.

3 Films transmitted under the 'Red Triangle' logo included Derek Jarman's *Sebastiane*, noted (indeed, notorious) for its treatment of gay themes.

4 The National Viewers and Listeners Association was the umbrella group headed by Mrs Whitehouse, set up to monitor and campaign against excessive sex and violence on British television.

5 The *British Humanities Index* surveys the content of 'quality' newspapers such as *The Times*, *The Guardian*, and *Observer*, and periodical publications such as the weekly *Spectator* and *New Statesman*. Articles are indexed according to whom, or what, they are about. While these titles certainly do not include all the relevant articles published in the British press over the period surveyed, nor all the print media, they do allow a clear trend to be discerned.

6 Appleyard, B., 'Listen, sex is not an issue', *The Independent*, 27 October 1993.

7 Rodwell, L., 'At crime's hard core', *The Times*, 31 July 1987. The documentary on child pornography appeared as part of the *Cook Report* series in 1987.

8 Levin, B., 'Of modern human bondage', *The Times*, 22 February 1988.

9 Levin, B., 'The hateful shame of pornography', *The Times*, 30 May 1986.

10 For a brief account of the purpose of and motivation behind the ordinance, *see* Itzin, C., 'The campaign trail starts here', *The Guardian*, 2 February 1988.

11 Wallsgrove, R., 'A law against it', *New Statesman*, 27 January 1984.

12 Weatherby, W.J., 'A trend towards fewer peeps', *The Guardian*, 3 July 1984.

13 Fullerton, M., 'Through a glass darkly', *New Society*, 8 March 1984.

14 This issue was a response to the 'moral panic' which developed around the phenomenon of 'video nasties' in the early 1980s, and the media-orchestrated anxiety that young children were being exposed to explicit sex and violence in videos rented by adults. For a detailed discussion of the Video Recordings Act (as it became) see Marsh *et al.*, 1986.

15 Kuhn, A., 'Covering up sex', *New Statesman,* 24 February 1984. For a more substantial examination of the role of the state in regulating sexually orientated material, *see* Cooper, 1993. For a feminist critique of the public sphere/private sphere dichotomy, and its implications for the pornography debate, *see* Lacey, 1993.

16 Coward, R., 'What's in it for women?', *New Statesman*, 13 June 1986.

17 Coward, R., 'Sexual outlaws', *New Statesman*, 9 June 1989. Coward cites in this connection American writer Kathy Acker's short story 'Male', published by the *New Statesman* on April 25 1986. 'Male' described such acts as the rape of a female child and male-male sex, in the context of an avant-garde commentary on militarism and male sexuality.

18 Wilson, E., 'Against Feminist Fundamentalism', *New Statesman*, 3 June 1989.

19 Galloway, J., 'The phoney search for women's erotica', *New Statesman*, 21 December 1990.

20 Iley, C., 'Why women are not pawns of porn', *Sunday Times*, 7 August 1994.

21 Cockerell, M., 'When does a boob become an error?', *Sunday Times*, 30 October 1988. For a television documentary account of the treatment of sexual themes on British television see Cockerell's *Sex on Television*, produced by Panoptic for Channel Four and broadcast on Wednesday 2 November 1988.

22 Edwards, M., 'The facts of life', *Sunday Times*, 5 March 1995.

23 Cosgrove, S., 'In the midnight hour', *The Guardian*, 6 March 1995.

24 From the critique of the *Red Light Zone* prepared by viewer Caroline Isle to introduce the *Right to Reply* debate broadcast by Channel Four on 6 May 1995.

25 *Fetish* (Robert Seurcomor, 1994).

26 *NYPD Nude* (Margo Harkin, 1994).

27 *Viva Tabatha!* (Fiona Ross, 1994).

28 *The Sex Shogun of Shinjuku* (Gwyneth Hughes, 1994).

29 Two of the programmes most vulnerable to charges of gratuituous female nudity, it might be noted, were directed by men – *Holiday Snaps* (John Quick, 1994) and *Go! Go! Archipelago* (Paul McGuigan, 1994).

30 Hughes-Hartlett, L., 'Sex in a bold climate', *Sunday Times,* 12 April 1992.

31 For an account of the circulation battles between the top selling women's magazines, *see* Reid, S., 'Sexual Politics', *Sunday Times*, 16 July 1995.

32 Compton, E., 'Suburban sex scandal', *Company*, January 1995.

33 Blakeley, K., 'Is one woman's sexuality another woman's pornography?', *Ms*, 13 (7), April 1985.

34 *See*, for example, Elmer-Dewitt, P., 'On a screen near you: cyberporn', *Time*, 3 July 1995.

35 *See*, for example, Polskin, H., 'TV's getting sexier...', *TV Guide*, 7–13 January 1989, and Frankel, M., 'What's the sexiest scene in film?', *American Film*, September 1990.

36 Iannone, C., 'From 'Lolita' to 'Piss Christ', *Commentary*, January 1990.

37 *Newsweek*, *Time* and *People Weekly* were among those mainstream periodicals which covered extensively Madonna's use of sexuality in December 1990.

38 MacKinnon's book *Only Words* was published in early 1994, producing a flurry of reviews and commentaries on the continuing campaign to censor and ban pornography.

39 'The selling of sex', *Newsweek*, 2 November 1992.

4

Sexual representation, from antiquity to the Internet: history, definition, regulation

Destigmatized or not, sex in the media – particularly pornographic representations of sex – remains the object of legal and moral sanction in both Britain and the United States. At the same time, and despite nearly 150 years in which something called 'pornography' has circulated in capitalist societies, it remains curiously difficult to pin down as a category. 'I may not be able to define it precisely,' United States Justice Potter Stewart is famously reported to have said, 'but I know it when I see it'.[1] It has also been defined as 'books that one reads with one hand' (Polsky, 1967: p. 189). Both remarks, though light-hearted in tone, have the serious purpose of highlighting the difficulty of defining the key term around which the debates addressed in this book revolve. Sexuality in the media has become a public issue, principally, because of its allegedly pornographic quality. Yet, as the above statements imply, what *is* pornography, exactly? When does the media representation of sexual behaviour, the public articulation of sexual identity, the cultural expression of sexual desire, become subject to the contention and moral-legal regulation which we associate with the term 'pornography'? This chapter attempts to answer that question by reviewing and assessing the competing definitions of pornography which have, historically and currently, circulated in the public domain.

In providing a definition of pornography, we must also investigate the meanings associated with two other terms: first, obscenity, a concept frequently regarded as synonymous with pornography (most of the legislation which has been used to restrict or ban the pornographic does so on the grounds of its 'obscene' qualities; but, like pornography itself, as we shall see, precisely what constitutes obscenity defies neat definition); and, second, erotica.

If pornography and obscenity are, as it were, the 'evil twins' of the sexuality debate, the word erotica is frequently deployed as a positive counterweight, connoting the healthy, legitimate representation of sex. Once again, definitions vary and, alongside pornography and obscenity, we shall identify and seek to make sense of them in this chapter. Each of the terms is loaded with political, moral and aesthetic overtones, depending on who is doing the defining, and we will aim, by the conclusion of this chapter, to suggest definitions which can be consistently applied to all the categories of representation with which we are concerned. Before doing that, however, it is useful to note that while the twentieth century, with its dramatic developments in the sphere of communications technology, has been one in which debate about sexual representation has become intensely politicized and fractious, images of human sexuality and debate about their cultural significance are as old as civilization itself.

Sexual representation: an historical overview

As the Reagan administration's Meese Commission noted in its final report, sexuality has been a subject of human cultural expression 'almost since the beginning of recorded history' (1986: p. 235), a fact reflected in the artifacts of civilizations as old as those of ancient Greece and Rome. It was indeed the discovery by nineteenth century archaeologists of Greek and Roman pottery, and other relics depicting sexual behaviour in graphic images, which served as the catalyst for subsequent debates about and campaigns around pornography.

From the sixth to the fourth centuries BC sexually explicit pottery, depicting such activities as heterosexual copulation, orgies, and male homosexual bonding (although the depiction of oral or anal penetration was rare[2]) was being produced in Athens and Attica (Sutton, 1992; Shapiro, 1992). In Indian and Chinese civilizations of the first centuries AD, sexual behaviour was depicted with relative explicitness, as anyone who has read the *Kama Sutra* will know.

Arguably, however, the first true pornographer was the Italian artist Pietro Aretino, who in the 1530s wrote a series of sexually explicit sonnets, which were later illustrated with engravings. The resulting images, which came to be known as *Aretino's Postures*, are especially important in the history of sexually explicit representation because, in Lynn Hunt's words, '[he] brought together several crucial elements to form the basis of the pornographic tradition ... particularly the explicit representation of sexual activity . . . and the challenge to moral conventions of the day' (1993a: p. 26).[3] Aretino laid the ground for the expansion of pornography in Europe over the next two centuries by 'charting the terrain in which [it] was formulated, and by setting the parameters of its subject and the techniques of presentation' (Findlen, 1993: p. 107).

These engravings, and the texts which they illustrated, were probably the first images which could be described as pornographic in the modern sense of the term. Copies and imitations spread throughout Europe in the decades and centuries after their appearance, circulating among the relatively small male elites of political rebels and libertines. The nature of Aretino's audience, indeed, is important in understanding the social meanings of early pornography.

While there was already, by the sixteenth century, a tradition of sexual representation in European art (Lucie-Smith, 1991), the *Postures* presented an altogether more flagrant and shocking image of human sexuality, deliberately intended to flaunt the social and sexual mores of the time. Early pornography was sexually arousing to the point of inducing masturbation, as Samuel Pepys confessed rather shamedly after reading *L'Ecole Des Filles*, but it was also openly subversive, using sex as a satirical vehicle to attack the political establishment of early modern Europe. *L'Ecole Des Filles* (1655), the first acknowledged example of French pornography, presented 'a blend of philosophical and sexual subversiveness' (de Jean, 1993: p. 116) and commenced a tradition which culminated in the works of the Marquis de Sade who in the eighteenth century 'took the politically and socially subversive possibilities of pornography to their furthest extreme' (Hunt, 1993b: p. 330). In Restoration England too, sexually explicit novels tended to have the quality of political satire, being written and read by those who, though privileged members of the ruling elites, were infected by the radicalizing influence of emerging materialist and bourgeois philosophies.

Pornography, capitalism and the technology of reproduction

'The history of pornography and efforts to suppress it', it has been observed, 'are inextricably bound up with the rise of the new media and the emergence of democracy'.[4] The circulation of any sexual representation, pornographic or otherwise, was constrained until the eighteenth and nineteenth centuries by the undeveloped state of the media, and the lack of means of mechanical reproduction. *Aretino's Postures* and other early examples of the pornographic were produced and copied by hand. Only with the inventions first of printing and later of photography did sexually explicit works such as James Read's *Fifteen Plagues of a Maidenhead*, editions of Boccacio's *Decameron*, and John Cleland's *Memoirs of a Woman of Pleasure* (also known as *Fanny Hill*) begin to circulate in multiple reproductions.

Fanny Hill, which circulated in the late eighteenth century in relatively large quantities due to the new possibilities offered by the medium of print, also signalled the emergence of a more recognizably modern pornography, in so far as it had little or no political agenda, but pursued the aim of sexual arousal alone (Hunt, 1993b; Gordon, 1980). After the French Revolution and into the nineteenth century, apolitical pornography became the norm, although explicit sexuality continued to be used on occasion as a satirical or aesthetic tool with subversive potential. The commercialization of sexually explicit media on the one hand, and its depoliticization on the other, may be compared with the early history of journalism which, in England and elsewhere, had a radical anti-establishment function until the consolidation of capitalism and the bourgeoisie as its ruling class in the late eighteenth and early nineteenth centuries.[5]

The mass reproduction of visual pornography began with the invention of photography in the early nineteenth century, and the subsequent development of film. Images of sexual activity were part of the photographer's repertoire from the outset,[6] as they were of the early cinematographers. Linda Williams (1990) argues that modern film pornography grew indirectly out of Edward Musbridge's stop-motion experiments, published as *Animal Locomotions* in the late nineteenth century, which not only pioneered the technology and aesthetics of the moving image in general but also, she suggests, first 'fetishized' the female body for the benefit of the male viewer. Early 'stag'[7] films were being made and shown in public as early as 1904, to wealthy clients in brothel-type establishments (Koch, 1993).

Thereafter, as each new medium of reproduction emerged, it was used as a means of circulating images of sexuality. In the 1970s, video pornography (both in the sense of being shot and viewed on video-cassette) appeared and has since come to dominate the market. In the 1990s technologies such as CD-rom and the Internet are increasingly being adopted for use by the producers and consumers of pornography, producing new problems for those who would regulate such material (*see* below and Chapter 7).

What pornography is

Thus far, while using the adjective 'pornographic' to describe such works as *Aretino's Postures* and Cleland's *Fanny Hill*, we have avoided a definition of the term. The word pornography derives from the Greek *porne* and *graphe*, combined to form *pornographos*. *Pornographos*, as used by the Greeks, did not have the contemporary meaning of 'pornography' but referred to 'a specific subcategory of biography – tales of the lives of the courtesans – which may not contain any obscene material at all' (Parker, 1992: p. 91).[8] Henry argues that the Greek philosopher and writer Atheneus, active in the period AD 200–300, used the term 'pornographer' to mean someone who 'represents [prostitutes] in speech or in pictorial form, [who] admits knowledge of prostitutes and shares it publicly' (1992: p. 263), a usage which prefigures and anticipates contemporary antipornography feminist approaches. By the late eighteenth century *pornographe* was being used in France to refer to 'writing about prostitutes', or what one source describes as 'the depiction of whores' (Rabinowitz, 1992: p. 37).

The earliest modern usage of the term, to describe material 'associated with immorality and the need to protect society' (Hunt, 1993a: p. 14), has been traced to 1806 in France, and Etiene-Gabriel Peignot's *Dictionnaire* of sexually explicit books, among which he included *L'Academie Des Dames* (1660), *L'Ecole Des Filles* (1655) and Sade's *Justine* (1791). The term first appeared in the *Oxford English Dictionary* in 1857. Today it is listed as 'sexually explicit material ... intended to arouse'.

I will suggest here that the label 'pornography' signifies: a) a particular *content* with b) an *intention* to produce c) a particular kind of *effect*. In the remainder of this section we focus principally on the content and intentionality of pornography, while Chapter 5 below is devoted to the question of effect.

The liberal perspective

Our starting point will be the content of pornography since this is, in one sense, its least contentious quality. Irrespective of how one defines the significance or connotative meaning of pornography, most agree that its content is sex. Although Susan Sontag, in her influential essay on the subject, argues that 'what pornography is really about, ultimately, isn't sex but death' (1982: p. 105), the denotative content of images defined as pornographic is clear: human beings, individually, in couples, or in groups, engaged in sexual behaviour.

This initial, if misleadingly simple, statement of what constitutes the pornographic allows us to include the masturbatory poses and topless displays of men's magazines and tabloid newspaper pin-ups; depictions of simulated and actual sexual intercourse between couples and groups of all permutations; and the more exotic practices signified by the term 'deviant sexuality'. In the great majority of definitions one encounters, however, pornography not only depicts these activities but it does so explicitly. Here we come to our first etymological problem.

'Explicit' is defined in most dictionaries as 'plain', 'open', 'not merely implied'. These are all subjective concepts, the interpretation of which may vary from one individual to another. Thus, one writer defines pornography as 'the presentation in verbal or visual signs of human sexual organs in a condition of stimulation' (Peckham, 1969: p. 47). For others, the mere display of a vagina, penis, or breasts (regardless of whether or not they are 'in a condition of stimulation') can be pornographic to some people in certain conditions, as was made clear in the British debate about the banning of 'page three girls'.[9] Pornography, in other words, can refer to representations in which sexual penetration is connoted, as well as denoted; in which sexual activity is merely implied, rather than shown.

In acknowledgement of this fact, most commentators do not refer to 'pornography' alone, but to pornographies of the softcore and hardcore variety, where 'soft' is less graphic, and more connotative of sexual activity than 'hard'. Bill Thompson notes that definitions of soft and hard vary between cultures, reflecting particular histories and traditions. Thus, in the United States, softcore pornography corresponds to what would be regarded in Britain as hard, while American hardcore refers to 'images which show more than vaginal and oral sex, and all other minority-interest material' (1994: p. 2) (*see* Chapter 7 for a more detailed description of these materials).

What makes the relatively less explicit (or indeed implicit) representation of sexual activity nonetheless pornographic is its intention to arouse. The image of a topless woman in a television documentary about breast cancer is not pornographic, if there is no intention on the part of the producer to induce sexual arousal in his or her audience. A 'page three girl' in a British tabloid newspaper, on the other hand, is intended to have the effect of stimulating the viewer, as might the images in a men's magazine specializing in large breasts. To describe such images as explicit would be a misuse of the term. Arousing, on the other hand, they certainly are for some, and are intended to be.

The same condition of intentionality should be applied to all representations defined as pornographic. Graphic images of male-female penetration during sexual intercourse are frequently used in the context of sex education in schools, and on television. They are not pornographic, even if some viewers should find them arousing, if it is not their intention to arouse.

While, of course, the intention to arouse will normally be evident from the context in which a text is produced and distributed, it may not always be so. Sometimes the issue of intentionality will deliberately be blurred. Many of the 'safer sex' educational videos produced in the course of the HIV/AIDS epidemic contain scenes of male-female, male-male, and female-female sexual intercourse.[10] These depictions are intended not only to educate in the techniques of safer sex but also to convey the notion that such practices can be sexually satisfying (*see* Chapter 6). Thus, they are shot in such a manner as to be arousing for the communities to which they are addressed. Such films are an example of the increasing difficulty, in the post-AIDS environment, of separating the pornographic from the nonpornographic in a simple and unambiguous way.

Definitions of the pornographic as that mode of (more or less) explicit sexual representation which is intended to arouse were favoured by the first major official investigations of the subject: the Johnson Commission in the United States and the Williams Committee in Britain. The appeal of such a definition in those relatively liberal times lay in its neutral, nonjudgemental tone, reflecting the increased social tolerance of sexual diversity and adventurism which prevailed in those years. Those who seek to retain the spirit of that time retain the 'liberal' definition, or variants of it. King, for example, defines pornography as 'sexually orientated material of a graphic nature designed for recreation rather than education' (1993: p. 57). In a recent essay, Lynn Segal links this and similar definitions with what we can call the 'liberal' or 'libertarian' perspective in the sexuality debate: one founded on the belief, correct or otherwise, that pornography is harmless and should be more or less freely available (1993).

The radical feminist perspective

As we saw in Chapter 2 the liberal perspective has, since the mid-1970s, been challenged from two directions: the radical or cultural feminist position; and that of moral conservatism. These two perspectives accept, in broad terms, definitions of pornography as sexually explicit, intentionally arousing material, but dispute the liberal implication that the effects of this arousal, when it occurs, are harmless. Pornography, it is widely agreed, is a representation of sexual activity which positions the viewer or reader as a *voyeur*. The human subjects depicted in pornographic texts are objectified as purely sexual animals, their beings stripped down to the sexual essence for the voyeuristic pleasure of the spectator. This is particularly true of visual pornography (as opposed to literary texts, where conventional narrative plays a greater role in the structure of the work) and – within visual pornography – of photography and film especially. Linda Williams, as we saw, suggests that modern pornography really began with the invention first of photography, then of experiments with moving image, such as Musbridge's *Animal Locomotions* in the 1870s. These experiments endowed representations of the human body with 'a quality of credibility absent from other picture-making' (1990: p. 186). At the same time as objectifying the human body, photography made possible the heightened fetishization of the female, and positioned the male viewer (and the male photographer) as 'seeker of knowledge'.

The 'maleness' of pornography is of course what has given it its special place within the radical/cultural feminist worldview. Pornography represents sex, and seeks to arouse, but it does so in the social context of patriarchy. The objectification and fetishization of women present in much pornography is a reflection of male dominance, endorsing and reinforcing it. Its explicitness (however we may define that term) and its intention to arouse are not neutral characteristics of the text but demonstrations of male power. The images, and their arousals, are produced by and through the physical abuse and exploitation of the women whose bodies they depict.

The arousals of pornography, by dehumanizing and objectifying women, induce misogyny, with all this implies for male behaviour (in the sexual and other spheres). Thus, this branch of feminism rejects the liberal, nonjudgemental assessment of pornography, and replaces it with a focus on the violent, oppressive nature of the material. As Diana Russell's influential definition goes, pornography is 'material that explicitly represents or describes degrading or abusive sexual behaviour so as to endorse and/or recommend the behaviour as described' (1992: p. 315). In this sense, pornography's intended effect of arousal is at the same time an incitement to woman-hatred, an arousal which would 'bring harm to others, in particular to the women and sometimes children who are represented as the object of male arousal' (Cowrie, 1992: p. 132).

Perhaps the best-known definition of this type is the one developed by Andrea Dworkin and Catharine MacKinnon as they campaigned through the United States legal system to restrict the availability of pornography. In attempting to implement the Minneapolis Ordinance they proposed the following definition of pornography (Itzin, 1992: p. 435), the production and distribution of which should, they argued, be subject to civil litigation.

> Pornography is the sexually explicit subordination of women, graphically depicted, whether in pictures or in words, that also includes one or more of the following:
>
> i) women are presented as dehumanized sexual objects, things or commodities; or ii) women are presented as sexual objects who enjoy pain or humiliation; or iii) women are presented as sexual objects who experience sexual pleasure in being raped; or iv) women are presented as sexual objects tied up or cut up or mutilated or bruised or physically hurt; or v) women are presented in postures of sexual submission; or vi) women's body parts – including but not limited to vaginas, breasts, and buttocks – are exhibited, such that women are reduced to those parts; or vii) women are presented as whores by nature; or viii) women are presented as being penetrated by objects or animals; or ix) women are presented in scenarios of degradation, injury, abasement, torture, shown as filthy or inferior, bleeding, bruised, or hurt in a context that makes these conditions sexual.

Here, and in similar definitions, the explicit character of pornography is hardly as important as its degrading, humiliating, subordinating content, which may be present in soft- and hardcore pornography in equal measure. Pornography, for Dworkin, uses 'the medium of sex', in whatever form – print, photography, film, or video – to depict patriarchal hierarchy, objectification, submission and violence which, in the pornographic text, 'all become alive with sexual energy and meaning' (1991: p. 59).

The moral conservative perspective

From the moral conservative perspective pornography is distinguished not by its representation of misogynistic and patriarchal sexual behaviour but by the decontextualized, morally subversive character of its images. As the Longford report, driven by this perspective, put it in 1980, 'pornography is a representation which isolates one physical activity – sex or violence – from the social context which would justify it as an activity or portray its consequences' (quoted in Ellis, 1992: p. 150).

Moral conservatism in western societies is founded on adherence to Judaeo-Christian family values, which stress the virtues of the nuclear family, monogamous sexual relationships within marriage, and the reproductive rather than recreational functions of sexual behaviour. Pornography, of course, violates these values. The effects of pornography, on the nuclear family among other things, are considered in the next chapter. Here, we acknowledge the undeniably hedonistic quality of pornographic texts, celebrating as they do behaviours that are not only, in many cases, fantastical and removed from the real sexual experiences of most users, but precisely opposed to the constraints and restraints on sex lives which moral conservatism demands. Pornography generally represents sexual activity in every conceivable situation except that of monogamous marriage, and in circumstances where the reproduction of the species is hardly a major consideration. While this, for many, is a large part of its appeal, it clearly requires a negative response from religious or morally conservative views.

Definition and effect

Definitions of the pornographic, then, are closely connected with competing perspectives on the meaning and function of sexual behaviour, the significance of its representation, and notions of impact and effect. The moral neutrality of the liberal definition implies a 'weak effects' model, allied to a defence of individual rights and autonomy in choice of sexual lifestyle. Those liberal perspectives which are also feminist, and variants which have been adopted by large sections of the gay community, go further and assert (*see* Chapter 6) a strongly pro-social role for pornography in the affirmation and strengthening of minority or subordinated sexual identities. Radical feminism and moral conservatism, on the other hand, identify pornography (albeit for different reasons) as a fundamentally amoral/immoral category of representation, deeply implicated in negative social phenomena.

Pornography and the erotic

The radical/cultural feminist definition of pornography begs the question: can there be any mediated sexuality, in the context of a patriarchal society, which is not misogynistic, hierarchical or subordinating to women? For the majority of radical feminists, the answer is 'yes'. Pornography is a male creation, and thus a reflection of (misogynistic) male desires and fantasies. Not all representations of sexuality need articulate maleness in this way, however. Another category – erotica – can represent sexuality in nonhierarchical, nonsexist, nonsubordinating ways. Sensitive to accusations that they are fundamentally antisex, radical feminists have stressed the possibilities of erotica which, in their positioning of the viewer, and the construction of meaning within the structures of the texts concerned, are the opposite of pornography's brutalizing masculinity.

For Gloria Steinem, whose distinction between the two categories of representations has been influential, 'erotica is about sexuality, but pornography is about power and sex-as-weapon' (1980: p. 38). Implicit in Steinem's statement, and in all similar attempts to separate the erotic from the pornographic, is the view that sexuality is not, and never should be, about power, and that the exercise of power cannot be truly sexual. Where pornography is about violence, domination and lack of choice, erotica signifies mutuality, equality, and choice. Erotica can be as sexually explicit as pornography, but will lack 'the sexualized and sexually explicit dominance, subordination and violence' (Itzin, 1992: p. 18) of the latter.

Erotica has also been defined as a category of representation which, unlike pornography, accurately or authentically reflects the sexuality of the observer (Smith, 1988). This allows a distinction to be made, for example, between an image of lesbianism produced for men (a frequently recurring image in mainstream heterosexual pornography) and a (denotatively) similar image produced for lesbians or bisexual women. By this definition the British magazine *Lesbian Lusts*, published by a company associated with British pornography 'king' David Sullivan and 'intended to explore the language of female desire, of fantasy, of sexual and sensual contact between women', is pornography, since its main market is clearly male. The images in *On Our Backs* and *Lezzie Smut*, on the other hand, both magazines produced by and for women, are erotica (*see* Chapter 7). Erotica is defined, in this instance, not by its manifest content but in the context of its reception, i.e. women performing, as equals in the sexual stratification system, for other women, as opposed to being constructed as plaything-objects for men.

The deployment of the term 'erotica' to distinguish a politically correct sexual representation from one which is implicated in the maintenance of patriarchal oppression has become widespread, although it is a misleading usage. By 'erotic', psychiatrists and others who study the mechanisms of human desire mean that which induces sexual arousal. There is, however, no necessary connection between arousal and the representation of sexual behaviour between human beings. Leather, as is well known, can be deeply arousing for some men and women. Neither it, nor its representation, is thereby pornographic. Similarly, images of women's high-heeled shoes are erotic for some, but hardly pornographic.[11] In short, the pornographic and the erotic are entirely distinct categories, which overlap only to the extent that most people, whether they admit to it or not, find depictions of sexual activity arousing.

Pornography, erotica and mass culture

Despite this fact, the two terms have become commonplace in debates which attempt to separate 'legitimate' from 'illegitimate' sexual representations. For the feminist views referred to above, the dichotomy turns on the depiction and exercise of sexual power. Other, equally influential, approaches have used the concept of erotica to make aesthetic judgements about the 'artistic' quality of sexual representations, and to construct taste hierarchies based on these judgements. Feminist novelist Erica Jong has stated her view that 'erotica celebrates the erotic nature of the human creature ... and does so artfully, dramatically. Pornography, on the other hand, serves simply as an aid to masturbation, with no artistic pretensions and no artistic value'.[12]

One approach, heavily influenced by the Frankfurt School and mass society theorists of communication, views pornography as the mass cultural, commoditized form of sexual representation, implicated in the alienation and anomie which, according to this perspective, have characterized capitalism in the twentieth century. For Barbara Smith, 'pornography does not describe sexuality, it describes sexual *acts*. It solidifies white, male, heterosexual fantasies, and then commoditizes them' (1988: p. 179), as all culture has the tendency to be commoditized in capitalism. Erotica, on the other hand, is the authentic, uncommodified form of sexual representation: Art with a capital 'A'. Smith again: 'Erotica is sexualized Art and pornography is sexualized capitalism.' Mass-produced and consumed by the masses, pornography is that form of sexual representation manufactured principally for profit. From this perspective pornography is an economic, as well as a moral or political, category. Both pornography and erotica are defined 'in terms of their means of distribution and consumption and their place within the cultural spectrum' (Smith, 1988: p. 179), the former being part of the general system of mass culture, the latter distinguished by its artistic value. As Joel Korel puts it, 'pornography is the mass-cultural mode of sexual representation, which channels, directs and codifies the taboos and boundaries according to which desire is deployed. ... The erotic is also a mode of cultural representation, although ... it is not mass cultural' (1990: p. 161). For Korel and others of a similar view, eroticism can be subversive of dominant sexual values, while pornography is almost always pro-systemic and narcoticizing.

These distinctions lead us into a wider debate within cultural studies about the nature of aesthetic judgements, in which (in this specific context) the pornographic is viewed as 'trash' (low culture) while erotica can be defined as 'art' (high culture) and thus be deemed acceptable as an object of aesthetic analysis and discernment. Although Susan Sontag, in her seminal essay on 'the pornographic imagination', argued that some pornography could be viewed as interesting and important 'works of art' (1982: p. 86) more common is the effort to keep pornography separate from the culturally validated realm of Art.

D.H. Lawrence, writing in the 1930s, and himself strongly associated with the artistic exploration of sexual themes in novels which were denounced on their publication as pornographic, sought to distinguish between erotica and pornography in the following terms:

> In the first place, genuine pornography is almost always underworld, it does not come into the open. In the second, you can recognize it by the insult it offers, invariably, to sex, and to the human spirit. Pornography is the attempt to insult sex, to do dirt on it (1936: p. 23).

For Lawrence, in a variant of the mass-culture approach, mainstream bourgeois society, by driving sex underground, had by the time he was writing created a class of 'pornographic people' for whom 'the sex flow and the excrement flow is the same thing. ... It happens when the psyche deteriorates, and the profound controlling instincts collapse. This is the source of all pornography' (1936: p. 27). For Lawrence, as for many others, pornography was a dirty, degrading, humiliating representation of sex, a deviation; while erotica was valid, healthy and natural. As John Ellis observes, pornography was then, and largely remains, 'the pariah of representational practices' (1992: p. 158).

Pornography denotes the sexually explicit, but it connotes the forbidden, the shameful, the that-which-should-remain-hidden. Although, as Chapter 3 noted, it can be argued that a general cultural destigmatization of the sexually explicit has been under way since the 1980s, the dimensions of shame and taboo remain central to all debate around the pornographic. To use pornography, or to defend its use, has not historically been something one could do openly, in public. Even today the vast majority would deny any interest (other than public-spirited or scholarly) in the subject.

This debate is not a new one, and it applies not only to pornography. For cultural critics of the postmodern school it is simply another example of the recurring elitist attempt to distinguish aesthetically between high and low culture; to impose taste hierarchies on society as a whole which devalue the popular. As such, the pornography/erotica dichotomy is a false one, and the emergence of pornography as a cultural category is best understood as an attempt by the bourgeoisie of nineteenth-century Europe to contain and control 'mass' (in the sense of popular) culture, in the face of the threat posed by new and democratizing communication technologies.

I described earlier how explicit representations of sexual activity were known in the cultures of ancient Greece and Rome as long ago as 500 BC. The word 'pornography', however, was not commonly used in English until the discovery by archeologists in the mid-nineteenth century of sexually explicit paintings and artifacts at Pompeii and other sites which were then catalogued and removed from public view. At this time 'pornography' meant 'a genre of [sexually explicit art] available to bourgeois men who could declare that their interest was scholarly. What defined it from the start was that it was forbidden to the general public' (Rodgerson and Wilson, 1991: p. 18). Early pornography, from the engravings of Aretino to the first sexually explicit novels, had an exclusive, elite audience of scientists and art connoisseurs who could justify their looking at such images. Exclusivity could not be maintained, however. By the end of the nineteenth century, with the growth of the urban proletariat, literacy was spreading rapidly and developments in print and photographic technology were expanding the possibilities of image reproduction. In the words of the US Attorney-General's Commission:

> As printing became increasingly economical, printed materials became more and more available to the masses. Thus, the kind of sexually explicit material that had circulated relatively freely in England among the elite during the eighteenth century now became more readily available to everyone. With this increased audience came an increase in demand, and with the increased demand came an increase in supply. ... And because the audience was more broad-based, the material itself became not necessarily more explicit, but certainly briefer, simpler, and more straightforward (Meese, 1986: p. 261).

In keeping with the 'Victorian values' of the time, the cultural elite which had hitherto monopolized the consumption of sexually explicit material developed a fear of the growing urban mass and its potential for moral degeneration. As pornography became more widely available to 'the great unwashed' in the form of sexually explicit books and photographs, so the fear grew that it would 'corrupt the minds and morals of those into whose hands it might come' (Kendrick, 1987: p. 188). Thus a 'discursive distinction' (Kipnis, 1993: p. 138) began to take shape, with sexual representation being separated into the legitimate and the illegitimate, the worthy and the unworthy – categories related not to manifest qualities of the images in question but to the socio-economic status and assumed corruptibility of those most exposed to them. For Kendrick, 'the [subsequent] history of pornography has been a vast, frustrating endeavour to separate the valuable from the worthless' (1987: p. 158) – to clearly distinguish the artistically valid representation of sexual behaviour from the publicly sanctionable zone of the pornographic. From this point of view, and without regard to the message-content of the image, the emergence of pornography as a cultural and legal category was a part of the process whereby the dominant moral values of the time were imposed upon the public as a whole, and the subordinate working masses in particular. In Bill Thompson's account the growing 'problem' of pornography was, like the campaign against prostitution which also took place in nineteenth-century Britain, part of a 'crusade' by society's moral arbitors and cultural elites 'to promote and determine society's unofficial but 'public' attitude toward all sexual behaviour, especially that of women' (1994: p. 9).

Pornography, obscenity and the law

The progress of this crusade, if such it was, was marked by the state's adoption from the seventeenth century onwards (in Europe and later the United States) of a steadily more interventionist posture towards sexually explicit material than had been the case before the eighteenth century. As part of this process the concept of obscenity emerged to become virtually synonymous with pornography. In 1580, as part of the English state's campaign against the developing 'free press', an Obscenity Bill was passed, outlawing 'licentious' material. It did not function effectively, however, and early sexually explicit works, such as James Read's *Fifteen Plagues of a Maidenhead* survived attempts at prosecution. The first conviction under this legislation was of a Sir John Sidley of London in 1633, not for publishing an obscene book, but for having urinated from his balcony onto the crowd passing in the street below (Goldstein and Kant, 1971). Notwithstanding the comic mental picture conjured up by this event, it signalled the onset of what Foucault calls 'the great prohibitions' on sexual expression and behaviour which accompanied the seventeenth century (1990: p. 114), as the embryonic bourgeois state strove to extend its control over human sexuality.[13]

The first conviction for the offence of 'obscene libel', setting the precedent for the successful prosecution of a number of sexually orientated books and pamphlets in the first half of the eighteenth century, was secured in 1728 against Sir Edmund Cull's *Venus in the Cloisters*. By the nineteenth century, sexually explicit materials were being regularly and effectively suppressed on the grounds of their obscenity.

The 1857 Obscene Publications Act defined obscenity as 'something offensive to modesty or decency or exposing or suggesting unchaste or lustful ideas or being impure, indecent, or lewd' (quoted in Thompson, 1994: p. 14), establishing as sanctionable 'those things considered disgusting, offensive, filthy, foul, repulsive', and 'making public that which society decrees should remain hidden' (Downs, 1989: p. 9). With this legislation the state, and moral campaigners such as members of the 'vice' societies established by Willam Wilberforce in the late nineteenth century, implemented a far-reaching censorship of sexually orientated materials, allied to the dissemination of ideas about sexuality and sexual behaviour which had a major impact on women in particular. The dichotomy of 'good girl/bad girl' dates from this period, as does the effort to control and regulate 'wayward' female sexuality by such means as incarceration in mental institutions. Literary novels by Flaubert, Maupassant and others were also censored, as the moral crusades continued into the twentieth century. In the United States, moral campaigner Anthony Comstock set up 'Societies for the Suppression of Vice' and launched a personal crusade against all manner of sexual discourse. In Britain, the sex-educational books of Marie Stopes, intended to help women control their reproductive functions, and the novels of Lawrence and Joyce were attacked.[14] Then and since, the United States constitution has permitted legal assaults on the sexually explicit if they could be shown to be 'obscene', i.e. if:

> 1) the average person, applying contemporary community standards, would find that the work, taken as a whole, appeals to the prurient interest; and 2) the work depicts or describes, in a patently offensive way, sexual conduct; and 3) the work, taken as a whole, lacks serious literary, artistic, political, or scientific value (Meese, 1986: p. 241).

The British legal system defines obscenity in the 1964 Obscene Publications Act as material the effects of which 'if taken as a whole [are] such as to tend to deprave and corrupt persons who are likely, having regard to all the relevant circumstances, to read, see, or hear the matter contained in it' (Hawkins and Zimring, 1988: p. 70). This amended the 1959 Obscene Publications Act which, in response to the zealotry of some moral campaigners, followed the US model by enshrining in law a distinction between obscene materials and sexually explicit 'art' (of redeeming value and thus protected from censorship). This explains why, in Britain, the extremely explicit works of the Marquis de Sade (as well as graphic sexually orientated novels by contemporary writers like Nicholson Baker and Thomas Pynchon) can be bought in respectable bookshops throughout the country.

Both definitions reinforce the highly subjective nature of the pornography debate. In the US case, terms like 'average', 'contemporary community standards' and 'prurient' have culturally specific meanings, so that standards of obscenity in Texas or Arkansas will differ greatly from those of California and New York. Definitions of the 'obscene' are relevant only to particular communities at particular times, while a sexually explicit image may only be sanctioned as 'obscene' if the community within which it is circulated declares it to be so. In Britain, too, continually shifting notions of depravity and corruption, as well as the fluid nature of the art/porn dichotomy (*see* Chapter 8), make objective, rational judgements on allegedly obscene materials difficult to make.

The difficulty of legislating around concepts of such ambiguity and relativism, combined with the impact of the sexual revolution, led to the liberalization of sexual censorship regimes from the 1950s onwards, fuelled in the United States by the 'weak effects' findings of the Johnson Commission, and in Britain by the Williams Committee. While Britain remains considerably more illiberal than America in what is considered by the law to be acceptable for public consumption (the erect penis remains wholly beyond the pale, for example) it cannot be argued that the moral conservative crusades of the post-World War II period, in contrast to their pioneering antecedents of the nineteenth and early twentieth centuries, have succeeded in their objectives. Indeed, as Bill Thompson has argued, the most powerful and effective lobby for the banning and censorship of pornography in the last decades of the twentieth century has been the feminist movement. In the United States, as we have seen, Catharine MacKinnon and Andrea Dworkin led the way with the Minneapolis Ordinance, which sought to make the production, sale and use of pornography an actionable civil offence. In Britain, feminists in the Labour Party and elsewhere have campaigned vociferously against 'top shelf'[15] magazines and 'page three girls' in the tabloids, although without success.[16]

While there have clearly been some unexpected and uncomfortable alliances between sections of the feminist movement and the moral conservative lobby, it is obvious to anyone who studies the views of both groups that their reasons for opposing pornography are completely different: for the moral conservatives, the longstanding concern of the religious bourgeoisie to regulate sexual behaviour in the interests of social stability; and, for the feminists, the belief that the depiction of women in pornography plays an important part in the continuing survival of misogynistic ideas and behaviours.

Towards a working definition

The history of pornography's emergence as a cultural category, and subsequent efforts to formulate a serviceable definition of it, show above all that the term is political in the broadest sense. Its first modern usage in the nineteenth century, and its subsequent evolution as a moral and aesthetic category, can be clearly linked to developments in the economic, social, technological and cultural lives of the societies in which something called 'pornography' has circulated. No definition can be fully understood without first situating it in the context of public debates about the role of women, or the nature of art, or the moral rights and responsibilities of a community.

Pornography, and the elements said to comprise it, are shifting, slippery things, changing their content and meaning over time and between cultures. Even the most 'neutral' attempt to define pornography in terms of its content and intention implies some communal agreement as to the meaning of 'sexually explicit'. Linking pornography with obscenity, as many courts have found, is by no means a straightforward process, given that community standards of offensiveness, to the extent that they can be fully known, are constantly changing. Efforts by cultural commentators to fit pornography into the high culture/low culture dichotomy are as elitist and questionable as similar efforts in other areas of media production.

In bringing this account of a concept and its evolution to a close, I will present pornography in relation to a series of categories around which the debates outlined above have been organized. I began by seeking to define pornography in terms of its manifest content (sexually explicit), its intention (to arouse) and its effects (the harms which it inflicts on society). Alternatively, pornography may be described in terms of the following categories: aesthetic, moral, legal, and political.

As an aesthetic category, pornography is that type of sexually explicit image which lacks the qualities of art, however they may be defined, in literature, photography, cinema, or any other medium in which the pornographic can find expression. While erotica is, for many commentators, the artistic expression of sexuality, pornography is trash, produced for profit rather than cultural enlightenment, to stimulate only on the level of physical sexuality, as opposed to the intellectual, life-enhancing qualities of the truly erotic. Porn is mass culture, while erotica is sexually explicit art for the cultural elite.

As a legal category, pornography is closely linked, if not always synonymous with, the obscene. Not all that is obscene belongs to the realm of pornography, but, to the extent that pornography is subject to legal control and sanction, it is because of its perceived offensiveness to contemporary community standards of what can be depicted in public about sex.

From the moral viewpoint, pornography is that which subverts the dominant moral values of a community: in western capitalist societies, the values of family and religion. Moral lobbies have campaigned so vociferously against pornography because it is believed to be the antithesis of family-based, reproduction-orientated sexuality.

Finally, as a political category, pornography is indicted as a key instrument in the patriarchal struggle for the subordination of women. Pornography is offensive to feminism not because of its assault on family values but because of its indirect and direct violation of women as a social stratum.

Around each of these categories debate rages about the meaning of pornography and the harms which it causes. My intention in this chapter has been to set the terms of that debate by outlining the currently dominant positions within them: aesthetic, legal, moral, and feminist. In subsequent chapters the merits of the protagonists will be examined in more detail. In doing so, we must examine more closely the debate about pornography's negative effects, on the one hand, and its positive 'uses and gratifications' on the other.

Notes

1 Justice Stewart stated, in his 1964 judgement on material accused of obscenity, 'I shall not attempt further to define the kinds of material I understand to be embraced within that shorthand description; and perhaps I could never succeed in intelligently doing so. But I know it when I see it' (quoted in Hoff, 1989: p. 22).

2 Various forms of nonpenetrative sex between males were commonly depicted, such as one man putting his penis between the closed thighs of another.

3 Aretino also used 'the form of the dialogue between women [and] the discussion of the behaviour of prostitutes' (Hunt, 1993: p. 26) identified by Hunt as defining characteristics of the earliest pornographic writings.

4 Elmer-Dewitt, P., 'On a screen near you: cyberporn', *Time*, 5 July 1995.

5 For a discussion of the historical development of journalism in England, *see* McNair, 1996.

6 For examples of early pornographic photographs, *see Caught looking* (Ellis, ed., 1986).

7 The name given to short pornographic films addressed to a male audience, and usually consumed in all-male contexts such as 'stag parties', strip shows, and reunions.

8 Parker notes that another ancient Greek genre – *an-aiskhunto-graphii* ('writers of shameless things') – was more 'pornographic', as we understand the term today, than *pornographos*, comprising as it did a form of early sex manual.

9 In 1986, British Labour MP Clare Short introduced a bill to parliament which would have banned the photographs of topless models that appear on page three of several tabloid newspapers. For an account of the origins of 'page three', *see* McNair, 1996.

10 *See*, for example, *Well sexy women: the lesbian guide to sexual health* (Pride Video Productions, 1993), *Getting it right: safer sex for young gay men* (Pride Video Productions, 1993), and *Seriously sexy: safer sex for young people* (Paradox Films, 1993).

11 Some individuals find conventionally nonsexual objects, such as dead bodies, amputated limbs and autoasphyxia, sexually arousing, i.e. erotic. The clinical term for this condition is paraphilia.

12 Quoted in 'The place of pornography', a round-table discussion spon-

sored and published by *Harper's* magazine, November 1984. Italian political sociologist Norberto Bobbio, in a contribution to the debate written in 1961, takes a rather different tack, associating erotica not with 'quality' artistic endeavour but with bourgeois decadence. 'Eroticism', he writes, 'has always been in every epoch the unfailing fruit of the economically untroubled lifestyles of the idle rich.' For Bobbio all culture, whether art or trash, is awash with 'unbridled eroticism. ... We have lost any capacity to distinguish between freedom of artistic expression and pornography' ('Bad sex makes for bad politics', *The Guardian*, 12 October 1990).

13 For Foucault, the emergence of capitalism and the corresponding intensification of state regulation of behaviour was not an attempt to stop public discourse of, and participation in, sex, but to rationalize that discourse and place sex within the realms of science, law and management. From the seventeenth century, sex became the object of scientific exploration, and legal, moral and hence social regulation.

14 For an account of the moral outrage against Stopes' *Married Love* in 1923–24, *see* Rose, 1992.

15 The softcore magazines sold in mainstream newsagents throughout the United Kingdom, so called because they are displayed on the top shelves of magazine racks, out of reach of children.

16 Rejecting the feminist argument that this lobbying is grounded in a progressive political struggle against cultural sexism and misogyny, Bill Thompson connects it directly to the 'four-hundred year old crusade of the middle classes to label various kinds of sexual material 'obscene', 'offensive' or 'pornographic' ... in order to imply [that] they possessed some innate and dangerous quality ... and must, therefore, be outlawed' (1994: p. 6). For Thompson, the post-1970s radical feminist rationale for censoring pornography is 'really religious' (1994: p. 40).

|5|

The harms pornography does: causes and effects

Since pornography began to be perceived as a public issue in the nineteenth century, the debate has centred on its causative role in a variety of undesirable social phenomena: its negative effects on individual behaviours and group values; its capacity to stimulate antisocial responses in those exposed to it; and the impact which it may have on the urban environments where it is sold. One's attitudes to these and other alleged effects largely determines how one views the validity of legal, moral and political campaigns to restrict or ban pornography and other media depictions of sex. This chapter discusses the range of pornography's alleged effects, and the nature and quality of the evidence used in proving or disproving them. Not all discussion about the harms and benefits of pornography can be incorporated within the cause-effect paradigm, of course, and the next chapter will continue the discussion with a review of current writing on the uses, gratifications and meanings of pornography. Undoubtedly, however, the cause-effect paradigm has been dominant in this debate, and has structured the greatest proportion of empirical research undertaken on the subject.

The effects debate, as it relates to pornography, can be grouped into five broad categories. First, there are assertions about effects on *behaviour*, and pornography's power to stimulate behavioural responses. Second, there is the issue of pornography's effects on *morality*, i.e. the extent to which individual and group values can be shaped by the consumption of pornography. Third, the relationship between pornography and *ideology* may be examined. In so far as an ideology of patriarchy is still prevalent in modern capitalism, countered by an ideology of feminism through which women struggle and compete for equality and power, what role does pornography play in reproducing and reinforcing these systems of ideas? A fourth category of effect concerns the impact of pornography on the lives of those who are employed, manipulated or coerced as performers into making it. The fifth category, finally, is *environmental*, concerned with pornography's effects on social structures such as the 'combat zones' and 'red light districts' of inner cities where it is typically displayed and sold.

In examining the nature and extent of these effects, three types of evidence are routinely deployed: the results of experimental studies normally conducted in controlled laboratory conditions; anecdotal evidence obtained in interviews and personal testimonies; and statistical data purporting to show links between the existence and availability of pornography and certain (anti) social phenomena. As we shall see, each of these types of evidence has problems of reliability and applicability associated with it, a methodological fact which has undoubtedly contributed to the difficulty of resolving the pornography debate satisfactorily.

Pornography and behaviour

Systematic scientific research into the effects of pornography on behaviour began with the work of the US Presidential Commission on Obscenity and Pornography in 1968 (the Johnson Commission), and has since been one of the main foci of empirical social science in the western world, generating many hundreds of research papers and books.[1] Some have found in this vast body of work 'firm data as to what kinds of effects to expect from what kinds of erotica on what kinds of individuals under clearly specified conditions' (Byrne and Kelley, 1984: p. 9). The British researcher Hans Eysenck has concluded that 'there is now very little doubt that the portrayal of sex ... in the media does have some important effects on at least some people' (1984: p. 317).

On the contrary, substantial doubts remain, and the status and meaning of the data which have been collected are rather more contentious than these authors allow.

Stimulus-response

Research into the effects of pornography on behaviour can be divided into two phases. The first, beginning in the 1960s, and driven by the proliferation of explicit sexuality in the media which was a feature of that decade, supported the sexual liberalism of the period by appearing to show that there was no link between the availability of pornography and antisocial or criminal behaviour. The key statement of this finding was contained in the Johnson Committee's report, published in 1970 during the first Nixon administration. Reviewing the research evidence on effects on a variety of

levels, the members of the Commission reported that they could 'not conclude that exposure to erotic materials is a factor in the causation of sex
crimes or sex delinquency' (quoted in Baird and Rosenbaum, 1991: p. 24).
In the Commission's assessment there was no evidence of a correlation
between the performance of crime, sexual or otherwise, and exposure to or
use of pornography. Indeed, 'available research indicates that sex offenders
have had less adolescent experience with erotica than other adults' (Baird
and Rosenbaum, 1991).[2] The Commission went further, and suggested that
there was evidence of a negative correlation between the availability of
pornography and the incidence of sex crime, i.e. as the quantity of pornography in circulation increased, the rate of crime went down.

The main evidence cited in this connection was the work of the Danish
researcher Kutchinsky, who argued that following the liberalization of
pornography in Denmark in 1962, and the resulting 'porno-wave' which
engulfed the country, the incidence of serious sex crimes – rape in particular
– did not increase. Discussing his findings in a later article, Kutchinsky
asserted that 'during the same period there was a strong increase of nearly
all other crimes, including nonviolent sexual crimes, while all other sexual
crimes decreased. The same is true in Sweden, where pornography was also
legalized and became abundantly available at the same time as in Denmark'
(1990: p. 244). In Germany too, Kutchinsky argued, the incidence of rape
went down as access to pornography became easier. Thus, 'while no one
claims it was pornography that led to the decrease, these developments leave
hardly any doubt that pornography does *not* cause rape' (1990: p. 245).

This optimistic reading of the evidence was echoed in another key document, the UK government-commissioned Williams Report, published in
1979. Sexually explicit material – whether labelled as pornography or erotica – did not appear to be the cause of antisocial behaviour. Both the
Johnson and Williams investigations lent support to the relatively liberal
regimes of censorship which had emerged in most western capitalist societies following the sexual revolution since, without clear evidence of harm,
there was little justification for the restriction of sexually explicit materials.
With the rise of feminism on the one hand, however, and the moral conservative lobby on the other, these conclusions were cast into doubt.

Two strategies were adopted by the opponents of liberalism. Firstly, the
quantity and quality of the evidence marshalled to support the liberal perspective was questioned. It was argued, for example, that the Johnson and
Williams reports were written when research into the effects of pornography was still relatively rare. That which was available, such as Kutchinsky's
correlational study, had 'serious flaws' (Court, 1984: p. 147). Contrary to
his claims, Kutchinsky's work had not proven a decline in sex crime after
pornography became widely available in the Scandinavian countries. The
reduction in the incidence of *recorded* sex crime was mainly attributable, it
was argued, to the removing of certain minor offences from the statute
book.

The second strategy employed was to argue that the nature of pornography had fundamentally changed since the late 1960s and early 1970s. Specifically, pornography had become much more violent, linking sex and aggression in unprecedentedly explicit and direct ways. From the outset, social science research on pornography had distinguished between the effects of violent pornography and that in which violence was minimal or absent. The first category had always been regarded as potentially much more dangerous, on the grounds that if there *were* discernible behavioural effects of exposure to media, combining sex and aggression in pornographic images might link the two in the fantasy worlds and real-life behaviours of some individuals (Malamuth and Donnerstein, 1984). The association of sex and violence found in some pornography, it was feared, could encourage or stimulate (male) users to associate the two in real-life social contexts, and thus cause physical harm to others in the pursuit of sexual satisfaction.

The increasing emphasis on the distinction between violent and nonviolent pornography which characterized the debate in the 1980s was clearly related to the ascendancy of feminist definitions of pornography as the representation of abusive or degrading sexual activity (*see* Chapter 4), and as that which communicates 'rapist values and ways of abusing women' (Dworkin, 1990a: p. 32). It also coincided with the political ascendancy, in the United States especially, of a conservative moral lobby concerned to halt what was seen as the corrupting spread of pornography, and which embraced the violence issue as a weapon in its armoury.

In the key document of this phase, the report of the Attorney-General's Commission on Pornography (Meese, 1986), an attempt was made to develop a typology of pornography which allowed reconciliation of the earlier research findings with a contemporary agenda of censorship and restriction. For the Meese Commission, pornography could be divided into three categories, defined in order of their alleged dangerousness as: sexually violent; nonviolent but degrading; nonviolent, nondegrading.

Meese acknowledged (on the basis of some 20 years of research evidence) that the latter category of material was not a cause of antisocial behaviour. 'From a purely social scientific perspective there is no cogent evidence that materials in this class have a predominantly negative behavioural effect' (Meese, 1986: p. 28). Again: 'there is no persuasive evidence to date supporting the connection between [this] material and acts of sexual violence' (p. 337). Donnerstein *et al.*, leaders in this field of research, agreed that 'the data, overall, do not support the contention that exposure to nonviolent pornography has significant adverse effects' (1987: p. 85) and that there was 'no evidence for any 'harm'-related effects from sexually explicit materials' (Donnerstein and Linz, 1990: p. 233).

Material in the first category, however, in which images of sex and violence are combined, was not viewed so benignly. Reviewing the available social scientific literature, such as that assembled by Donnerstein *et al.* (1987), the Meese Commission found evidence that sexually violent material tended to stimulate an aggressive response in the viewer/reader who, it was inferred, would then be more likely to commit real-life acts of violence. As the report put it, 'depictions of sexual violence increase the likelihood that rape myths [i.e. the belief that women who say no to a sexual advance really mean 'yes'] are accepted and sexual violence towards women condoned' (Meese, 1986: p. 1032). This type of material caused sexual violence by normalizing it for the viewer, breaking down his inhibitions and increasing his propensity to behave violently in a sexual context.

Material which was, by the Commission's categorization, 'non violent but degrading' had a tendency to produce similar effects, though not as strongly.

By the mid-1980s, then, social science research had advanced beyond the 'weak effects' conclusions of the 1960s and 1970s to present a more complex hypothesis focusing on the adverse effects of exposure to images of sexual aggression. From this perspective there was an important distinction to be made between a category of harm-free (in behavioural effects terms) pornography and one which induced aggression in the process of consumption, leading ultimately to real-life sexual violence and coercion. A related conclusion of the Meese Commission was that men predisposed to aggressive and violent sexual behaviours such as rape were more likely to be aroused by the 'forced sex depictions' (1986: p. 1031) of pornography, which in turn could trigger real-life rape attacks.[3]

The emergence of a 'strong effects' hypothesis in relation to (violent) pornography was the product, as we noted earlier, both of political feminism, which linked pornography directly to the oppression of women within patriarchy, and the moral conservative and religious right, which blossomed and found expression in the United States in the years of the Reagan administration. However, the fact that the assertion of pornography's strong negative effects on male sexual behaviour has politico-ideological roots does not, in itself, provide grounds for its dismissal. As the Meese report acknowledged, evidence and proof in such a debate can never be fully conclusive, and if even one individual in a society, or 10, or 100, was 'stimulated' by the viewing of pornography to commit a sexual assault, rape or sexual murder, this might be thought sufficient justification to restrict further or even ban the circulation of such material.

In assessing the respective validities of the 'weak' and 'strong' effects hypotheses, as they are applied to sexually explicit materials, we have to consider the quality of the evidence advanced by their protagonists, such as statistical data of the type assembled by Kutchinsky in Denmark, and criticized for the reasons already noted. The old adage that there are lies, damned lies and statistics is no less true in the pornography debate than in any other sphere of social reality subject to statistical analysis. Numbers can be manipulated to prove that sex crimes have gone up since the post-1960s spread of pornography, or down. Some figures show that convicted sex offenders use more pornography than the average male; others that they use less. As a rule, protagonists in the pornography debate select those statistics which reinforce their case, and reject contradictory evidence. This is an inevitable feature of social scientific debate, and one which should lead us to regard all figures with a degree of scepticism and caution.

Less open to challenge might be thought to be the recorded statements of convicted sex murderers, such as Ted Bundy in the United States, who have testified to their interest in the use of pornography before, during, and after the commission of a crime. Caputi cites Federal Bureau of Investigation figures that 81 per cent of serial killers questioned had an 'interest' of this kind in pornography (1992: p. 205). As with statistical evidence, however, analysts are required to be sceptical of the sex offenders' own accounts of why they offended. Criminals often employ rhetorics of justification and vocabularies of motive as part of a defence strategy to suggest diminished responsibility. Cameron and Frazer argue, from an avowedly antipornography feminist position,[4] that the 'porn-blaming' (1992: p. 378) of Bundy and others is no more than the self-justification of an individual selecting a plausible 'reason' for his deviance (since there are so many who believe that pornography has such effects) from those available in the public sphere. We have already noted the evidence of some studies that sex offenders consume less pornography than the average nonoffending male. Kutchinsky, on the other hand, detects some correlation between the use of pornography and sexual deviance (as opposed to sexual offending), but argues that the relationship is not one of cause and effect. 'Sexual deviants', he suggests, 'become users of pornography not because they are sexually deviant, but because their sexual deviance makes them sexually lonely' (1990: p. 239). Pornography, for this group, is a substitute for real sex.

The most controversial, yet apparently most 'scientific', data used in the debate on pornography's behavioural effects are those contained in the vast number of laboratory-based studies conducted by social scientists in the United States. This research, as presented by Donnerstein, Linz, Penrod, Malamuth, Zillman, Bryant and others in hundreds of books and articles since the early 1980s has provided the main empirical support for the thesis that violent pornography stimulates real-life aggression.

In evaluating this research, one must begin by acknowledging the ethical and methodological difficulties which arise from efforts to measure levels of aggression and propensity to violence in individuals. It is practically impossible to conduct group experiments on the effects of exposure to pornography outside a laboratory (who will allow a Donnerstein or a Malamuth to observe them in the privacy of their own bedroom, particularly if violence or coercion is involved?). Laboratory research is therefore essential. Inside the lab, however, subject groups tend not to be representative of the population as a whole (students are often recruited) and realistic experiments difficult to design. The research cannot permit a real act of sexual violence to occur, so artificial substitutes, or indicators that sexual violence would occur in comparable circumstances outside the laboratory and in the absence of the researcher, have to be found. These include the use of aggression indices measured by physiological factors such as pulse, and behavioural responses such as a subject's willingness to inflict electric shocks on a 'victim'. A typical experiment might seek to show that pornography combining images of sex and aggression can be arousing to a 'normal' man, i.e. one who has no record of sexual aggression or violence. A simple device measuring penile tumescence will enable this physiological reaction to be assessed. Another might investigate the link between arousal and aggression by first showing subjects examples of pornographic material, and then inviting them to inflict electrical shocks on female researchers (the shocks are not real, of course, although the subject is assumed not to realize this). The female researcher's involvement as 'victim' in the experiment will be disguised, so that the subject believes the 'punishment' to be real. Thus, a capacity to inflict pain by this means can be read as a propensity to commit violence, after stimulation by sexually explicit material, in the real world.

Given that ethical and practical considerations constrain the design of more realistic experimental procedures, the artificiality of those which are routinely used greatly limits their applicability to social reality. Firstly, the levels of aggression which have been observed in laboratory conditions cannot be equated with real, actual aggression in the world outside because they are 'allowed or encouraged by an experimenter with the guarantee that no punishment will ensue' (Downs, 1989: p. 169). Subjects may believe – quite correctly – that no real harm comes from their displays of aggression, and thus the routine social inhibitors on aggressive, antisocial behaviour are absent. In other words, the social meaning of aggressivity when displayed in a sanctioned laboratory environment is very different from that of real aggression, directed at real people, with flesh and blood consequences.

Lynn Segal (1993) adds the further objection that laboratory evidence ignores or understates the complexity of the relationship between fantasy, psychic arousal and behaviour. The role of fantasy in the use of pornography is examined in Chapter 6. Here we note the obvious but important fact that an individual whose deviant or perverse sexual fantasies are aroused in a laboratory context will not necessarily transfer those fantasies into deviant sexual behaviour in the real world.

Critical attention has also been drawn to the potentially distorting impact of the 'experimenter demand effect' in which, as Donnerstein *et al.* put it, 'subjects attempt to guess and then confirm the experimenter's hypothesis' (1987: p. 12).

Many of the laboratory studies have been conducted within what psychologists refer to as the Buss paradigm. A subject is first angered by a female researcher, then exposed to pornographic material. He or she is then invited to display aggression towards the female researcher, usually by the aforementioned means of inflicting fake electric shocks. Several such studies have found that subjects so predisposed to aggress display consistently higher levels of aggression following exposure to pornography, and that 'being predisposed to aggress (angered) is crucial for exposure to sexual materials to have an effect on aggression' (Donnerstein *et al.*, 1987: p. 45).

The problem with this procedure, methodologically, is that it cannot distinguish between a subject whose aggression is heightened by exposure to pornography and one aroused merely by the fact of being deliberately provoked beforehand.

Categorizing pornography

A further, and even more fundamental difficulty arises with laboratory methods of this type: that of categorization. Firstly, it is not universally agreed as to what such labels as 'violent' or 'degrading' mean in the context of pornographic representations. They have been applied at various times to simulated acts of sado-masochism, or merely to the performers' wearing of black rubber or PVC. It may mean a woman on her knees performing fellatio ('degrading' in the Dworkin-MacKinnon definition discussed in the previous chapter). For Donnerstein *et al.*, degrading means 'the depiction of women as willing recipients of any male sexual urge or as oversexed, highly promiscuous individuals with insatiable sexual urges' (1987: p. 4), although why sexual willingness, promiscuity or even insatiability should be viewed as inherently degrading is not explained.

'Violent' and 'degrading' may refer to materials which explicitly condone sexual violence against and degradation of women (however we may define those terms); but they may also refer to images of women (rather than men) in dominant sexual positions. In other words, the violent or degrading content of a particular image, to those who view it, will depend largely on its context of reproduction and reception. The Meese Commission categories, and similar typologies developed by other researchers[5] ignore this context.

Allowing for the moment that we can agree about what constitutes violent and degrading material, both the antipornography feminists and moral-conservative positions go on to assume that there has been a dramatic increase in the quantity of such material in circulation since the 1960s. In fact, no such increase can be shown. Several observers, from a range of positions, agree that 'none of the wealth of scientific literature on the subject support the claim that sexual imagery today is more violent than the pornography of twenty years years ago' (Pally, 1993: p. 5). Donnerstein and his colleagues acknowledge that 'we cannot legitimately conclude that pornography has become more violent since the time of the 1970 obscenity and pornography commission' (1987: p. 91). Violent pornography remains, as it always has been, a small proportion of total pornographic output, usually addressing a specialist s/m audience within the gay and straight communities. The 'spiral of depravity' identified by one observer in relation to the UK pornography market – by which was meant a flood of legally available, particularly violent and degrading videos and magazines – simply does not exist.[6]

In any case, as a number of commentators have pointed out, the physical harms with which the consumption of pornography is most frequently associated – rape and the sexual abuse of women – are crimes as old as human civilization itself, long predating the development of the media forms utilized by the contemporary pornography industry. Robert Stoller asserts that 'though porn might incite to masturbation, the argument that it incites to bodily harm is propaganda; for without pornography, most societies in the world have nonetheless promoted rape' (1991: p. 223). Walter Kendrick finds 'a strange incongruity in tracing a violence said to be endemic in Western culture back to some pictures and films that could not have existed a century ago and that have been promiscuously on sale for only about twenty years' (1987: p. 232), while Donnerstein *et al.* note that 'ideas about rape are so pervasive in our culture that it is myopic to call them the exclusive domain of violent pornography' (1987: p. 109). To the extent that rates of serious sexual offences have increased in postwar capitalist societies, there is no clear correlation between that phenomenon and the increasing availability of pornography. In Japan, for example, where explicit images of a sado-masochistic, violent nature are commonplace, the reported incidence of rape and other serious sex crimes is only one third that of the United States (Abramson and Hayashi, 1984).[7] We have already cited Kutchinsky's analysis of the Danish data. Bill Thompson (1994) makes the additional point that, where the incidence of sex crimes has increased in parallel with an increase in the availability of pornography, this may be a factor of increasing population, improved police techniques, and women's growing readiness to report rape.

For all these reasons, and we have by no means exhausted the list of methodological objections to behavioural effects research and its attempt to correlate consumption of pornography with antisocial behaviour, its results, even when clear and consistent, are of limited value. As it is, and methodological problems aside, the results are often contradictory.

Drawing conclusions

Despite the uncertainty of the evidence, some researchers, such as Dolf Zillmann, have developed an 'addiction model' of pornography use. For Zillmann, 'prolonged exposure to sexually explicit materials produces a tendency to seek out more deviant and extreme forms of sexuality' (Linz and Malamuth, 1993: p. 17). Donnerstein and Linz report some evidence that exposure to pornography 'desensitizes' the user, a process which is then 'significantly correlated with assignment of greater blame to the victim [of rape]' (1990: p. 229).

Elsewhere, however, Donnerstein, while advancing the link between violent pornography and aggression levels, qualifies this by stating clearly his view, based on his own research, that 'it is the aggressive content of pornography that is the main contributor to violence against women. In fact, when we remove the sexual content from such films and just leave the aggressive aspect, we find a similar pattern of aggression and antisocial attitudes' (1984: p. 79). Others have agreed that the key content factor in promoting misogynistic behaviour by males towards women is in fact violence rather than sex.

While the status of this evidence can be no less secure than that which we have already criticized for its artificiality and lack of context it seriously undermines, if valid, all antipornography views based on the behavioural effects model.

More recent research has found that men's 'usual response [to depictions of sexual cruelty] is ... one of anxiety and depression, of revulsion rather than arousal' (Segal, 1993: p. 14). Thelma McCormack's detailed review of the experimental evidence reaches a similar conclusion: 'what the aggression studies show is that there can be both an increase and a decrease of a tendency towards aggression as a direct result of exposure to aggressive stimuli' (1985: p. 188). While exposure to erotic stimuli may lead to short-term sexual arousal, and a concomitant increase in sexual activity in the immediate post-experimental period, this will take place 'in a manner consistent with the subject's usual practice' (1985). Exposure may induce fantasies of rape and other violent or antisocial sexual behaviours, but not the implementation of fantasy.

The uncertainty of the experimental evidence, even for those who endorse its methodological and epistemological underpinnings, is reflected in the Meese report itself, which despite its generally assertive tone of moral condemnation and outrage is unable to go beyond such conclusions as 'some forms of sexually explicit materials bear a causal relationship to sexual violence' (1986: p. 309), while acknowledging at the same time that the 'etiology of deviance still remains to be answered' (1986: p. 974) and that 'certain socio-cultural mediating circumstances may be involved' (1986: p. 206). For Edward Donnerstein himself, who has devoted the bulk of his academic career to reaching it, 'a straightforward, definite conclusion on the relationship between pornography and aggression against women is difficult to make' (1984: p. 78). Moreover, in work published in 1987, following the appearance of the Meese report, and in response to what they felt to be the commission's misuse of their expert opinions (to assert a cause-effect relationship between pornography and sexual aggression or violence) Donnerstein and his colleagues denounced the report's findings as 'unwarranted' (1987: p. 172). Echoing Bernard Berelson's famous formulation, they presented their conclusions on the behavioural effects of pornography as follows:

> Some forms of pornography [for them, only that which is violent], under some conditions [when an individual is *already* predisposed to aggress], promote certain anti-social attitudes and behaviour (p. 171).

Despite the ambiguity of the evidence, antipornography campaigners – feminist and moral conservative alike – routinely draw such straightforward conclusions as the following by Diane Russell (1992):

> Pornography can induce a desire to rape women in males who had no such desire previously (p. 325).

Or, again (Weaver, 1992):

> Contemporary sexually explicit materials may be ... a potent catalyst for sexually abusive behaviours such as rape (p. 307).

Naomi Wolf's *The Beauty Myth* (1990) characterizes the chain of cause and effect thus:

> What is happening is that men and women whose private psycho-sexual history would not lead them to eroticize sexual violence are learning from such scenes to be interested in it. In other words, our culture is depicting violence so *that* men and women will become interested in it (p. 106).

On 25 July 1994, leading antipornography feminist Catharine MacKinnon was interviewed on Channel Four television's *The Vision Thing*. I quote from the interview at some length because it illustrates the reliance on sweeping generalization and extrapolation which characterizes the views of many proponents of this perspective. In the exchange quoted here, presenter Sheena MacDonald hints gently that MacKinnon's view of a pornography-infested society does not square with her own experience. In reply, MacKinnon paints a picture of a world in which all (or most) men are porn-users, sexual abusers and potential rapists, and goes further to suggest that MacDonald may herself have been abused as a child (with the implication that her relatively liberal views may be a consequence of this).

> SM: I'm a woman who lives in a nice area. To the best of my knowledge my husband doesn't use pornography. I don't see pornography. My newsagent doesn't stock it. I don't watch anything on television that could remotely be construed as pornographic. I don't actually feel that I am subordinated by sexually explicit material, directly, in my life. How does what you're saying affect me?

> CM: Well, first of all, you didn't cover what happens to her [sic] when she was a little girl, a child. A really considerable proportion of women are sexually abused as children.

> SM: Okay. I don't remember that I was sexually abused as a little girl.

CM: That's also possible – that it happened but you don't remember it. But let's assume that you weren't.

SM: But I might find it offensive that you would suggest that I was.

CM: Offensive? Most women I've talked to don't.

SM: I love my father. I love my male relations, my female relations. The idea that any of them would abuse me in that way I would find very upsetting.

CM: Well, indeed it's upsetting, and it should also be noted that a lot of people who were sexually abused by their relatives loved them, and continue to love them, and so that isn't a contradiction at all, it's just part of the problem here. The other thing to point out is that she's living in a neighbourhood surrounded by people who have a lot of money. It's those people who use pornography the most, simply because they have the most access to the money to get it. That also means that they have the best access to the pornography that is least visible, and in this country that means the most violent. So there is an inverse relation to class structure. The more money you have, the more you can get the worst pornography the easiest.

SM: So you're suggesting that as I go through this world, as this fictional woman, my teacher may be using pornography, my dentist may be using pornography. . . .

CM: Your doctor or your therapist may be using pornography. Somebody can be using pornography as you walk down the street – any street, anywhere – but in particular places where women are being prostituted you can be taken for one of them. Men who rape women select, often on the basis of the pornography they consume, they figure out what woman they want to use, and any woman is being used in the pornography, so there's an image of all of us in there. That means we are all being targetted, a target drawn on each of us for some particular group of consumers.

In the book which this interview was promoting, MacKinnon links pornography to the conflict in the former Yugoslavia. 'Just prior to the Serbian war . . . pornography was everywhere. . . . Linear causality is not all that rare and difficult to prove' (1994: p. 25). On the contrary, causality, in the sense intended by MacKinnon, is so rare as to have eluded proof entirely, despite some 30 years of scientific efforts.

Scripting abuse

If the capacity of pornography to stimulate aggression and hence rape or sexual assault is unproven, there is no doubt that it is frequently used as an accompaniment to, and instrument of sexual abuse within relationships. One writer notes that while '"experts" debate the impact of pornography, you have only to talk to battered women to know that it is used as a recipe book for violent scenes in the home. Many battered women report that their husbands keep pornographic magazines beside the bed, and consult them as they proceed step by step to "have sex"' (Jones, 1990: p. 65). In this sense, it is argued, pornography provides the script for abuse, functioning as 'a source of narratives' (Cameron and Frazer, 1992: p. 377) through which men sexually subordinate their partners. Pornography has been similarly implicated in abusive relationships between lesbians and between gay men.

The evidence of such a role for pornography, given the private and hidden nature of the abusive behaviour involved, can never be anything but anecdotal. It is, nonetheless, overwhelming. Many couples use pornography in their sexual lives consensually (and, in the case of s/m devotees, this could be interpreted, wrongly, as abuse). In other cases the subordinate partner (in a straight or gay context) may be coerced into following the script. The key issue here is: does pornography cause the abuse, and would the abuse be reduced in the absence of the script provided by pornography? From the antipornography feminist perspective, the answer to both questions is yes, since pornography not only normalizes and legitimizes abusive behaviour but, it also intentionally encourages it. Pornography 'predisposes men to act out the behaviour' depicted therein (Wyre, 1992: p. 238).

For Catharine MacKinnon, as we have seen, 'the message of these materials is "get her", pointing to all women' (1994: p. 15). The chain of causation is direct and unambiguous. By legitimizing the fantastic, the violent, the abusive in sexual behaviour, pornography negatively shapes the sexual realities of those whose partners use it.

Pornography, however, has not been shown to be the cause of sexual abuse within the domestic, private sphere, but rather an accessory, used by some individuals in the commission of their abusive behaviour, just as other objects can be used. Not all men (nor women, for that matter) who use pornography proceed to abuse their partners. Those who do, it is reasonable to suppose, would commit acts of abuse whether they had access to pornography or not. As Lynne Segal (1992) has argued, pornography's misuse is a function of the social context within which the sex act takes place, and will be associated with a relationship which is abusive and exploitative in many ways other than sexual. The man who burns his wife with a lit cigarette when drunk is likely to be the same man who beats her for failing to prepare his meals the way he wants them, for coming in late from a night out with girlfriends, or for not looking like his favourite 'page three girl'. He may also take pleasure in forcing the behaviour depicted in pornography upon her in bed – as an expression of his power over her, rather than for his own sexual satisfaction. The scripted abuse to which pornography contributes is one element in a larger picture.

Pornography and performance

In recent years, as the difficulty of proving negative behavioural effects on those who consume pornography has become clear, so antipornography campaigners have shifted their attentions to the harms done to those involved in its production. In this strand of the debate, pornography is viewed not only as endorsing and provoking violence toward, and abuse of, women by those who use it for sexual satisfaction, but as an act of violence and abuse in itself, against the women, children and, in the case of gay porn, men who perform in it. The argument is extended to the involvement of women in live sex performances, strip shows, and other nonmedia contexts where individuals simulate or perform sex acts for money. The damage which such performances inflict is increasingly asserted to be 'the real issue'.[8]

Arguments of this type frequently focus on child pornography[9] in which, by definition, those involved as 'performers' are nonconsenting adults. Such images, as Nick Davies puts it, are themselves 'records of crime – rape, bodily harm, child abuse',[10] and are frequently used as manipulative tools in the commission of further child abuse by paedophiles. As Kelly notes, however, 'child abuse is not "caused" by child pornography, rather the pornography is the record of abuse which has already taken place. It may then be used to justify and/or facilitate further abuse which in turn may result in the production of more child pornography' (1992: p. 121).

As records of criminal behaviour, moreover, examples of child pornography are already illegal, certainly in Britain and the United States, and punished severely when their production, distribution or use is discovered. As Linda Williams notes, 'there is no commercial market for kiddie porn. If an occasional underage performer is discovered, it is a source of great scandal and embarassment to the industry' (1992: p. 263). In Britain, as of late 1994, some 4000 men were reported to be under criminal investigation for their suspected involvement in child pornography.[11]

Snuff

Frequently cited alongside child pornography in this connection is the phenomenon of the 'snuff' movie, i.e. images depicting real violence and even murder. These images, fictionalized in Bret Easton Ellis' *Less Than Zero* (1985),[12] represent records of violent crime and are by definition, like child pornography, illegal. That said, substantial doubts exist as to whether 'snuff movies' are real, or are a kind of urban myth developed in the heat of the pornography debate. The feature film *Snuff*, released in the United States in the 1970s, was an extremely gruesome and misogynistic example of a 'slasher' movie, different only in degree to those made by such respected directors as John Carpenter, Abel Ferraro, and Brian de Palma for the mainstream cinema. The argument of many feminists and moral conservatives that thereafter 'real' snuff movies circulated in the pornographic underworld has yet to be substantiated. 'Snuff' movies may exist, but as time passes the phenomenon begins to take on the character of a 'moral panic' around which public outrage and political action is periodically organized. An influential article by antipornography feminist Beverley Labelle acknowledges this when she writes that:

> whether or not the death depicted in *Snuff* [and by extension the phenomenon of 'snuff' movies] is real or simulated is not the issue. That sexual violence is presented as sexual entertainment, that the murder and dismemberment of a woman's body is commercial film material is an outrage to our sense of justice as women, as human beings (p. 192).

Here we see another example of the conflating of two quite different phenomena which characterizes much of this debate. Sexualized violence is not the same thing as pornography (although some pornography may contain images of violence), and has been part of the cinematic repertoire throughout the twentieth century. In this context, *Snuff* is a particularly graphic example of a long-established subgenre (a 'video nasty', to use the term which became popular in the early 1980s). It is undoubtedly true, and may be a cause of regret to many, that sections of the audience find such material entertaining, but the existence of *Snuff* the movie is not evidence for the existence of a pornography in which real people are murdered.

The performers

If child pornography and 'snuff' are extreme cases of the argument that pornography *is* violence against those who appear in it, more problematic is the status of performances in sexually explicit materials undertaken by consenting adults. On the one hand, antipornography campaigners assert that the women who perform in pornography are essentially victims of abuse. They may be coerced into having sex, drugged into submission, or forced into the industry as a consequence of economic hardship. In none of these contexts can it be said that women freely consent to their involvement. In every case exploitation is present. For this reason 'a great deal of pornography is the recorded physical and sexual abuse of women' (Itzin, 1988: p. 56).

In addition to the issue of exploitation, pornography performers may also be exposed, in the normal course of their work, to sexually transmitted diseases such as gonorrhoea, syphilis and, most seriously, HIV infection.

Where a woman appears to be performing voluntarily, it is argued, this is likely to be the product of a history of child sexual abuse. Itzin (1988) cites US statistics indicating that 75 per cent of females involved in pornography are incest survivors. Robert Stoller's ethnographic study of 'who does what, how, when, where, why and therefore to whom in porn' (1991: p. ix) finds that many female performers *are* voluntarily involved, but links this volunteering to the psychological condition of hysterical personality, i.e. individuals who 'think and feel erotically day and night and have consciously done so since early childhood' (p. 24). Such women are 'profoundly exhibitionistic' and likely to have been sexually abused by, or erotically attached to, their fathers. 'Early sexual experience is the distinguishing characteristic of the person most likely to become a part of the sex industry or a sex performer' (p. 156). In this sense, a woman's 'choice' is really no choice.

Opposed to the view of females involved in pornography as victims are those who argue that, in many cases, such involvement *is* truly voluntary – the product of entirely rational financial, personal and sexual choice. For Gayle Rubin, pornography is not necessarily, nor ever exclusively, 'a document of abuse' (1993: p. 32), but a means for some women to explore their sexuality or, more mundanely, to make relatively good money. Lynne Segal (1993) describes as 'offensive' the view that women involved in the production of pornography are, by definition, exploited and abused, any more than are workers in any other industry.

The evidence cited by the protagonists in this particular debate is, once again, largely anecdotal. On the performer-as-victim side of the fence, Linda Marciano (formerly pornographic movie star Linda Lovelace) is frequently enlisted as an example of a woman who, by her own account, was enmeshed in an abusive relationship with the man who later introduced her to the pornographic film industry.

Evidence for the opposing viewpoint is provided by women such as the pornographic film actress quoted in Delacoste and Alexander's collection of interviews, who 'finds performing in sexually explicit material satisfying on a number of levels' (1988):

First, it provides a physically and psychically safe environment for me to live my exhibitionist fantasies. Secondly, it provides a surprisingly flexible and supportive arena for me to grow in as a *performer*, both sexually and non-sexually. Thirdly, it provides me with erotic material that I like to watch for my own pleasure. Finally, the medium allows me to explore the theme of celebrating a positive female sexuality – a sexuality heretofore denied us. In choosing my roles and characterizations carefully, I strive to show, always, women who thoroughly enjoy sex and are forceful, self-satisfying and guilt-free without also being neurotic, unhappy or somehow unfulfilled (her emphasis).[13]

Rather than enter the futile debate about who among these conflicting voices is lying, misled or confused (since one or other must be), I will suggest that, since the pornography industry, like most others, is organized on capitalist principles, it can be more or less exploitative and abusive, depending on other factors such as the legal environment within which it operates or the personalities of individual entrepreneurs. The production of pornography is an industry in which involvement can be a rational choice for some, an irrational one for others, and an unwelcome imposition for still others.

Pornography as ideology

So far in this chapter I have examined a range of perspectives on the physically observable, behavioural effects of pornography: its effects on those who produce it, its users, and those sexual partners for whom it becomes part of an experience of abuse. In this section, I turn to the question of pornography's function and impact as ideology. What are the ideas and values reproduced and reinforced by pornography, and what effects do these ideas and values have on the social structure? For some commentators this set of questions is ultimately of more importance than the behavioural effects debate, which has proven so difficult to ground empirically and continues to evade resolution. From this perspective pornography's moral harms provide an alternative route of attack.

Pornography's alleged ideological effects can be addressed on two levels, reflecting two very different approaches to the issue. First, we can speak of pornography's morally disintegrative effects – the assertion that pornography undermines and destroys the moral structure on which a civilized, ordered society must be built. Second, there are the ideologically integrative functions of pornography – the extent to which it is implicated in the maintenance and reproduction of patriarchal ideology, and thence of patriarchy itself. The latter concern is of course that of antipornography feminism, while the former reflects the moral agenda of those groups who aspire to the conservation of existing social structures and values, and even to the restoration of those which prevailed in earlier, less permissive times.

The moral conservatives

For this group the primary threat posed by pornography is to the traditional structure of the nuclear family. Emphasizing the strongly religious underpinning of this perspective is the following statement, given in evidence to the Meese Commission by a Father Bruce Ritter (quoted in Meese, 1986):

> To me, the greatest harm of pornography is not that some people are susceptible to or even directly harmed by the violent and degrading and radically misleading images portrayed all too graphically by mainstream pornography. Rather pornography's greatest harm is caused by its ability – and its intention – to attack the very dignity and sacredness of sex itself, reducing human sexual behaviour to the level of its animal components. The greatest harm of pornography does not lie in its links to sexual violence or even its ability to degrade and indignify individuals. . . . Pornography degrades sex itself and dehumanizes and debases a profoundly important, profoundly beautiful and profoundly, at its core, sacred relationship between a man and a woman who seek in sexual union not the mere satisfaction of erotic desires but the deepest sharing of their mutual and committed and faithful love (p. 99).

In response to the liberal and optimistic tone of the Johnson Commission report, prominent moral conservative and Nixon administration advisor Charles Keating Jr stated to the Meese Commission his view (quoted in Baird and Rosenbaum, 1991) that:

> if man is affected by his environment, by circumstances of his life, by reading, by instruction, by anything, he is certainly affected by pornography. The mere nature of pornography makes it impossible for pornography to affect good. Therefore, it must necessarily affect evil. Sexual immorality, more than any other causative factor, historically speaking, is the root cause of the demise of our great nation and of all great peoples (p. 30).

The Meese Commission report, itself driven by a strongly moral conservative agenda, echoes this assessment of pornography's effects in its conclusion that exposure to sexually explicit materials 'appears to impact adversely on the family concept and its value to society'(Meese, 1986: p. 29).

In so far as such a value-laden perspective can ever be supported by evidence, it has come from the work of such as Zillman and Bryant, who have sought to show that pornography, by its apparent endorsement of casual, often deviant sex, thereby induces promiscuity and marital instability. In one paper they write that 'those massively exposed to pornography will become distrusting of their partners in extended relationships. ... Another likely consequence ... is a growing dissatisfaction with sexual reality' (1990: p. 216), leading, they imply, to an enhanced willingness to experiment sexually, outside the nuclear family if necessary. Other researchers have argued similarly that exposure to pornography 'fosters a lack of respect for social institutions such as the family and traditional sex roles for women'(Linz and Malamuth, 1993: p. 17).

The methodological basis on which such conclusions have been drawn has been widely criticized. It is of course true, as moral conservatives often point out, that rates of marital breakdown have steadily increased since the sexual revolution of the 1960s; but this is more the consequence of women's growing economic and legal autonomy, it might well be argued, rather than their husbands' or their own exposure to pornography. Few would doubt today that the rate of marital breakdown was artificially depressed before the 1960s principally by patriarchal legal and moral sanctions against women who decided to leave the family.

Contemporary moral conservative criticisms of pornography's negative ideological effects are founded firmly on the Judaeo-Christian proposition that sexual activity is only legitimate within the confines of the heterosexual nuclear family, monogamy and reproduction of the species. In so far as pornography rarely depicts sex in these contexts[14] it inevitably offends the moral codes of many Christians.

AIDS and the morality of safer sex

Before the discovery of HIV/AIDS, the moral conservative position on these matters was regarded by most moderate Christians and nonbelievers, heterosexual or gay, as hopelessly outmoded. Feminists too, whose views on pornography's ideological effects will be examined shortly, regarded anything which reinforced the bourgeois nuclear family as reactionary and inherently patriarchal. Since HIV/AIDS has become a factor in the debate, however, a concern with monogamy and relationship stability (marital or otherwise) has moved from being the province of moral crusaders alone to the realm of public health policy. In the post-AIDS environment promiscuous casual sex *is* dangerous, and if pornography could be shown to cause it, or even to encourage it, this would be an important consideration in assessing its place in society. Denis Altman notes with some concern, of gay male-orientated pornography in particular, that 'the role of pornography in changing sexual behaviour is tricky. The AIDS epidemic seems to have coincided with a boom in gay pornography, the great bulk of which represents sexual acts which are considered "high risk".[15] What is not clear is whether pornography encourages people to be careless or provides a safe outlet for fantasies that most people recognise cannot easily be acted out in real life' (1986: p. 158).

From this viewpoint, pornography, while depicting unsafe sexual scenarios, may make it easier for couples who use it (and this of course applies to hetero- and homosexual couples equally) to maintain satisfying sexual relationships. Far from breaking families apart, it may help to bond them together.

In assessing the morally disintegrative effects of pornography, one can do little more than to apply one's own moral values to the issue. If monogamous sex, in the missionary position, for the purpose of reproduction, is regarded, based on one's sincerely held religious beliefs, as the only legitimate sexual lifestyle (and recent years have shown that a number of prominent Christians, in a variety of denominations, are less than consistent in this respect) then pornography will justifiably be viewed as an unwelcome temptation to the extent that it may arouse or suggest nonreproductive behaviour. On the other hand it can be argued, as Burstyn does, that 'the philosophy underlying the conservative evaluation of sexually explicit materials is rooted firmly in a *harsh interpretation* of biblical ideas, an interpretation that defines sexuality in the first instance as a problem: a dangerous, corrupting force that must be contained within the framework of marriage' (1985: p. 17) (my emphasis). Outwith this context, it seems feasible that pornography could be just as beneficial to a loving sexual relationship as it could be damaging.

Pornography and patriarchy

While moral conservatives complain that pornography is destroying patriarchy some feminists maintain that it upholds it, and that this is the most important aspect of pornography's negative effects, from which all others stem. Although feminists and moral conservatives have worked in alliance to campaign against pornography, this should be viewed as a tactical relationship only, since the bases on which the two groups oppose pornography are fundamentally different, and their beliefs ultimately irreconcilable. While the moral-conservative perspective strives to maintain the male-dominated nuclear family structure (and thus, too, male domination in the wider political, economic and social spheres) and attributes its postwar decline at least partly to pornography, the feminist political project has been one of liberating women from male domination and ending sexual stratification. Pornography, it is argued, has played and continues to play a key role in the reinforcement and reproduction of the values which make male domination – patriarchy – possible. Pornography in this sense is patriarchal ideology in its purest form, representing and defining women in ways which make their subordination and oppression seem normal; 'teaching' both men and women how to behave sexually, and what their respective roles are within sexual relationships.

The theoretical basis of this view is that gender roles are socially rather than biologically constructed. At birth males and females are, apart from the obvious anatomical differences, identical in terms of their potential ability to develop successfully into adulthood. There are no significant differences in intelligence between the sexes, and no biological reasons why male and female children should not grow into maturity as sexual equals. The process by which they are separated into masculine and feminine roles, and thence into dominant and subordinate positions in the socio-economic hierarchy (a continuing structural feature of all advanced capitalist societies) is one of education and learning, centred first on the family, then the formal education system, and increasingly, the mass communication media. As the media have expanded in the twentieth century they have become increasingly important as the source of the information and values around which we organize and regulate our lives. In so far as femininity and masculinity can be taught, they are taught not only by parents to their children, and teachers to their pupils, but in the content of advertisements, television drama, cinema and popular fiction. Men and women learn from these sources what it means to be masculine on the one hand, feminine on the other, with all the implications for lifestyle and lifechance which follow.

So how does pornography fit into this ideological effects model? From the feminist perspective, patriarchy's survival as a social system depends upon the acceptance by society as a whole of the sexual stratification on which it is founded. The idea of women's subordination, and the male's right to dominate, must be 'commonsensical'; it must be naturalized to seem inevitable and immutable. This is true in the political, economic, social and *sexual* spheres, the latter of which determines the position of women *vis à vis* the family, their male partners and their children. In so far as pornography expresses an ideology of female subordination in sex, it therefore contributes to the maintenance of patriarchy as a whole. As Shere Hite puts it in her survey of women's attitudes to sexuality, 'pornography as we know it – as, indeed sex itself – is a reflection of society. . . . The fact that men dominate women in most of these pictures is such a commonplace that it is not seen as remarkable. . . . Pornography reinforces in men so many of the old and stereotyped attitudes to women and toward themselves that have done so much damage' (1993: p. 232). For Clark, pornography is simply and unambiguously 'a method of socialization . . . the tangible, palpable embodiment of the imposition of the dominant sex system' (1983: p. 53).

As Chapter 4 observed, feminists of this persuasion define pornography as, at its most benign, that sexually explicit material which degrades, objectifies and dehumanizes women; which reduces women to the status of sexual object, available for the pleasure and gratification of men. At worst, as Catharine MacKinnon puts it, 'pornography sexualizes rape, battery, sexual harassment, prostitution and child abuse; it thereby celebrates, promotes, authorizes and legitimizes them. . . . It eroticizes dominance and submission' (1992: p. 461). Given that one of the key functions of ideology is to legitimize oppression or exploitation by making it appear natural or normal, pornography is thus revealed as the ideology of male supremacy. When consumed by men, it sanctions their abusive treatment of women. When consumed by women, it 'teaches' them acceptance of their sexual subordination.

Alongside Catharine MacKinnon, perhaps the best-known exponent of this perspective is Andrea Dworkin, for whom 'the major theme of pornography as a genre is male power' (1981: p. 24). For Dworkin, pornography is the mediated essence of patriarchy, reflecting men's domination of women in its form and content, and in its production and distribution. For Dworkin, pornography is not merely one aspect of patriarchal ideology, but central to it, in so far as its content expresses patriarchal hierarchy, dehumanizes women and turns their sexuality into a commodity for purchase by men, and imposes submission on all women (particularly those who perform in it). Pornography expresses the violence of patriarchy, the essentially oppressive nature of male sexuality, 'the brutality of male history' (p. 69). For Susan Brownmiller, responding to the suggestion (*see* Chapter 6) that there can be a nonsexist, nonexploitative pornography, 'pornography is the undiluted essence of anti-female propaganda' (1991: p. 38).[16]

With the emergence of radical/cultural feminism in the late 1970s and 1980s the assertion of pornography's special role in the reproduction of patriarchal ideology became for a time dominant within the feminist movement as a whole, and has remained so for those who assert the fundamentally exploitative, abusive nature of male sexuality. For this group, pornography is both a reflection and a major cause of patriarchy. If all (hetero-) sexuality in patriarchy is antiwoman or exploitative, pornography is particularly abhorrent because it so graphically and coldly displays that sexuality and gives it voice.

The migration of pornography

Having developed this analysis of pornography's ideological effects, feminists then began to extend it to materials which were not in the conventional sense pornographic, such as advertising and mainstream Hollywood feature films. Pornography came to be seen as the extreme case of a much more pervasive cultural misogyny. Jennifer Caputi identified a new category of 'gorenography', by which she meant 'materials that, although not sexually explicit enough to qualify as pornography, nonetheless are like pornography in that they present violence, domination, torture and murder in a context that makes these acts sexual' (1992: p. 210). Examples of 'gorenography' were 'slasher' films such as *Halloween* and *Friday 13th*.[17]

Mainstream advertising was also implicated in patriarchal oppression and the communication of 'femicidal ideology' 'when it borrows the pornographic conventions of showing a woman visually dismembered and reduced to a body part' (Caputi,1992: p. 212). Naomi Wolf has argued that in the 1970s and 1980s the conventions of pornography crossed over to women's magazine ads, as 'beauty pornography' and 'beauty sado-masochism' in which women learnt that 'no matter how assertive she may be in the world, her private submission to control is what makes her desirable' (1990: p. 106).

In Britain, as was noted in Chapter 4, antipornography campaigners, such as Labour Party MPs Clare Short and Dawn Primarolo, attempted to introduce restrictions on the tabloid newspapers 'page three girls', on the perfectly consistent grounds that if objectification of women was the issue in hardcore pornography – which was and remains illegal and relatively difficult to obtain in the UK – then it was even more dangerous when presented to the family in the form of topless models with their morning newspapers.

Ironically, perhaps, a similar point is made by those feminists who from the mid-1980s onwards were publicly refuting the antipornography campaigners. For writers such as Gayle Rubin the attempt to specify pornography as an especially vicious or violent expression of patriarchal ideology was erroneous, since 'what distinguishes pornography from other media is the level of sexual explicitness, not the quantity of violence in its imagery or the quality of its political consciousness' (1993: p. 26). If indeed pornography is misogynistic and sexist, then so are all other forms of cultural expression in patriarchal societies. As Rubin puts it, 'sexism is no more intrinsic to pornography than it is to fiction. Gender inequality and contemptuous attitudes towards women are endemic to this society and are consequently reflected in virtually all our media. ... They do not originate in pornography and migrate from there into the rest of popular culture' (p. 25).[18] 'Sexist and violent materials are symptoms of a sexist and violent society,' argues Dority, 'not their causes' (1991: p. 113).

From this perspective, and to the extent that pornography is expressive of patriarchal ideology, it is so only in the materialist sense that all cultural production in a patriarchal society reflects social reality. Pornography is not, in and of itself, sexism, unless one believes that the explicit depiction of sexual behaviour is always and everywhere bound to be sexist. For (feminist) critics of the antipornography feminists this is a fundamental point, since it opens up the possibility of non-sexist, nonmisogynistic pornographies. If there can be cinema, and advertising, and literature which is subversive of dominant ideologies and values (and who would deny it?), so too can there be subversive pornography (in addition to the traditional category of erotica, already accepted as a possibility even by antipornography feminists).

Misreadings

A second criticism of the antipornography feminist view is that statements such as Shere Hite's quoted above – 'men dominate women in most of the pictures' – are not borne out by analysis. Content analyses of pornographic magazines do not show that men are present, let alone dominant over or violent toward women in the majority of images (Thompson, 1994). The definitions of dominance, degradation, and objectification formulated by antipornography campaigners are highly subjective, and ignore the semiological complexities associated with the interpretative dimension of communication. Gayle Rubin challenges the antipornography feminist view that a) all pornography depicts violence, and b) that such depictions necessarily mean or signify woman-hatred.

> The pictures of fucking and sucking that comprise the bulk of pornography may be unnerving to those who are not familiar with them. But it is hard to make a convincing case that such images are violent. All of the early anti-porn slide shows used a highly selective sample of s/m imagery to sell a very flimsy analysis. Taken out of context, such images are often shocking. This shock value was mercilessly exploited to scare audiences into accepting the anti-porn perspective (1984: p. 298).

In a later essay she again challenges the assumption that pornography is intrinsically sexist. Empirical content analysis, she argues, shows that pornography is not especially violent when compared to other genres, and that even sado-masochistic materials are relatively innocuous. 'SM materials are aimed at an audience that understands a set of conventions for interpreting them. Sadomasochism is not a form of violence, but is rather a type of ritual and contractual sex play' (Rubin, 1993: p. 22).

More fundamentally, the assertion that male sexuality is intimately bound up with violence is condemned by another strand of feminism as naively essentialist, as is the converse notion that female sexuality is inherently nonviolent, spiritual and nurturing. From this perspective the views of Dworkin and others 'really offer nothing more than women's traditional sexual values [the good girl/bad girl dichotomy] disguised as radical feminist sexual values' (Echols, 1984: p. 64). The campaign against pornography is viewed here as an attempt to impose a restrictive and reactionary code of sexual conduct. For Lisa Duggan, antipornography feminism wrongly presents 'a vision of sexuality as a terrain of female victimization and degradation' (1988: p. 84) and 'pornography as the monster that made it so' (Duggan *et al.*, 1988: p. 75). For this writer and other like-minded feminists the sexual sphere, like others in patriarchal society, should be viewed as a site of struggle, entered by women as active agents constructing antipatriarchal images, rather than passive victims of the sexist *status quo*. The antipornography campaign reinforces, from this perspective, nothing less than the patriarchal stereotype of female sexuality.

The critique of ideology

A final criticism of the ideological effects model as described here relates to the concept of ideology itself. Just as links between the consumption of pornography and the adoption of antisocial behaviour patterns are unproven and likely to remain so, the notion that the consent of the oppressed to their oppression can be secured by propaganda, ideology, or any other form of false consciousness disseminated through the media has increasingly been criticized as simplistic and patronizing. The view that women in patriarchy are 'kept in their place' by pornography (and its impact on men's and their own attitudes and values) is no less crude than vulgar marxist theories of mass culture and capitalist brainwashing. Conceptually, it is now acknowledged by most serious scholars of communication that media audiences are relatively active in relation to the messages they receive, i.e. they have the power to resist dominant ideas, in so far as these are present in the message. Audiences decode messages differently, depending upon their individual social circumstances, and, while they are never totally 'free' in this respect (given the overdetermining constraints imposed by their particular socio-economic and educational histories), a certain amount of autonomy and distancing is always present at the receiving end of the communication process. Thus, the thesis of a dominant patriarchal ideology, unproblematically transmitted to the masses through pornography and other means, raises more questions than it answers. As Altman puts it:

> if ... the ideology of a dominant repressive culture is in some way present in 'popular' images and texts, how does it get there? How do we account for the fact that such repression is less than total, and that alternate, conflicting sets of representations coexist at the same time, in the same place, under the same political system? How can we acknowledge and analyse the diversity with which women respond to such representation? And finally, what is the relationship between ideology, as we can analyse it through representation, and actual behaviour? (1984: p. 127)

Even if pornographic messages were intrinsically misogynistic, and did have the power to shape the beliefs of those exposed to them, the vast majority of citizens in a country such as Britain neither consume, nor have access to, the hardcore images implicated in patriarchy by antipornography campaigners. Patriarchal ideas are widespread, but pornography is not and never has been. Indeed, as several observers have pointed out, if pornography is so central to the maintenance of patriarchal culture, why is its consumption so stigmatized (rather than being vigorously encouraged by the patriarchal establishment), and why is it so ferociously opposed by those in the moral-conservative camp who wish nothing more than to keep women the subordinate partners in the family, and in society as a whole?

Pornography and the environment

Finally, in this review of pornography's effects, we come to the issue of the environmental harm allegedly inflicted by the retail industry which exists to distribute sexually explicit materials and otherwise service the demand for sex-related commodities. In the Meese Commission report this was identified as an important category of effect, and in Britain too concern about the impact of sex shops, cinemas, and strip clubs on an urban environment such as Soho in London has driven much of the legislation restricting their operations. Those who assert a negative effect in this regard link the appearance of a retail sex industry with an increase in prostitution, sex-related crime, and a general lowering of an area's reputation (followed by declining property values and deterioration of buildings, etc.) as it attracts the worst elements of contemporary urban society. Even one sex shop opening in a city such as Glasgow or Portsmouth has generated fierce opposition on these grounds from local politicians, police and public figures, often leading to their closure. As a result the retail sex industry has tended to concentrate in ghettos, such as London's Soho, New York's 42nd Street, or Paris' Pigalle, where it often acquires the status of a risqué, slightly dangerous tourist attraction.

In this category of effects, as in the others we have discussed, the chain of causation is difficult to untangle. Does the opening of sex shops and strip clubs lead to a district's decline, and turn it into a 'no-go' area for women, or does an area's decline make it more attractive, because cheaper, to the sex industry?

On the question of crime, there are no clear correlations between the incidence of crime in an area and the size of the sex industry there, but beyond that it is difficult to say very much that is meaningful. Here, as in many of the examples given above, public perceptions of 'a problem' are what often makes it so.

Conclusion

Despite the substantial expenditure of research time and resources which has been made, and the many approaches which have been adopted, it has to date proved impossible to resolve the cause-and-effect debate in the sphere of the pornographic. It is, as one observer remarks, a 'sterile debate',[19] which seems unlikely to advance much beyond the continuing exchange of pseudo-scientific evidence on the one hand, and bitter polemicizing on the other. Cameron and Frazer put it well when they write that 'human behaviour is not determined by laws analogous to those of physics. It is not deterministically "caused". It needs to be explained in a different way, by interpretation of what it means and elucidation of the beliefs or understandings that make it possible and intelligible' (1992: p. 368).[20] For these authors pornography can never be conclusively shown to be the cause of sexual violence, although it may at times articulate and give unwelcome expression to the 'Sadean' philosophy of transgression and transcendence which underpins some of the most notorious cases of male sexual violence against women.

For gay activist and safer sex educator Simon Watney, attempts to extend legal concepts of obscenity to wider and wider categories of material – whether emanating from feminist or moral-conservative positions – 'share a common determination to iron out all inconsistencies and complexities within current legislations surrounding sexuality, and to replace them with fixed codes regulating the production, distribution and consumption of all sexual materials according to strict universalizing content-based definitions of "pornography"' (1987: p. 59). As such, they should be resisted with a counter-attack which emphasizes the positive 'uses and gratifications' to be drawn from the production and consumption of sexually explicit material. In the next chapter, I examine what these might be.

Notes

1   For a review of this material, and of the effects research tradition in general, *see* Morley (1980) and Cumberbatch and Howitt (1989).
2   Some 20 years later there was still 'a fairly strong consensus among researchers that sex offenders invariably [have] less exposure to pornography than the average male' (King, 1993: p. 72).
3   This finding was drawn from Donnerstein *et al's.* (1987) research, which found that men predisposed to rape enjoyed violent pornography more than the control group.
4   They hold the view that 'the prototypical stories told in pornographic fiction are narratives of male transcendence and mastery', and that 'we must be critical of pornography'(1992: p. 378).
5   Donnerstein *et al.* (1987) used the following six categories to test effects, based on degrees of violent, explicit, and degrading content: i) nonviolent, low degradation, sexually explicit; ii) nonviolent, high degradation, sexually explicit; iii) violent pornography (depicting

sexual coercion in a sexually explicit manner); iv) nonexplicit sexual aggression; v) sexualized explicit violent; vi) negative-outcome rape depictions (in which a woman is first depicted as resisting rape, then succumbs and enjoys sexual satisfaction from the experience).

6 Davies, N., 'Under cover kings', *The Guardian*, 28 November 1994.

7 Sallie Tisdale (1995) notes that Japanese 'erotic' magazines have a hero known as 'Rape Man', and that, while the depiction of pubic hair is forbidden, Japanese pornography deals largely in scenarios of rape, bondage, coercion and female submission.

8 *See*, for example, Davies, N., 'Dirty Business', *The Guardian*, 26 November 1994, and the research by Diane Russell on which it is based.

9 For an account of the child pornography industry, *see* Tate (1990).

10 Davies, N., 'Dirty business', *The Guardian*, 26 November 1994.

11 Davies, N., 'Red light for Blue Squad', *The Guardian*, 27 November 1994.

12 Ellis (1985) describes a scene in which the Californian rich kids who populate the novel watch a 'scratchy', 'black and white' video of a black man sexually assaulting and murdering two white teenagers (p. 153). Here, as in the novels of James Ellroy, Andrew Vaachs and others, the 'snuff movie' is treated as an authentic phenomenon, symbolizing the sexual (and from the above scene, one could infer, racial) degeneracy of American culture.

13 Sallie Tisdale's *Talk Dirty To Me* (1995) includes an interview with Alex, a San Franciscan prostitute who strongly defends her right to engage in such work, while explaining the sexual and financial pleasures and benefits she derives from it. Alex describes how, as a teenager, she 'was aware of having this sexual power that people wanted, and that I could use it to my advantage to get things I wanted. I was so sick of being poor all my life, and I wasn't looking forward to a whole life of being poor like my parents and grandparents had been'(p. 132).

14 Zillmann and Bryant note, with some justification, that 'pornography appears to thrive on featuring social encounters in which women are eager to accommodate any and every imaginable sexual urge of any man in the vicinity' (1990: p. 209).

15 'High-risk' sexual behaviour includes unprotected penile penetration, particularly anal, and any other activity which may involve the passing of one participant's bodily fluids into the bloodstream of the other.

16 As an example of what is meant by such statements, we can refer to a recent edition of *Hustler* magazine (UK edition), advertising a forthcoming short story, described in the text as 'gore fiction' with the following extract: 'The chainsaw sliced easily into Sally's flesh. Each pass sent a thin spray of blood splattering across the wall. "If that won't teach the bitch to step in line, nothing will."' (December 1994).

17 Both are examples of movies in which young females, during or shortly

after participation in sexual intercourse, meet with violent ends at the hands of knife-wielding psychopaths.

18 The philosopher Fred Berger agrees that 'in so far as it arises in a social context entirely infused with male sexism, much [pornography] reflects the worst aspects of our society's approved conception of sexual relations. Too often, the scenes depicted involve male violence and aggression towards women, male dominance over women, and females as sexual servants. ... [But] this is not necessary to pornography as such; where it is true, this reflects social and sexual attitudes already fostered by other social forces' (1991: p. 151). If, argues another analyst, 'the iconography of heterosexuality [from advertising through the spectrum of representational forms to hardcore pornography] is, by definition, a representation of dominance/submission, activity/passivity, power/ powerlessness' (Kostash, 1985: p. 33), why single out pornography as the enemy *par excellence*, and attribute to it all (or at least a large part) of the ills of patriarchy?

19 Davies, N., 'Dirty business', *The Guardian*, 26 November 1994.

20 The same point is made in a Dissenting Statement to the final report of the Meese Commission by two of its female members, Judith Becker and Ellen Levine, who made clear their view that 'human behaviour is complex and multi-causal. To say that exposure to pornography in and of itself causes an individual to commit a sexual crime is simplistic, not supported by the social science data, and overlooks many of the other variables that may be contributory causes' (Meese, 1986: p. 206).

|6|

Consuming pornography: uses, gratifications and meanings

Some years ago James Halloran wrote that 'we must get away from the habit of thinking in terms of what the media do to people and substitute for it the idea of what people do with the media' (quoted in Morley, 1980: p. 12). This statement, and the 'uses and gratifications' approach to the media which it encapsulates, was viewed by many communication scholars as a rather disingenuous attempt to evade the question of media effects: to place an inordinate emphasis on the individual consumer of media rather than the socially determined *process* of media consumption; to be stating the obvious, and adding little of value to the debate.[1] In relation to sexual representation and pornography, however, the uses and gratifications approach offers an alternative route to answering some of the questions raised in the previous chapter. As was argued there, the debate about the effects of explicit sexual representation is so bound up with the pursuit of moral and political agendas as to have become sterile and circular. For every piece of evidence 'proving' an effect of some kind there is a counter-argument disputing it on methodological or other grounds. The study of how people use pornography, on the other hand, the gratifications which they derive from that consumption, and the meanings which sexual representations have for them, allows us to cut through the mystifications of behavioural psychology and statistical social science to reach the level of individual experience and to ask: what does mediated sex mean to people in the context of their actual lives and experiences?

This chapter explores that question. First I examine the attempts by some scholars to describe the characteristics of pornography as a genre, comparable to other genres. Then I consider the uses made of pornography and other forms of sexual representation by a variety of sexual communities – gay and straight men, gay and straight women – and the meanings which these materials might have, in the context of a post-AIDS environment characterized by the intense politicization of sexual identity.

Pornography as meaningful communication

An important step in the movement away from viewing pornography as a fundamentally (im-) moral category of sexual representation, uniquely damaging in its effects on society, was taken by John Ellis in his 1979 essay 'On pornography', reprinted in the Screen reader on *The Sexual Subject* (1992). The section of the reader in which his essay was included announced its intention to look at pornography 'as representation' and stressed 'the importance of studying the various codes, narrative structures and forms of identification which characterize pornography' (p. 129). While Ellis' essay does not itself attempt to articulate the conventions of pornography in depth, by asserting the possibility and scholarly legitimacy of doing so he linked the study of pornography to the wider field of critical cultural studies, in which emphasis shifts from the analysis of manifest content to the construction of meaning, and to the polysemic potential of texts.

The variety of antipornography perspectives discussed in Chapter 5 share a view of pornography as bearing a unitary meaning – antiwomen, in the case of the feminist movement; antifamily for the moral conservatives. For both groups, only one reading of the pornographic text is possible. For Ellis, on the other hand, and the semiological school from which the study of linguistic conventions and codes derives, all texts including pornographic ones bear a plurality of meanings: they are polysemic (Kuhn, 1995). For Maurice Peckham, anticipating this approach in his study of art and pornography, 'the meaning of a [pornographic] term is any response to that term' (1969: p. 142), suggesting that the meaning of sexually explicit material is not only that which a particular campaigning group attaches to it but also a much more complex and multifarious collection of responses emerging from the many and diverse contexts in which the pornography is used, consumed and experienced.[2] The pornographic text is a complex sign, operating at many levels of meaning: denotative, connotative, and ideological.[3]

Film-maker Bette Gordon justifies her use of sexually explicit images in what are presented as feminist texts in the following way: 'pornography is not a monolithic construction but consists of a variety of practices operating across various institutions, places and times. ... The codes and conventions which characterize particular pornographic representations, construct sexual difference, and order ways of seeing can be analysed' (1984: p. 194). Pornography, in short, like any other media text, is 'imbued with theoretical and semiotic complexity' (Kipnis, 1993: p. 138), and carries within it a multiplicity of meanings. It can be read (decoded) and produced (encoded) from differing perspectives and positions.

Pornography as subversive text

The semiological approach to pornography has been given its most systematic application to date in the work of Linda Williams, who combines it with psychoanalysis to argue that the construction of meaning in sexually explicit material is not exclusively that of the female positioned in subordination to the dominant, exploiting male, and that the male gaze is not the only one possible in pornography. While, as she concedes, 'there is no escape from the power and dominance of the masculine heterosexual norm, it is precisely in the proliferation of different pornographies that opposition to the dominant representations of pleasure can emerge' (1992: p. 262). She acknowledges that pornography has tended to present an ideal of pleasurable sexual behaviour as seen from the perspective of the powerful male, but argues that it need not be so narrowly reflective of patriarchal sexual and social relations. Pornography should be analysed within the social and politico-economic context of patriarchy, but it is neither the essential expression of male sexuality nor the cause of it. Pornography is 'fundamentally a discourse, a way of speaking about sex' (1990: p. 228), in which patriarchy is over-represented, but open to colonization by nonsexist, nonpatriarchal voices.

In Williams' view the impact of the feminist movement, and the sexual revolution as a whole, has gradually been felt on the content of pornography, which has with time become more representative and expressive of the sexual identities of newly visible sexual communities ('liberated' women, gay men and women, nonsexist men, etc.). For Williams pornography 'has become an important means of representing a wide range of sexual identities once labelled deviant – gay, lesbian, bisexual, sadomasochist, not to mention the female sexuality which has functioned throughout Western civilization, and certainly in much pornography, as the basic deviation from the male "norm"' (1993a: p. 47).

Assiter and Carol go further, questioning the antipornography feminist assumption that all mainstream male-orientated material is inherently sexist. As they see it, 'the hard core porn men see principally shows equal relationships in which no-one particularly dominates anyone', while s/m material – the most sexist of all for many antipornography campaigners – shows 'a far higher proportion of stories in which females are dominant' (1993: p. 16). Indeed, 'given the number of porn films and magazines in which men perform as objects or as virtual sex slaves to women, it is hard to believe anyone could get the message of male dominance from modern porn' (1993). Ann Snitow suggests that pornography is not simply an expression of male sexual power and gender imbalance: 'it is also all those imbalances run riot, run to excess, sometimes explored and ad absurdum, exploded. Misogyny is one content of pornography; another content is that universal infant desire for complete, immediate gratification' (1983: p. 269).

This, suggests Williams and others, is not a recent phenomenon associated with the post-1960s politics of sexual liberation, but part of a deeper historical trend in which capitalism has liberated sexuality from the sphere of the exclusively reproductive, allowing for its commodification and mass reproduction. The expansion of pornography from the late eighteenth century onwards parallels 'a shift in emphasis from the reproductive and communal interests of society to the fullest expression of individual concerns' (Arcand, 1992: p. 175); a shift from what Williams calls 'the productivist mentality of work' with its associated conservatism and austerity in sexual and social relationships, towards a 'consumerist mentality of unending pleasure, shifting gender relations, and a desire for self-abandon' (1992: p. 273).

Applying the theoretical and analytical frameworks of Freudian psychoanalysis to pornography, Williams argues that the question of sexual agency (who is exploiting whom, and the meaning of that exploitation), in pornography of even the most apparently violent and degrading kind (e.g. s/m) is far from unambiguous but open to negotiation. Anne McLintock argues that 'identification [by the viewer] in porn can be multiple and shifting, bisexual and transexual, alternately or simultaneously – although context can limit or prohibit the degree of transgression' (1992: p. 125). For these authors pornography has the potential to be a subversive text, expressing ideas and values not those of the dominant patriarchal culture.

The sexually (and thus socially) transgressive nature of pornography is what gives it its appeal for many. As Murray Davis puts it, 'female characters are not the only ones sexually abused and humiliated ... male characters are commonly exploited as well. ... Pornography is extremely democratic in that it strips the false facades from everyone, not just from women; it peels away the crust of character, formed by society or even by the human condition itself to reveal people's authentic inner core' (1983: p. 182). While some find this 'ethic of transgression' – tipping as it often does into Sadean scenarios of pain and abuse – dangerous and disturbing, Davis and others welcome its subversive potential. For Scott Tucker, pornography, 'like any other human product ... can take forms which are more or less malignant or malign' (1990: p. 267). Pornography is not, *per se*, bad, but a 'form of story which both replicates sexual and social roles and also subverts them. ... Pornography gives us a glimpse of a world in which the erotic erupts into everyday life, in which people break out of family, work, school and passion; in which forbidden territory is trespassed' (p. 268). For Ellen Willis, applying a Freudian schema, pornography is 'the return of the repressed, of feelings and anxieties driven underground by a culture that atomizes sexuality, defining love as a noble affair of the heart and mind, lust as a base animal urge centred in unmentionable organs' (1983: p. 83). From this perspective pornography's subversive potential lies in its unearthing of (unnaturally) repressed sexual desires and fantasies.

The application of concepts and analytical tools drawn from semiotics, structuralism and psychoanalysis is of course a well-established approach to the academic study of media texts. It is, however, relatively new to the analysis of pornography in particular, and signals a major shift away from the concern with what pornography does to those who are exposed to it towards acceptance that it can, in theory and increasingly in practice, be adopted positively as one means of articulating forms of sexual behaviour hitherto excluded from public discourse. Even the conventional signifiers of male heterosexual pornography, this approach implies, such as objectification, dominance and submission, may acquire new and often subversive connotations in certain contexts. In short, this approach permits the subversive decoding of mainstream (male heterosexist) pornographic texts, as well as the subversive encoding of pornographies which challenge the patriarchal norm in their form and content. Pornography should be viewed as 'a site of feminist exploration into what it has to say about desire, what kinds of fantasies it mobilizes, and how it structures diverse sexualities' (Gordon, 1984: p. 191). This statement also applies to male hetero- and homosexual pornographic 'explorations' assuming, of course, that male sexuality is not of itself to be predefined as exploitative and violent.

Williams' *Hardcore* (1990) applies this approach to some examples of contemporary pornography which exemplify the positive articulation of gender roles and identities she wishes to emphasize, such as hermaphroditism and transsexualism. In the remainder of this chapter, I consider the possibilities of the subversive encoding/decoding of pornography, and the uses and gratifications associated with its consumption by, first, 'mainstream' heterosexuals, then the lesbian feminist, and, finally, gay male communities.

How men use porn

I will begin this section by restating the important fact that pornography can be and is used by many men (and some women) as an accessory to their sexual abuse of others. Chapter 5 highlighted the methodological difficulties associated with proving that pornography causes such abuse (in the sense of triggering the desire to abuse when no such desire or pattern of behaviour existed before). Abuse happens nevertheless, and pornography is often part of the process, 'scripting' particular acts. In the case of children, the making of pornography is both the act and the record of abuse. Such use (abuse) of sexually explicit material is already illegal in some cases (child sex abuse) and in others, as noted in Chapter 5, part of a broader social context in which abuse of all forms may be present. Few would suggest, however, that it is representative of how most men experience the consumption of pornography.

Maurice Peckham argues that pornography, as mediated sexuality, functions mainly as a means of teaching the sex roles which are central to human sexual behaviour in advanced societies. Pornography 'consists principally of the exaggeration of culturally standardized sexual cues' (1969: p. 170). It confirms genital response (arousal and penile erection, in the male case) to those standardized roles, and leads the user through a process of initiation. It may also be used as a substitute for real sexual activity with a partner, or for forms of sexual activity which may be thought of as dangerous, impractical or stigmatized. For many boys, pornography is the source of their first sexual experience. It is thus 'a central source of material that instructs young men about the relationship between their sexuality and their masculinity. [It] shows men what it means to be a real man having sex. Pornography is an important part of the male sexual script, which, in turn, is a vital confirmation of masculinity' (Kimmel, 1990: p. 12).

Scott Macdonald, in his bravely titled 'Confessions of a feminist porn watcher', agrees that men use pornography for educational purposes, and also to permit the observation of sexual behaviour without intrusion – a necessary element, he implies, of social learning. It enables men 'to deal periodically with the cultural context which mitigates against their full acceptance of themselves as sexual beings' (1990: p. 41). For Michael Kimmel, pornography's value lies in the fact that 'it brings the hidden, private world of male sexual pleasure into the public arena of political discourse' (1990: p. ix). It also functions as a necessary outlet for the expression of sexual fantasies.

To the extent that the use of pornography is associated with a process of socialization or integration into dominant male sex roles, from the feminist perspective this is of course an important reason for attacking it. Sara Diamond argues, however, that 'while the voyeurism that pornography encourages is an ideological confirmation of men's power, it is also a contemporary way of fulfilling curiosity about sex, and about other's sexual activities' (1985: p. 44). In this sense pornography not only expresses and reflects male power but in its private and furtive process of consumption also reflects male inadequacy, passivity and sexual timidity. In so far as the heterosexual male's use of pornography is bound up with socialization, or instruction into patriarchal conduct and norms of sexual behaviour, it performs precisely the (antisocial) ideological functions described in Chapter 5: pornography teaches men how to be sexist, and provides cultural legitimation for sexist behaviour. As was pointed out there, however, the teaching of such values is present throughout the apparatus of cultural production: within the family and at school; in popular feature films and drama; in comic books and pop music. Pornography therefore is not unique in reflecting the prevailing values of the society in which it circulates. It *is* uniquely sexual, of course, and provides, as Scott Macdonald suggests, a private sphere in which the male of the species can negotiate his desires and fantasies. Not all relationships are suited to or can accommodate such exploration, and not all men (nor women) have stable sexual relationships in any case. In these circumstances, it can be argued, pornography may have a socially useful role to play, precisely in its 'objectification' of sexual desire. Indeed, the 'learning and teaching' function of pornography now plays an increasingly important public health role in the context of HIV/AIDS (*see* below).

Women and porn

When the Johnson Commission undertook research on the use of pornography in the United States in the 1960s, it was found that virtually all sexually explicit materials were made for, and used by men.[4] The Meese Commission report, published 15 years later, found that the proportion of women reporting use of pornographic material had increased dramatically (to about two thirds of the level of male use, according to one 1985 Gallup poll) (1986: p. 904). While by far the largest proportion of pornographic material in circulation can still be defined as 'straight male-orientated', i.e. produced for a male, heterosexual audience, women in the 1980s were increasingly finding uses for sexually explicit material. Female-orientated pornography is now commonplace, part of the 'flourishing growth of popular sexual entertainment for women', identified by many cultural analysts (Ross, 1988: p. 191).[5]

Women are also able, it is argued, to read male-orientated pornographic texts in ways which allow them to derive pleasure and benefit from the experience. Carol Clover's introduction to *Dirty Looks* observes that 'there is no single "right reading" of pornography, and even the most standard forms of heterosexual pornography confess a deeply complicated relation to women and femininity, to men and masculinity, and to the terms of sexual difference that order our everyday lives' (Gibson and Gibson, 1993: p. 4). In any case, argues Marcia Pally, what's wrong with a bit of objectification now and then? 'It cannot', she writes, 'be a goal of feminism':

> to eliminate moments during the day when a heterosexual man considers a woman, or women as a class, to be sexually desirable. Feminism seeks to expand the roles accessible to women, including the role of voyeur and sexual subject. It is a feminist goal for women to recognize the objects of *their* desire and partake of them without a fall from good-girl grace. That means more sexual imagery by and for women, not less for men (1993: p. 6).[6]

As Chapter 2 suggested, the impact and influence of feminism has been reflected in the increasing tendency of women to express their sexuality in ways which would have been socially unacceptable prior to the sexual revolution. This has included acknowledging the existence of 'active' feminine sexuality, as well as its more conventionally passive dimension. The work of Nancy Friday has been influential in this respect, revealing in the form of interviews the highly instrumental, frequently aggressive and dominance-orientated sexual fantasies experienced by many women.[7] Friday's interviews expose 'the ambiguous and complex relationship between sexual pleasure and danger in women's lives and in feminist theory' (Vance, 1984: p. 3), challenge antipornography feminist assumptions about the nature of female sexuality, and make quite intelligible the notion that women can enjoy an activity defined by the former as the 'essence' of maleness. They may, as Friday's work shows, even enjoy fantasies involving scenarios of rape, submission and degradation.

Linda Grant's review of post-World War II sexual history links this movement with the development of the Pill in the 1950s and 1960s, and the subsequent sexual revolution (1993). The 1960s, as we have seen, was a decade in which images of sex became mainstream, sexual relations were liberalized, and women emerged as an active sexual community. Women's magazines such as *Nova* and *Cosmopolitan* began to change their content, reflecting the needs of a new generation of educated, economically independent, sexually assertive women. In the 1970s complex and sophisticated discourse about sex became a feature of women's magazines, and 'porn for women' appeared in the form of *Playgirl*. Grant goes on to argue that this development in women's readiness and ability to discuss and articulate their sexuality in public was interrupted by the influence of cultural feminism on the women's movement, with its over-arching characterization of pornography and male sexuality as inherently misogynistic. In the 1980s and 1990s, however, and as Chapter 3 showed, women returned to the public exploration of sexual identity and experience. There was an 'explosion of female sexuality' in these years (1993: p. 256), exemplified in the work of mainstream pop icons such as Madonna (*see* Chapter 8) who understood, as Grant sees it, that women 'must come to an accommodation with porn' (1993: p. 258). For Grant, the Madonna phenomenon was part of a second sexual revolution, in which women would 'reassert the gains made in the sixties and vanquish the New Right; abandon the sex-negative cul-de-sac along which feminism had taken female desire in the seventies; and formulate an overdue sexual language for the clitoris' (1993: p. 259).

Lisa Duggan and her colleagues, while accepting that much pornography represents a danger to women, argue nevertheless that 'its existence serves some social functions, which benefit women' (Duggan *et al.*, 1988: p. 74). By challenging Judaeo-Christian ideals of what sex is for and how it should be organized (i.e. exclusively within marriage and monogamy), pornography subverts the very patriarchy which so disadvantages women.

> Pornography carries many messages other than woman-hating: it advocates sexual adventure, sex outside of marriage, sex for no reason other than pleasure, casual sex, anonymous sex, group sex, voyeuristic sex,

illegal sex, public sex. Some of these ideas appeal to women reading or seeing pornography, who may interpret some images as legitimating their own sense of sexual agency or desire to be sexually aggressive. Women's experience of pornography is not universally victimizing (1988).

For these authors the sexual sphere is not one of unremitting, overwhelming male power, but can be 'actively contested': 'women are agents, and not merely victims, who make decisions and act on them, and who desire, seek out and enjoy sexuality' (Duggan, *et al.*, 1988: p. 75). Ellen Willis argues that:

> A woman who is raped is a victim; a woman who enjoys pornography (even if that means enjoying a rape fantasy) is in a sense a rebel, insisting on an aspect of her sexuality that has been defined as a male preserve. Insofar as pornography glorifies male supremacy and sexual alienation, it is deeply reactionary. But in rejecting sexual repression and hypocrisy – which have inflicted even more damage on women than on men – it expresses a radical impulse (1984: p. 85).

Assiter and Carol, following this line, suggest that 'the real threat [of porn] is in subverting the myth that women are largely asexual creatures who dislike sex' (1993: p. 16).

For antipornography feminists such an optimistic perspective is wholly misplaced and naive, deriving from a fundamental misinterpretation of the meaning of contemporary sexual culture. Just as the 1960s' sexual revolution amounted, for women, to little more than a 'free love' charter of advantage principally to men, the 'second' sexual revolution is taking place within parameters set by patriarchy, and thus can be of little benefit in the struggle against sexism. As Susan Faludi expressed it in her influential book (1991), the 'explosion' of sexually explicit imagery represents nothing less than a patriarchally inspired and directed 'backlash' against the gains of women since the 1960s. The post-1960s prevalence of sexually explicit imagery, particularly that (allegedly) growing proportion with a violent or sado-masochistic content, 'help to counterbalance women's recent self-assertion' (Wolf, 1990: p. 60). In Susan Kappeler's view (1992) the pro-pornography arguments of such organizations as Feminists Against Censorship, and of 'post-feminist' intellectuals like Camille Paglia, represent nothing more than an attempt to win acceptance from, and incorporation into, the still-dominant patriarchal culture. From this perspective the pro-pornography movement, even when it involves women who would define themselves without hesitation as feminists, amounts to a backlash against 'real' feminism comparable in its function to that which occurred alongside the first wave of feminism in the early 1920s. Women who publicize the pleasures of heterosexuality – and even, as we shall see in the next section, some forms of lesbian sexuality – are simply 'internalizing their oppression' and 'eroticizing their subordination'. The 'pro-sex tradition', as Susan Jeffreys calls it, 'turns out to mean pro-sexual dominance and submission' (1990a: p. 25). Women's consumption of pornography, and the championing by some of such practices as sado-masochism, represents complicity in patriarchal oppression, a complicity which Kathleen Barry finds 'intolerable' (1979: p. 252).

Such views do not deny 'the potential seductiveness of pornography for women' (Carola, 1988: p. 173), but insist that such a preference is not freely chosen. How could it be, in a cultural environment shaped from birth by patriarchal values? Women who use pornography, or defend its use, are victims of patriarchy, not rebels against it. The 'pro-sex', 'social constructionist' viewpoint, as Dorothy Leidholdt terms it, ignores the reality of sexual experience for the great majority of women, in which the imposition of deviance, coercion and exploitation is commonplace. To participate in that experience, either in the consumption of pornography or the acting out of behaviours depicted therein, is not the free exploration of female sexuality, but old-fashioned submission to male ideals.

> The sexuality our culture offers women today through pornography is not new, not avant garde, not revolutionary. It's the same sex male supremacy has always forced on us; being used as the instrument of someone else's sexual agency – the instrument of someone socially male. ... To speak powerfully in favour of sexual pleasure while blithely ignoring the fact that this pleasure is usually achieved through women's subordination and violation is to speak powerfully in favour of a system that keeps all women down (1990: p. 131).

Women's consumption and enjoyment of porn is, then, tantamount to support for patriarchal sexual relations, 'a part of the phenomenon of identification with the oppressor, much like that of some concentration camp prisoners with their jailers' (Stock, 1990: p. 150). As Susan Brownmiller once put it in an influential essay, 'there can be no "equality" in porn, no female equivalent, no turning of the tables in the name of bawdy fun. Pornography, like rape, is a male invention, designed to dehumanize women, to reduce the female to an object of sexual access' (1991: p. 38).

Here we arrive at the central division within feminism about the meaning and significance of pornography: on one side the radical feminists, strongly antiporn, who believe it capable of being accurately read only one way – as the essence and exemplification of male sexual oppression. For a woman to challenge this reading is to be complicit in her own oppression, and to share responsibility for the survival of patriarchy as a social system. On the other side are those pro-porn feminists who assert the multiplicity of meanings and readings to be derived even from mainstream male heterosexual pornography; the importance of fantasy and play in sexual desire and behaviour; and pornography's subversive potential to challenge dominant sexual values (which, all feminists agree, disadvantage women).

Contained in this latter constellation of views is not only a refutation (at least partial) of the thesis of pornography's antisocial, antiwomen effects, but a 'postmodernist' challenge to the attempt by some feminists to erect a monolithic worldview and theoretical apparatus for interpreting the pornographic. Gayle Rubin, for example, wants to 'challenge the assumption that feminism is or should be the privileged site of a theory of sexuality' (1984: p. 307), and to argue that cultural feminism, rather than advancing female rights and opportunities, undermines them by closing off whole areas of sexual expression. Antipornography feminism, from this perspective, seeks to impose an authoritarian, 'politically correct' ideal of what female sexuality should be, in isolation from what women actually feel and desire in the sexual sphere. For Rubin and other feminists of this persuasion pornography can be, in some circumstances, an instrument for the expression of an authentic female sexuality. As Carol and Pollard put it, 'our [female] sexuality has always been defined for us by others. As yet, we have not learned enough about who we are or can be to identify *any* authentic female sexuality, let alone its limits. Our only legitimate option is to let each woman explore as she pleases, and define for herself where she wishes to draw the line' (1993: p. 56).

If, these authors assert, women wish to use pornography as a means of exploring their own and their partners' sexual identities and preferences, then this should be accepted as compatible with feminism's strategic objective of delivering female equality. To argue otherwise is to support a biologically determinist, 'Victorian' conception of female sexuality as essentially asexual.

Pornography, then, can and should be one means by which heterosexual women (I shall examine the uses of porn by lesbians in the next section) can express and explore their sexuality. On one level, they can read mainstream pornographic texts subversively (many, as already noted, show women in dominating positions over men). On another, women can influence and participate – as full agents – in the production process of pornography. Furthermore, recognition of the existence of a female market for pornography has influenced male producers. Since the 1960s, pornography has ceased to be exclusively the secret, furtive object of an all-male sexual subculture, becoming instead mainstream entertainment for mixed-sex couples, both on video and in cinemas. As women have become more politically vocal and sexually demanding, men can 'no longer make porn without taking into account the complications of women's desire' (McLintock, 1992: p. 120). Now female sexuality, 'in particular the clitoral orgasm ... haunt[s] male pornography as a central problematic' (1992: p. 120). To deny this development, as cultural feminists do, is to close off opportunities for women 'to alter the shape of the industry on terms more suitable to our own uncharted pleasures' (1992: p. 131).

Notwithstanding the opposition of some feminist groups women *have* become increasingly involved in the production of sexually explicit material, not just in their traditional capacity as performers, but as producers and directors too (frequently combining these roles). In the United States Candida Royale's Femme Productions, and companies such as Fatale have pioneered a selfconsciously feminist pornography, by which is meant an approach that 'connotes women's empowerment, rather than victimization, on the sexual terrain' (McLintock, 1992: p. 75). Magazines such as *Quim*, *Bad Attitudes* and *On Our Backs* have expressed a similarly pro-pornography position (*see* Chapter 7 for a discussion of the content of these and other examples of 'porn for women').

Lesbians and pornography

One explanation frequently advanced to explain the sudden intensification of the pornography debate in the 1980s, and the public fragmentation of the feminist movement which accompanied it, was the fact that some of the most 'violent', 'objectifying' and 'degrading' material available was that used by lesbians in the context of sado-masochistic sexual behaviour. The lesbian s/m movement first emerged publicly in San Francisco in 1976, demanding the right to use pornography which reflected the sexual lifestyle of its members (Califia, 1982). Other lesbians, and feminists in general, were confused and disturbed by this 'sleeping with the enemy'. For Linda Williams, 'the feminist lesbian sadomasochist has arguably been the key provoking agent of these [intra-feminist] wars, unsettling all the comfortable received opinion about sexual power, pleasure and perversion' (1992: p. 248). Lesbianism, while representing the politically correct ideal for many feminists, challenged in its sado-masochist variant dominant feminist assumptions about the nature of female sexuality. If hierarchies, dominance and submission, and physical coercion in sex were all the product of patriarchy and symptoms of misogyny, how could it be that some lesbians – radically separatist and antipatriarchal – appeared to endorse and enthusiastically participate in such behaviours? How to make sense of lesbian pornography in which women were tied up, beaten with whips and other objects, penetrated by dildos, and 'forced' to undergo other equally objectifying and degrading treatment?

For the antipornography feminists s/m lesbianism, and the sexually explicit materials used by women in that context, were, like porn for straight women, defined as a kind of internal colonialism of the female psyche by patriarchal norms and values. Women were not 'naturally' sado-masochistic, but were merely appropriating values and practices learnt from the dominant patriarchal culture. The 'butch-femme' roles[8] affected by some lesbians were a pathetic mimickry of the hierarchical relationships formed by straight couples. The practices of s/m lesbians – 'libertarianism', as one writer called it – were fundamentally apolitical: 'a sexual preference without a feminist politics' (Raymond, 1992: p. 166), distinct and distant from ideologically sound, campaigning feminism. While some sought to define lesbian s/m and the pornography associated with it as a radical social force it was in reality a politically bankrupt sexual lifestyle, which attempted to ignore socio-sexual reality.

For the 'libertarians' themselves this was a patronizing, authoritarian stance, which denied women the autonomy and agency to develop and articulate their own sexual preferences. Far from being an apolitical, valueless practice, 'sadomasochistic fantasy recognize[d] the role of power in the woman's often circuituous route to pleasure' (Williams, 1990: p. 228). As photographer Grace Lau put it, 'there are women who are tremendously aroused at the sensation of being in a powerless position, but that is because in reality they have power, they have made a choice. I believe women today who have absorbed the feminist analysis, and feel they know themselves and their sexuality, make an educated and independent choice about how they want to experience the erotic'.[9]

One of the most damaging aspects of antipornography feminism, from this perspective, is its tendency to isolate and stigmatize 'deviant' sexualities, such as s/m lesbianism. Having only recently emerged from legal, political and medical persecution and discrimination lesbians and other sexual minority communities (such as gay men) now find their rights to expression attacked by an influential strand of the feminist movement, often in alliance with moral conservatism. In this sense 'the [antipornography] discourse on sexuality is less a sexology than a demonology' (Rubin, 1984: p. 301), constructing a hierarchy of 'good' and 'bad' sexual identities, within which anything apart from monogamous lesbianism of the non-s/m variety is condemned as antifeminist. Concerning the 'violence' depicted in s/m pornography its defenders stress the role-playing, ritual dimension of such behaviour, and its fundamentally consensual character.

Of course, not all lesbian pornography has a sado-masochistic content. Much of the female-produced and directed material mentioned above is aimed at the lesbian market, and selfconsciously sets out to depict only sexual activities which would be defined as nonexploitative, noncoercive and nondegrading (*see* Chapter 7).

No matter how far removed from the patriarchal, misogynistic conventions of male-orientated pornography we may acknowledge such material to be, its very existence contradicts the view that all pornography is, by definition, patriarchal. For Gayle Rubin, Linda Williams and others, this is the key difficulty with antipornography feminist campaigning: it rejects the notion that female sexuality, like that of the male, can be hedonistic, lustful, self-gratifying, and instrumental, thereby replicating historically well-established notions of what women should and should not be, sexually speaking. In the context of patriarchal dominance – economically, politically and culturally – the phenomenon of lesbian (and female straight) pornography is

viewed from this perspective as a progressive-subversive political development, albeit one still restricted to the margins of cultural production. Failure
to recognize the empowering, subversive quality of some pornography leads
straight into the 'sex-negative cul-de-sac'. Consequently:

> our current sexual politics can no longer be that begun by Kate Millett
> and continued by anti-pornography feminists. This politics of con-
> demning the evil masculine 'other' feeds all too easily into the con-
> demnation of the deviant sexualities of 'perverse others'. Now that
> these perverse others take their place, not simply as freak contrasts to
> a dominant norm, but as authoritative subjectivities, both explicit and
> erotic, on the scene of sexual representation, the anti-pornography
> feminist reification of a vilified masculinity backfires as a strategy for
> the furtherance of feminist goals (Williams, 1993b: p. 59).

Pornography and the gay male

Many of the 'uses, gratifications and meanings' of lesbian pornography
apply also to the material used by gay men. Here, too, the debate has centred around the validity and political significance of sexual representation
for a minority which has historically been oppressed because of its sexual
preference. Added to this is the issue of HIV/AIDS. Does the presence of
HIV/AIDS, and the constraints it imposes on gay male sexual behaviour,
have implications for the meanings to be derived from gay pornography?

Simon Watney answers this question in the affirmative. HIV/AIDS, he
argues, has provoked 'a crisis of representation ... a crisis over the entire
framing of knowledge about the human body and its capacities for sexual
pleasure' (1987: p. 9). In relation to gay pornography, the crisis can be
defined as one in which the activities depicted are, in a large proportion of
the materials in circulation, precisely those which the professional medical
community has identified as 'unsafe' or 'high risk' – principally anal penetration of one male by another.

Two general responses are possible to this crisis: one, identified by Linda
Singer, Cindy Patton and other writers, is the appearance of an 'erotopho-
bia' in cultural life, defined as 'the terrifying, irrational reaction to the erotic
which makes individuals and society vulnerable to psychological and social
control in cultures where pleasure is strictly categorized and regulated'
(Patton, 1985: p. 103). Gay male sexuality, and the pornography which
articulates it, may be thought to be particularly vulnerable in this respect,
since the HIV/AIDS epidemic has been, and continues to be associated in the
public imagination with the gay male sexual lifestyle. Moral conservatives,
notes Steven Seidman, seized upon HIV/AIDS to 'rehabilitate' the notion of

male homosexuality as deviant, diseased and dangerous, while liberals used it to 'legitimate a sexual ethic of monogamy and romance' (1992: p. 156). From both directions the hedonism and self-centred instrumentalism of the gay male sexual lifestyle was attacked.

An alternative response, identified by Dennis Altman in 1986, has been to recognize the positive role – the uses – which pornography can play in the (safe) expression of gay male sexuality: providing an (albeit mediated) experience without the exchange of body fluids by which means HIV is transmitted. Altman, as we saw in Chapter 5 recognizes the difficulties in assessing the significance of this role: in particular, the extent to which gay porn 'causes' or condones promiscuous (and unsafe) sexual behaviour, or presents an outlet for fantasy.

While the uses of pornography in this respect are available for all sexual communities, they are of special importance to gay men, as already suggested. For this group in particular, any device which might reduce the risks attached to sexual activity must be welcome. Of course, while the viewing of pornography is 'safe sex' *par excellence*, those who perform in the material may be subjecting themselves to the risk of HIV transmission. It is significant therefore that gay male pornography (as well as straight) increasingly depicts safer sex techniques and messages. Moreover, there are now in circulation increasing numbers of 'educational' materials which offer instruction in safer sex, using images which, in other contexts, would be defined as pornographic (Patton, 1992). In Britain, Pride Video Productions has made *Getting It Right* and *Well Sexy Women* (both 1993) for gay men and lesbians respectively, depicting oral sex, 'rimming', fisting and other exotic practices, the showing of which would not be permitted in a non-educational context.[10] These films are part of the movement, now established as socially legitimate, because necessary from the point of view of public health, 'to develop images, languages, and practices which eroticize safe sex' (Singer, 1993: p. 70). The message of such material, as expressed by the makers of what they describe as 'safer sex porn' is that 'you can have hot sex without placing yourself at risk of AIDS' (Carlomusto and Bordowitz, 1992: p. 177).

In addition to the potential of gay male pornography as a risk-reducing form of sexual activity (and an educational tool), many would defend it as an authentic expression of a particular kind of sexual lifestyle. Like lesbian porn, that produced for and by gay men, in so far as it celebrates and articulates 'deviance', subverts and challenges the still-dominant homophobic culture, becoming to that extent a political text. Gay male pornography is, from this point of view, an important part of the struggle for social recognition and legitimation of a marginalized sexual community.

Against this view, John Stoltenberg – himself gay – condemns much of gay sexuality, and the pornography which expresses it, as lacking progressive and worthy features. For Stoltenberg the 'fast-lane' gay male sexual lifestyle, celebrating as it does promiscuity and hedonism, lacks integrity and should not be held up for emulation, while the pornography frequently reproduces conventional patriarchal roles and stereotypes. Just as the butch-femme lesbian lifestyle is condemned as a poor imitation of hierarchical het-erosexuality by cultural feminists, gay male parallels, in which dominance, submission, sado-masochism and exaggerated masculine/feminine distinc-tions are present, are no more worthy of political support than their straight antecedents. Male supremacy in a gay context is, for Stoltenberg, no more laudable than it is in a relationship between a man and a woman (1990; 1992). Gay pornography, like any other, institutionalizes and eroticizes male dominance and should therefore be condemned, a view rejected by Mandy Merck in the following terms:

> For every attempt ... to assimilate gay porn to a genre of allegedly unremitting patriarchal oppression (phallocentric, male-supremacist, sadistic, homophobic) come replies defending its crucial affirmation of homosexual identity, fluid role-reversals, multiple eroticism, subver-sive humour and educational necessity in the age of AIDS. Gay porn, like other forms of representation, includes work distinguished by misogyny, racism and homophobia, as well as invitations to non-macho identifications, satire of heterosexuality and safe-sex informa-tion (1993: p. 217).

Conclusion

Chapter 5 reviewed a complex and contentious debate centred on the status of various kinds of evidence, against which hypotheses about the harms caused by pornography – its negative effects – were reviewed and compared. In this chapter, by contrast, we turned our attention to the question of meaning, and the uses and gratifications obtained from the pornographic by those who choose to consume it. While emphasizing at the outset the poten-tial for abuse of pornography in relation to coercive sexual activity, the dis-cussion has proceeded from the assumption that, in many of the contexts in which it is used, pornography is neither the cause nor the conduit of antiso-cial or violent behaviour, but a form of sexual representation exposure to which is freely entered into. We then attempted to describe some of the 'uses and gratifications' which might be derived from that exposure.

The debate about meaning progressed on three levels. First, there is the central issue of the meaning of the sexual revolution as it has affected straight and gay men and women. From the perspective of some feminists the revolution has been misnamed, amounting only to 'more of the same', i.e. an excuse for patriarchal values and practices to find freer expression, to the benefit principally of men. It has also been viewed as a 'backlash'

(Faludi, 1991; Wolf, 1990). Even the gays who have developed their own pornographies on the back of this revolution are argued to have internalized their own oppression by aping patriarchal patterns of dominance and subordination. 'Libertarian' feminists, on the other hand, and members of the gay communities themselves, have asserted the subversive, even political character of their pornographies, just as they defend the validity of their lifestyles. From this perspective the sexual revolution has signalled a genuine advance in the rights and powers enjoyed by previously stigmatized and oppressed sexual minorities. Their production and use of pornography is part of that empowerment.

Second and related to the above, the debate has concerned the meaning of sexuality. On the antipornography feminist side divisions between the legitimate and the illegitimate in sexual behaviour tend to be clearly drawn so that sado-masochism, for example, is wrong. Its meaning is clear: violence, dominance, degradation and submission. By extension, any pornography which depicts it is 'eroticizing violence' and playing into the hands of the patriarchy. For the libertarians, on the other hand, the meaning of this and other sexual identities is considerably more complex, based on forms of role-playing, so that the violence and domination are not read as real coercive acts but the enacting of rituals, games and fantasies by consensual adults. To deny this, for Simon Watney, is to fail to understand the significance of sexual behaviour, and 'to confuse the simple yet central distinction between coercive and consensual forms of sex, sliding endlessly between "representation" and "real"' (1987: p. 71). For whatever reasons, shrouded in the mysteries of personal psychological history (including, in some cases, histories shaped by child sexual abuse) some individuals fantasize about and derive pleasure from performing sexual scenarios which may seem offensive or degrading to others, ranging from the extremes of violent s/m-type behaviour to the nonviolent, now relatively mainstream activities of oral and anal penetration. Before condemning such behaviour, the libertarians argue, its meaning to those engaged in it must be understood and, if it is genuinely consensual, its legitimacy allowed. To do otherwise is to impose one politically correct model of sexuality on diverse communities: precisely the objective sought by moral conservatives.

The third level, finally, on which this chapter has discussed meaning, is in the texts themselves. In the writings of Beverley Brown, John Ellis, Linda Williams, Annette Kuhn and others, we note the importation of critical communication studies into the field of the pornographic. With this movement pornographic texts cease to be carriers of uniform, universally agreed meanings, but polysemic, shifting signifiers. Gays can read straight porn, and vice versa; images can vary in their meaning according to the social semiotic of their reception; pornography can be decoded and encoded 'subversively'. For Gloria Steinem, whose seminal essay was adopted as a key text by antipornography feminists, sexuality could be, as well as the means of the biological reproduction of the species, a means of communication.

And, she conceded then, 'sex as communication [including the porno-graphic form of sexual communication] can send messages as different as life and death' (1980: p. 37). In this context, to argue as some feminists did that pornography was always and everywhere patriarchal and oppressive was to say that these negative qualities were inherent to sexual representa-tion, when in fact they were present only for those who read them in that way.

I conclude this chapter, then, by suggesting that the meanings, gratifica-tions and uses of pornography are many and varied. While some perspec-tives are clear in their denunciation of sexually explicit material as, in the context of contemporary patriarchy, essentially sexist and misogynistic, this particular reading does not correspond to nor incorporate the experiences of many men and women, gay and straight, for whom pornography is part of a sexual lifestyle. To this extent the antipornography feminist position is flawed because, as Andrew Ross puts it, it has 'no interest in the wide vari-ety of uses to which pornography [is] put by diverse consumers and taste subcultures ... [it] cannot account for the interplay between the complex constructions of representation and fantasy in the consumption of pornog-raphy' and it cannot 'accommodate the testimony of women who enjoy pornography' (1989: p. 188).

Notes

1   *See*, for example, David Morley's review of the effects debate in *The Nationwide Audience* (1980).
2   As Anna Marie Smith expresses it, 'no text has an "essential" meaning; even the most explicit sexual image may or may not have a *sexist* con-notation. The connotation of a sexual image depends on the ways in which multiple codes are intertwined together in that particular instance. As such, we cannot define sexist elements in abstraction. The distinction between non-sexist, sexually explicit material and sexist sex-ually explicit material must always be established with respect to par-ticular texts, and those texts must be evaluated in terms of their specific contexts' (1995: p. 200).
3   For a definition of these terms, and an introduction to the semiological school, *see* Fiske (1992).
4   Hawkins and Zimring report that at this time upwards of 95 per cent of patrons of pornographic bookstores were male (1988: p. 54).
5   Ross notes that 'the male strip joint à la Chippendales, the 'Tupperware' parties for buying sex accessories and paraphernalia, the vast readership for romance novels and literary erotica, and the rapidly growing female consumption of female pornography ... have all

become routine features of popular cultural life for women in the last fifteen years. Even s/m, once the privileged preserve of a wealthy male class, has become a typical post-camp pop fantasy, and a conventional, if not entirely common, practice in middle-class culture (1989: p. 191)

6   Kathy Myers (1995) argues similarly that there is a 'necessary objectification' involved in all acts of looking, whether by men at women, women at men, or any other form of voyeuristic experience. Objectification should not, therefore, be viewed as a necessarily negative phenomenon.

7   One chapter of *Women On Top*, for example, reflects the content of these fantasies in its title – 'Seductive, sometimes sadistic, sexually controlling women' (Friday, 1991).

8   In which one woman plays the dominant masculine role in a relationship, the other the submissive 'feminine' role.

9   Quoted in Neustatter, A., 'Guess who's coming to the erotic dinner?', *The Observer*, 25 November 1990.

10   *Seriously Sexy: Safer Sex For Young People* (Paradox Films, 1993) was produced by the same organization for young heterosexuals.

|7|

Pornography today

Pornography first emerged, as shown in Chapter 4, as a type of literary and visual image circulating more or less exclusively among the male elites of early modern capitalism. In this respect it may be compared to other media forms, such as journalism, the initial accessibility and dissemination of which were dependent on the consumer's possession of wealth, education and literacy. From the nineteenth century onwards, however, paralleling the development of journalism in this respect at least, pornography gradually became commodified – the commercial product of a growing industry, available to more and more people as the technology of text reproduction developed. By the latter part of the twentieth century pornography had become a mass-market phenomenon, consumed by millions and sustaining a multi-billion dollar global industry. This chapter reviews the development of that industry, and identifies its main contemporary players. I then examine the content of some of what they produce, selecting material representative of the variety of markets addressed by pornography.

The producers

The development of a pornography industry has, as one would expect, proceeded hand in hand with the invention of new forms of image reproduction, utilizing the opportunities for commercial exploitation of humanity's long-standing interest in depictions of the sexually explicit which each new invention has presented. While the content and stylistic conventions of modern pornography can be traced back to the seventeenth century (*see* Chapter 4) pornographic images became available for mass consumption only with the invention of photography in the nineteenth century. In Hebditch and Anning's account (1988) the first mass producer of pornography is identified as Englishman Henry Hayler, who manufactured and distributed sexually explicit images in large numbers in the 1870s. For his efforts he was targeted by the Society for the Suppression of Vice and raided by the police in March 1874.

Advances in the technologies of photography, film and publishing steadily increased the circulation of pornography in the late nineteenth and early twentieth centuries, although the production and consumption of sexually explicit materials remained illegal and heavily stigmatized in Europe and North America. Only with the sexual revolution of the 1960s did pornography move 'above ground' and acquire the status of a legally sanctioned, if still shame-evoking, element of western consumer culture. Prior to this point, images of nudity were limited to naturist magazines and pin-ups.

The modern pornography industry can be said to have been established, then, when the mass-reproductive power of media technology could begin to take advantage of the sexual liberalism associated with the late 1960s and thereafter. The first hardcore magazines were produced where sexual liberalization went furthest, fastest, in Sweden in 1967, using newly available colour-printing techniques. In Denmark and Germany, too, where the impact of the sexual revolution resulted in a dramatic loosening up of moral regulation and censorship, pornography of the most explicit varieties was pioneered. For this reason, these countries became the base for the first large-scale commercial producers of pornography: in Sweden, Berthe Milton, founder of the Private chain of magazines (and later video), which established conventions of hardcore pornography subsequently adopted elsewhere; the Theander brothers in Denmark, who founded the Rodox company, described by Hebditch and Anning as 'the largest pornography publishing house in the world' (1988: p. 53); Beate Uhse and Hans Moser in Germany. These individuals and the companies they established applied the new printing techniques to the climates of moral liberalism which existed within the countries where they operated, establishing a multi-national industry as their products were first exported abroad, then used as the templates for numerous imitations. Beginning with magazines, these European companies also pioneered the production and mass distribution of film and then video pornography, sex aid products such as vibrators and lingerie, and the sex shops in which this growing range of sex-related commodities were sold. In many countries hardcore pornography could, from the late 1960s onwards, be purchased in high-street bookstores and newsagents. Mail-order was also developed as a means of disseminating sexually explicit material.

The United Kingdom

Such liberalism in the production and distribution of pornography was not universal, of course. In Britain, one of the largest consumer markets in

Europe, material of the type produced by Private or Rodox has never been legal. When loopholes in the law are discovered, such as the possibility of circumventing obscenity legislation by subscribing to materials through mail-order, these have been closed off. When in the early 1990s it became possible for British satellite viewers to receive hardcore televisual pornography produced by the Red Hot Dutch company, the sale of the decoder required to unscramble the offending signals was prohibited.

As a result of this vigilance by the state, British pornography has always been less explicit than that available in continental Europe. It has nevertheless fostered a large and profitable industry selling, according to one estimate, 20 million copies of magazines in 1993, and making for its manufacturers a profit of £52 million.[1] The longest established and most successful of British producers is Paul Raymond, whose organization pioneered adult cinema clubs and striptease shows in London's Soho district in the 1950s, and established its first pornographic magazines in the 1970s (Itzin, 1992). By the 1990s Raymond was one of the wealthiest businessmen in Britain, with major holdings in the London property market and a personal fortune estimated at around £1.7 billion. Although property-dealing was the source of the largest part of his wealth, he was firmly associated in the public imagination with his adult theatres, such as Raymond's Revue Bar in London.

While still subject to occasional vilification in the press and elsewhere Paul Raymond represents, as Catherine Itzin's edited volume describes him, 'the respectable face of pornography in Britain' (1992: p. 78). Even by British standards the materials to which his companies put their name are 'soft'. His London theatres attract tourists in the same way as the Moulin Rouge floorshow in Paris. His magazines – the best-known is *Men Only* – are broadly comparable in their degree of explicitness with both Hugh Hefner's *Playboy* and Bob Guccione's *Penthouse* in the United States. In this sense he is part of what we might call a 'pornographic establishment' with its roots in the British tradition of dirty postcards and sexual innuendos rather than the in-your-face graphicity of continental European pornographers. While *Men Only* and its closest competitor, *Mayfair*, owned by Kenneth Bound, have undoubtedly become more explicit over time, they are part of a masculine culture of 'entertainment for men' which, like *Playboy* in the United States, predates the emergence of hardcore pornography into the mainstream marketplace, and the rise of feminism in the 1960s.

More controversial, in the context of the relatively strict censorial regime of the United Kingdom, has been the output of David Sullivan and his associates, notable in Britain for actively seeking to imitate the styles and content of hardcore European pornography. Sullivan has enhanced his reputation, and periodically provoked episodes of minor moral panic, by seeking to cross over from the production of pornography to the sphere of respectable newspaper publishing.

At the time of writing David Sullivan was the proprietor of the *News and*

Echo regional newspaper in the north of England, and had also been sub-stantially involved in the Portsmouth and Sunderland and Bristol *Evening Post* newspaper chains.[2] For a brief period in 1987 he joined forces with Express Newspapers to co-produce the *Star*. It is, however, as Britain's most outrageous pornographer that he remains best known.

Sullivan's success can be attributed in large part to his skilful manipula-tion of British antipornography legislation, which has allowed him since the 1970s to market his products as being on the very boundary of what is legally acceptable in the UK. By tapping into the frustrated British demand for material somewhat more explicit than *Mayfair* and *Men Only*, Sullivan made a fortune in the supply of 'hardcore' magazines and videos, and the establishment of a chain of sex shops in which to sell them and associated products. Using titles like *Private*, and the pirated covers of Rodox publica-tions, Sullivan was able to persuade enough of the people, enough of the time, that they were indeed purchasing European-type hardcore pornogra-phy from his Private Shop and mail-order companies. Such material is not legal in Britain, as we have stressed, and could never be sold 'over the counter'. As Mark Killick (1994) shows, however, from the early 1970s when he entered the market as a young businessman with a talent for mail-order selling to the present day Sullivan has successfully pursued a market-ing strategy of 'promising much but delivering less'. The strategy was not without risks, and Sullivan has throughout his career been subject to close policing by the police and regulatory authorities, with regular confiscation of his stock, and even on one occasion imprisonment for his alleged involve-ment in sauna clubs whose female workers were offering patrons more than a hot bath.

Sullivan first emerged in the early 1970s, inspired by the example of Bob Guccione's *Penthouse* in the United States. He began by distributing explicit (though not hardcore) photographs by mail-order, then progressing to the production of magazines and feature films. The Private chain of sex shops was established in 1978. After serving his prison term, and as he moved increasingly into mainstream newspaper publishing, Sullivan gradually cut off his formal connections to the pornography industry. He remains inti-mately involved with pornographic magazine production, telephone sex lines, and the Private shops, though his control is heavily disguised by opaque structures of ownership (Killick, 1994; Itzin, 1992).

Sullivan is notable in the UK context, not just as an entrepreneur who has been extremely successful in building a business empire around pornogra-phy, but in expanding the boundaries of the acceptable in British sexual cul-ture. Several Sullivan-established titles feature in the content analysis below. Here we observe that he injected into British pornography a raunchy, explicit quality absent from *Men Only* and *Mayfair*. Their production of pseudo-sophisticated 'entertainment for men' was joined in the sexual mar-ketplace by David Sullivan's 'cheap and nasty' approach. Sullivan's titles were, to put it simply, crude, visually and linguistically, and aggressively marketed as such. Where *Mayfair* and *Men Only* used soft-focus lenses and exotic foreign locations to photograph their models, Sullivan's were shot in everyday locations, in stark colour or black-and-white, vaginas and anuses held open to the (openly encouraged) leering gaze of the male viewer. Female genital depilation was frequently depicted, as were lesbian and heterosexual couples (though never, of course, erect penises). In using a title such as *Whitehouse* Sullivan also challenged, in a way which the old pornographic establishment did not, the moral campaigners.

Sullivan's titles remain prominent in the pornography market although, as already noted, the identity of their true owner is often obscured behind complex networks of obscure proxy companies. Few doubt that he remains an important figure in the UK industry, with the potential for further rapid expansion should the British regulatory regime ever be relaxed.

More recent entrants to the British pornography business include Northern & Shell (*Penthouse, For Men*) owned by Richard Desmond.[3] Desmond, to a greater extent than Sullivan, has achieved respectability in the wider UK publishing industry, enjoying good business relationships with the high-street newsagent chains and mainstream magazine distributors COMAG. Indeed, some reportage on the 'banning' of *Company* magazine's 'Suburban Porn Stars' issue in January 1995 (*see* Chapter 3) noted that the same stores happily stacked a number of Northern & Shell's pornographic magazines on their top shelves. Northern & Shell was further distinguished from David Sullivan's operation by publishing three of the UK's leading pornographic magazines targeted at the female market: *For Women, Women Only*, and *Women On Top* (the latter two titles are no longer on the market).

Comparable to Northern & Shell in turnover and profit is Galaxy Publications, producers of such titles as *Fiesta* and *Knave, Ravers* and *Two Blue*. This company, too, has achieved a measure of respectability, having its magazines distributed by leading regional publisher Argus Press.

The United States

The roots of contemporary mass-market pornography in the United States may be traced back to the postwar 'pin-up' magazines, in particular *Playboy*, established by Hugh Hefner in 1953. Like *Men Only* and *Mayfair* in the United Kingdom, *Playboy* was not simply about sex, but sold a lifestyle in which carefree, 'swinging' sex played a central role. Gail Dines notes that *Playboy* advocated 'the consumption of numerous upmarket commodities as a way of capturing the ultimate prized commodity: lots and lots of attractive, young, big-breasted women, just like the ones masturbated to in the centrefold' (1995: p. 255). *Playboy's* target market was the young, affluent American male, with plenty of disposable income to spend on the goods advertised in its pages.

Although containing images of objectified, sexually available women different from post-1960s pornography only in their explicitness, *Playboy* gradually became an accepted element of American male culture, to the extent that by the 1970s interviews could be found there with such pillars of the American establishment as President Jimmy Carter. Fidel Castro also consented to be interviewed in the magazine, aware that its vast and influential readership was a useful target for his antisanctions campaign. Dines remarks that Hefner is 'probably the only pornographer in America who has achieved celebrity status' (1995: p. 260), to the extent of making guest appearances on primetime situation comedy shows. By 1984 *Playboy* had a regular monthly circulation of some 5 million copies (Russo, 1987), falling to around 3.5 million by 1993.

The success of *Playboy* signalled the onset of postwar sexual liberalism in the United States (alongside Elvis Presley, Marlon Brando, the Beat movement, and other symbols of moral transgression), promoted and serviced by an increasingly explicit media of sex. In 1969 Bob Guccione established *Penthouse* magazine, which quickly came to rival *Playboy's* circulation with a similar mix of (somewhat more explicit) female nudes and current affairs/lifestyle editorial for men. Larry Flynt's *Hustler*, considerably 'harder' than either *Penthouse* or *Playboy*, was launched in the 1970s, achieving a lower, but still extremely lucrative, monthly circulation of 1.5 million by 1984 (Russo, 1987).

Following the the 'hands off' conclusions on sexual censorship and regulation reached by the Johnson Commission in 1970, genuine hardcore magazines flourished, as did the adult bookstore and mail-order networks through which they were sold. These publications matched Scandinavian and German material in their graphic displays of genital sex and specialist fetishes, and while they never attained the circulations enjoyed by *Playboy*, *Penthouse* and *Hustler*, collectively they came to occupy a substantial slice of the United States publishing industry. As of 1981, by one estimate, and before the advent of home video consumption on a mass basis, the manufacture of pornography generated some $7 billion of profit in the United States, 3 per cent of all corporate profits (Russo, 1987).[4] While the size of the pornography industry in the United States and elsewhere is often subject to exaggeration by antiporn campaigners there is no doubt that by the 1980s billions of dollars were being made in the sale of sexually explicit material to American consumers.

A major boost to the industry was provided by the development of video technology and its rapid penetration into the domestic consumer market. Hardcore pornography distributed in cinemas became commonplace in the late 1960s and 1970s with the infamous *Deep Throat* (1972) becoming the first mainstream feature, i.e. one which was viewed not only by the furtive denizens of peepshow booths and adult cinema clubs but 'normal' people on a night out at the movies. As early as 1976 Sony Betamax video-cassettes of *Deep Throat* and other hardcore feature films were making their way onto the market, and by the mid-1980s VHS tape players had become established as affordable consumer durables. In the United States (if not Britain, where hardcore material was illegal) many consumers marked their first purchase of a VCR by renting a pornographic tape from the local store.[5] In doing so they violated a fast-eroding cultural taboo and contributed to the creation of a large domestic market for hardcore pornography. This in turn encouraged the production of more films, and an improvement in their quality (as measured by production budgets). The old stag reels were replaced by glossy 90-minute epics costing on average, as of 1985, around $200 000 to produce; a minuscule sum by mainstream Hollywood standards, but enough to permit the incorporation into filmed pornography of half-decent scripts, special effects, and other 'quality' features suitable for the relatively affluent, middle class VCR-owner of mid-80s America.[6]

By taking film pornography out of the peepshow booth and into the American living room, video technology thus changed the nature of the audience. A 1986 survey of 1000 video stores in the United States reported that 63 per cent of tapes classified as pornographic were rented by women or couples.[7] The growing number of female users of pornography was noted in the previous chapter, as was the emergence of a distinct subcategory of pornography for women. In the United States the production of female-orientated pornography, or 'sexually explicit films made by women, for women and couples'[8] has been dominated since the 1980s by Femme Productions, established by former pornographic film actress Candida Royalle. Some titles from the Femme Productions catalogue were launched in the United Kingdom in the early 1990s, with appropriate cuts for the British censor, and sold in high-street shops alongside the *Lover's Guide* and other 'sex education' titles.[9] Pornography for gay women in particular has been produced for some years by the San Francisco-based Blush Entertainment and its video subsidiary Fatale.

'Porn for women', gay or straight, though a growing proportion of the US pornography market, remains marginal by comparison with the quantity of male-orientated material in circulation. In the United States the largest portion of hardcore male-orientated pornography is produced by the Cal Vista and Caballero companies in the sphere of video, while the production of magazines is the business of a wide variety of companies. Pornography for gay men is included in the output of many of these companies, who advertise it alongside their straight material. Gay male porn is sold through mail-order, and in the adult bookstores, as well as in specialist gay outlets.

The pornography industry and organized crime

A recurring theme in the arguments of those who support greater censorship and regulation of pornography is the alleged involvement in its production of organized crime. Volume two of the Meese Commission's report (1986) contains a lengthy analysis of the mafia's (Cosa Nostra) allegedly extensive role in the pornography industry, particularly in the retail and distribution ends of the business. In Britain, Richard Desmond and other 'porn kings' have been linked in the press to organized crime,[10] while David Sullivan's imprisonment for living off immoral earnings has already been noted. Such connections and allegations have reinforced perceptions of the pornography industry as a particularly sleazy and disreputable branch of international capital, and underpin much of the concern about the potential exploitation and abuse of those performers who earn their living from it (*see* Chapter 5). The violent death of US porn star John Holmes in 1990[11] further strengthened the pornography-crime link.

The earlier discussion of the harmful effects of pornography argued that, while many pornography workers have been exploited and abused, the majority who have made their views known through interviews, articles and books claim not to have been, asserting, often aggressively, the consensual, businesslike nature of their involvement. On the other hand, to the extent that the production and consumption of sexually explicit images (and live sex performances too) has been illegal or, at best, heavily stigmatized, the involvement of organized crime is hardly surprising. As in the supply of controlled drugs the very fact of illegality encourages an underground market in which organized criminal networks with little to lose inevitably become involved. It is easier, most sociologists would agree, to abuse workers, exploit consumers, and intimidate sellers if the production and consumption of a commodity is not regulated by the law and subject to the workings of the black market.

Conversely, when a hitherto illegal activity such as the manufacture and sale of pornography is decriminalized and becomes to a greater or lesser degree part of mainstream culture, regulations on hygiene, price and quality can be introduced and enforced. This process has already taken place in some countries where, as La Cicciolina and Tabatha Cash have shown,[12] legality and popular cultural acceptability brings not just wealth and fame to some star performers but also more power and control to all. Pornography, as has previously been argued, is a capitalist industry and therefore synonymous with every kind of exploitation for profit yet devised. Increasingly, however, it operates within the laws of 'respectable' western capitalism, which inevitably tends to reduce the involvement of mafiosi and other criminal gangs.

Pornography and new technology

No account of the pornography industry can neglect to mention the close connection between the spread of sexually explicit material in capitalist societies and the invention of new forms of information dissemination. I have noted, both in this chapter and in Chapter 4, how the development first of print, then of photography, cinema and video were the technological preconditions for successive stages in the emergence of mass-market pornography and the industry which produces it. As Pat Califia has observed, 'new technologies are always used for sexual purposes' (1993: p. 169).

Each new means of circulating information and images has increased the market for pornography, essentially by making it more accessible for private consumption. Video technology has also democratized, if that term is appropriate, the production of pornography. Many people use video cameras to make pornographic recordings of their own sexual behaviour, for their own private use. Independent film-makers and production companies exploit the relative cheapness combined with high quality of current video technologies to produce 'alternative' pornographies for sale and distribution in a commercial context. In this sense technology has shaped (and goes on shaping) the structure of the pornography industry, the make-up of its audience, and the content of what is produced, as well as making censorship more problematic.

Following the 'video revolution' of the 1980s, this process has entered a new phase, with the advent of the Internet and 'cyberporn'. September 1994 saw the publication in Britain of a new magazine, *Digital Dreams*. The magazine came with a CD-ROM, containing moving image versions of the nude stills on its pages, instructions on how to 'navigate' them, and coverage of other IT outlets for pornography. In July 1995 a flurry of articles appeared in the United States and Great Britain analysing the dangers of the spread of pornographic material through the global communications network known popularly as the Internet. In *Time* magazine a Carnegie Mellon study on 'The marketing of pornography on the information superhighway' formed the basis of a cover article on the growing use of the Internet to circulate sexually explicit text and pictures among computer-users, and children in particular – hence intensifying pressure from the Congress to censor the material.[13] British journalists followed the *Time* piece with articles of their own, relating the findings of the Carnegie Mellon study to the UK context.[14] Each of the articles acknowledged that cyberporn was a major dimension of the ongoing information revolution and that censorship, even if desirable from the moral perspective, was difficult to impose on such an open, interactive system. As to the content of cyberporn, it was similar to (indeed, frequently plagiarized and pirated from) that available on other more conventional means of pornographic communication.[15]

In fact, and despite the scale of the problem suggested by the flurry of articles, the Carnegie Mellon study reported that, as of 1995, only 3 per cent of material circulating on the Internet 'usergroup' network, itself comprising only 11 per cent of all Internet traffic, could be defined as pornographic. Private bulletin boards were also being used to download material, for a commercial charge.

Like home video before it, accessing pornography on the Internet has the benefit, for those respectable members of society who prefer not to frequent the combat zones and sex shops of the inner cities, of privacy (a computer terminal and a darkened room are all one needs); safety (HIV is one virus which computers are unable to transmit); and user-friendliness (many of the cyberporn services offer unprecedented selectability of material). For all these reasons, and notwithstanding the ability of unsupervised minors to access it, the Internet can be expected to increase in importance as a means of disseminating pornography.

Pornography today: content, styles and conventions

In the many hundreds of academic books and essays which have been written about pornography, one rarely encounters descriptions of what it looks or reads like. Many scholarly writers, as Sallie Tisdale and other journalists have observed, feel awkward in attempting seriously to analyse pornographic texts. Others, by choice or for legal reasons, may not have viewed such material.

Those accounts which have been provided often have a polemical function, as in Andrea Dworkin's influential *Pornography* (1981) with its stress on humiliation, rape and violence against women as the staples of pornographic content. Dworkin's examples are selected in order to substantiate her thesis, elaborated in this work and elsewhere over many years, that pornography *is* violence against women, and that 'the major theme of pornography as a genre is male power' (1981: p. 25). The reader of *Pornography* has no way of knowing whether the particular examples of pornography described in Dworkin's text are representative of sexually explicit materials as a whole, or whether her reading of the material is the only or most appropriate one to be drawn.

In reviewing the antipornography literature, one time and time again comes across references to a handful of images which are presented as evidence of the essential misogyny of pornography as a whole. They include the infamous cover of *Hustler* magazine's June 1978 edition, depicting a woman disappearing into a meatgrinder and emerging as 'mince' (this cover was a catalyst in encouraging the formation of the Women Against Pornography group in New York that year); a photoset, printed in *Penthouse*, of a female bound, gagged and suspended from a tree; and the photoset of a naked woman, bound to the hood of a car as the 'trophy' of two male hunters. These images, cited scores of times in the course of the pornography debate, have become metonymic – emblematic of the evils of all pornography, rather than particularly nasty examples of a particular category of sexually explicit material.[16]

Another source of accounts of the content of pornography, used extensively since 1986 by the moral-conservative lobby in particular, is the Meese
Commission report, several hundred pages of which comprise plot sum-
maries of films and novels, descriptions of photosets in magazines, and lists
of film and magazine titles. As Hunter Thompson noted at the time of its
publication (*see* Chapter 2) these pages of the report are themselves so sexually explicit that they could function like pornography, even if that was
clearly not the intention of the report's compilers. The Meese report is a useful guide, for the outside observer, to the range of pornographic material
available in the United States in the mid-1980s. Like the selections made by
Dworkin and others, however, it places an inordinate stress (i.e. one not justified by the proportion of such material in the totality of pornography in
circulation) on 'violent and degrading' depictions, categories which are
defined in the broadest and most simplistic of terms. As a result, some necessary and basic distinctions, such as that between real acts of violence
committed against real victims, and consensual acts involving bondage and
s/m rituals, are ignored. Reflecting the moral conservative makeup of the
Meese Commission, questions relating to the context and meaning of the
images described are passed over in the course of a more or less blanket
moral condemnation.

It is not my aim here to rectify these problems of contextualization and
sample bias in what are nevertheless valuable sources of information.
Rather, in the remainder of this chapter, I will describe the content and the
stylistic features of some examples of pornographic texts drawn from a wide
spectrum of material currently in circulation, and legally available in the
countries where it was obtained. While the quantity of material referred to
is minuscule in relation to the totality of pornography in circulation at any
given time, I have sought to make the selections representative of the various categories into which legally available pornography in Europe and
north America can be grouped.

Those categories distinguish material, first, according to the explicitness
of its content, with examples drawn from a continuum ranging from soft- to
hardcore. But the meaning of these terms varies from country to country, as
was noted in Chapter 4, so I have also distinguished between what is available in Britain, the United States and Europe (encompassing Scandinavia,
Germany, France, Spain and Italy). The material is also described in terms
of sexual orientation, of which four main categories can be identified: i) het-
ero-male; ii) hetero-female; iii) homo-male; iv) homo-female. These categories are not always mutually exclusive, nor is it always clear to which
category a certain representation might belong (images of transsexuality are
common in Italian pornography consumed mainly by heterosexual men, for
example). They enable us, nevertheless, to breakdown the vast output of
pornography as a whole into manageable bits.

I have excluded from the review examples of literary pornography – novels, short stories and poetry – for two reasons. First, it is often difficult to

clearly identify such a text as pornography, even when it has been written to be 'pornographic' in the sense of 'sexually explicit material intended to arouse'. Nicholson Baker's *The Fermata* (*see* Chapter 8), for example, contains some of the most explicit and arguably perverse sex scenes one could possibly imagine, as part of a novel intended to be, at least in part, a pastiche of and comment on pornography. Baker is widely recognized as a literary novelist, however; a celebrated *artist* who incidentally happens to treat sexuality as a theme in his work.

Second, the written word is not subject to the same moral regulation, in Britain or elsewhere, as visual publication. While the most explicit works of the Marquis de Sade are happily sold in the classics departments of Britain's high-street bookstores, any film-maker or magazine publisher who attempted to visually represent some of the acts described in *Justine* or *One Hundred Days of Sodom* would soon be in court. Contemporary pornographic novels, whether literary or 'trash' are similarly treated. While these texts are not insignificant in the debate about pornography's meaning and effects, this review concentrates on pornographic magazines, films and videos. The interested reader can find précis of some American pornographic novels in the Meese report (1986) and in Dworkin's *Pornography* (1981).

The United Kingdom

In Britain, visual representations of sexual activity cannot under the law extend to depictions of an erect penis or to penetration (vaginal, oral or anal). In this sense all legally circulating British pornography is 'soft' as Bill Thompson has defined it (1994). Although many antipornography commentators routinely use the phrase 'hardcore' to describe materials which they find particularly offensive, this is a reflection of moral outrage rather than an accurate description of what is contained in the material so labelled. The assessment of one writer that 'British pornography is bizarre and violent',[17] and has become dramatically more so in recent years is a value-judgement based on subjective definitions of what 'bizarre' and 'violent' mean.

That said, the British pornography market *can* be divided between materials which are more or less explicit, which are targeted at different socioeconomic groups, and which cater to particular sexual specialisms or fetishes.[18] While no producer can break the rules limiting which sex acts and body parts can be shown, there are of course many ways of connoting meanings around denotatively similar images.

Precise circulation and, for video, sales/rental figures are not available for most publications, but one can say as a generality that the 'softer' the material the more widely consumed and commercially successful it is. There exists, one might say, a hierarchy of respectability within which British pornographic materials are placed, both by moral arbiters and by consumers.

At the top of this hierarchy are the oldest and most-established male-orientated titles – *Mayfair, Men Only, International Club* and *Penthouse* are the market leaders – which combine their portrayals of nude females with articles and review features addressed to their young, relatively affluent male audience. In these magazines, sex is packaged as part of a broader male lifestyle. A 1995 issue of *Penthouse*, for example, published by Northern & Shell, included in addition to six photosets of solo nude females 34 pages of editorial, including an interview with film star Warren Beatty, reviews of CD releases by such artists as Frank Sinatra, Throwing Muses and Leftfield, and a regular feature on sports cars. The *Penthouse* ethos (and that of other magazines in this category) can perhaps be summed up in an advertisement for subscriptions: 'Fast lifestyle. Faster Women'.[19]

The nature of the intended audience for these magazines is reflected in the fact that they are packed with advertisements for expensive consumer durables such as Philips' hi-fi systems and Sega computer consoles. The photosets are shot in exotic foreign locations, depicting young women of a stereotypically beautiful type. The accompanying texts stress that the models are successful professionals; that they take pleasure in their work; that they are modest and unassuming; that they are, in short, 'nice girls'. In the issue of *Penthouse* already referred to model Dominique Carvasiglia is reported to have a boyfriend, to be wealthy (so she doesn't have to model for a living, but does it because she likes it), and is photographed in 'her beautiful Valencian garden'. In another photoset the model is described as 'one of the most charming and likable girls on the glamour circuit . . . one of the sweetest girls we have ever come across'.

By contrast, another subcategory of top-shelf British magazine is targeted downmarket, as reflected in a relatively low cover price and a distinctly cruder, more populist content. Titles such as *International Club, Escort* and *Razzle*, all published by Paul Raymond, retail for as little as £1.65 (1995 prices), their front covers describing the content within as 'now twice as dirty'; 'rude videos: home-made and horny', and 'the rudest wives you've ever come across'. Where *Mayfair* and the like construct their readers as relatively sophisticated 'men of the world', these titles assume a reader who wants his erotic object, and the representation of it, to be earthy, home-made, lacking in pretension, and presented with a light-hearted touch. Photosets are shot in starkly lit kitchens and bathrooms, featuring 'ordinary' women as opposed to the statuesque blondes and brunettes of the glossier titles. The models are often identified as local working-class girls.

The blue-collar market positioning of these titles is also reflected in the photography, in which 'reader's wives' and other home-made formats are prominent. In general, the photosets are shorter and 'dirtier' than those of *Mayfair* and *Penthouse*. In addition to standard poses of full frontal nudity the cheaper magazines routinely depict depilation, models covered in food or soapsuds, and being stretched into acrobatic positions suggesting maximum accessibility to the viewer. 'Lesbian' and group scenarios are common, and the models are depicted as uninhibited, eager, and highly sexed.

> Geordie Georgina spends her days building bricks and her nights building pricks as she swaps her Lego for a leg-over with any fella she fancies! 'You won't catch me settling down when there are so many new cocks to try', claims the 22-year-old Billington babe.[20]

As with other areas of magazine publication, then, pornography is target-marketed toward particular income, class and taste categories, the broad nature of which can be inferred from such features as the cover price, and visual and written style.

Titles associated with David Sullivan, although not necessarily owned by him any longer (*see above*) are distinctive in combining a 'dirty', downmarket style with higher-than-average cover prices. *Private, Blue Book* and others plagiarize the titles and style of European hardcore pornography with sufficient conviction to persuade purchasers to pay around three times what they would for *Escort*. For this premium readers are presented with sharply focused, brightly lit photosets, in colour and monochrome, of single females and female-female/female-male couples. The degree of explicitness (depictions of semi-erect penises, for example) comes close to the legally permissible limit of what can be shown in the UK. Editorial content is minimal, restricted to poorly written stories and obviously faked letters. To cut production costs the same models are used in different titles: 'Carole' in *Private* appears, in slightly different shots from what is clearly the same photoset, as 'Jacqui' in *Playbirds* and as 'Nicola' in *Blue Book*, all titles on sale at the same time in British newsagents.

Recent trends

Chapter 5 noted that the debate about pornography, in Britain and elsewhere, has been fuelled by the recurring claim that legally available material is becoming steadily more offensive, violent, and hence dangerous. One observer reports that some 68 new titles were launched on the UK pornographic magazine market between 1990 and 1994, and that most of these were appealing to more extreme and bizarre tastes.[21] While definitions of what is extreme and bizarre will inevitably vary we *can* say that new entrants have tended to follow the 'dirty', in-your-face style of *Razzle* and *Escort* rather than emulate the pseudo-sophistication of *Mayfair*. *For Men*, a new title published by Portland Publishing Ltd and distributed by Northern & Shell, is comparable to *Mayfair* and *Penthouse* in utilizing higher production values and including lifestyle and consumer coverage, but does so in the context of a much more explicit sexual content.

Some titles, such as *Eros* (published by Portland Publishing and distributed by Northern & Shell) target what they clearly assume to be a substantial market for images of sexual deviations and kinks – piercing, urolagnia (sexual pleasure associated with the act of urination) and leather fetishism have all featured in *Eros*. There have always been small-circulation specialist magazines legally available in the UK, such as *Janus*, which dealt with sado-masochism and other minority sexual practices, but *Eros* and similar titles have placed them on the top shelves to an extent that was not true previously. The UK censorship regime obviously forbids the visual representation of most of these practices, so they are explored in the context of 'agony columns' and readers' letters, which tend to discuss in reassuring terms the legitimacy of foot-fetishes and other 'perversions'.

Such content may not be to everyone's sexual taste, and seem bizarre to many, but it is not 'hardcore' pornography if compared with material so described in the United States and continental Europe. Neither is it noticeably violent. Of all the British titles reviewed for this section only *Hustler*, the UK-version of a long-established American magazine, contained images of sexualized violence against women (*see* footnote 16, Chapter 5). Representations of sexualized violence are more common, as many commentators have noted, in nonpornographic media (popular cinema and fiction, TV drama, tabloid newspapers, etc.) than they are in British pornography.

The most 'bizarre' titles tend, moreover, to be less crudely sexist than *Razzle*, *Raver*, and *Escort*, with the latter's routine depictions, visual and verbal, of women as insatiable 'sluts' and 'tarts'. The suggestion that British pornography is travelling along a downward 'spiral of depravity'[22] is one interpretation of the fact that the culture as a whole has become more explicit in representations of sex. When 's/m chic' has become an uncontroversial feature of fashion photography and television advertisements, and fetishism the subject of serious, nonjudgemental documentaries on Channel Four,[23] it seems less surprising that pornographers should reflect changing public perceptions of these practices by producing magazines and videos in which they feature.

Pornographic advertising

Much of the most 'bizarre and depraved' material in British pornographic magazines is contained in the advertisements which occupy a major proportion of all titles. Around 20 per cent of a typical magazine's pages will be devoted to the advertising of telephone sex lines, videos and magazines obtainable by mail-order or from sex shops, sex aids and lingerie, and contact addresses. These, very expensive, commodities are usually presented as being even more explicit or 'hardcore' than the magazine in which the advertisement appears. Telephone sex lines promising anal sex and 'golden showers' are common, for example, both practices which no British magazine will describe, in pictures or in words. If the phrase 'spiral of depravity' has any value as a descriptive term, it may be applied to these advertisements which, as the general sexualization of the culture proceeds, must entice purchasers for their products by seeming to offer ever-more authentic 'hardcore' material.

Porn in the USA

In the United States the range of sexually explicit material varies from the softcore of *Playboy* and *Penthouse*, comparable to British top-shelf magazines in their tone and content, to graphic depictions of penetrative sexual activity. As in the UK there is a spiral of increasing explicitness, with further divisions based on socio-economic category and sexual specialism.

Like the British market, the softest US titles are also those which enjoy the largest circulations, presenting the male consumer not merely with erotic imagery but current affairs and lifestyle material of the type also found in nonpornographic men's magazines. *Playboy* and *Penthouse* have become, as was noted earlier in this chapter, respectable institutions of American patriarchy, sufficiently so for appearances to be made in them by serving presidents and top film stars.

Harder in content and positioned considerably downmarket, while still claiming multi-million circulation figures, is Larry Flynt's *Hustler* magazine. Softcore in that *Hustler* photosets do not depict penetration and ejaculation this title, like its British namesake, delights in the adoption of an overtly sexist and misogynistic editorial stance, putting women – well-known women, and women in general – firmly in their place. Scatological, misogynistic humour has a prominent place in the magazine, with particular venom being reserved for attacks on 'political correctness'. Explicit stories and readers' letters focus on the themes of male dominance and female submission, with women reduced to 'cunts and bitches' throughout.[24] *Hustler* exemplifies American male-orientated pornography of the type most bitterly opposed by feminist campaigners: deliberately offensive and crude; often containing scenarios of undisguised violence and degradation; advocating misogyny as a lifestyle.

American hardcore

Moving along the continuum of legally available American pornography, we cross from soft- into hardcore material, in which models are depicted in the acts of sexual intercourse, masturbation, ejaculation and so on. While softcore pornography can visually suggest these acts, and will describe them in letters and stories, hardcore reveals all, usually culminating in the visible orgasm of the performers. In this sense it is 'genitally focused'.

As commodities, hardcore materials are more expensive than softcore and typically contain less advertising and written editorial. In many hardcore magazine titles advertising for sex lines, videos and other products may account for less than 5 per cent of available space. Consequently, cover prices may be higher by a factor of three or more, depending on the nature of the material, than *Penthouse* and *Hustler*.

Hardcore magazine pornography is presented in several formats. A title such as *Puritan International* parallels the style of more mainstream softcore titles by presenting a series of short photosets, alongside feature articles, stories and readers' letters. The photosets depict a full range of vaginal, oral and anal sex acts, involving homo- and heterosexual couples and groups. The approach is eclectic, rather than specialized.

Another format takes a single sexual preference (anal sex, for example), and depicts one or perhaps two or three scenarios in which it is explored. There are no stories or letters, the photographs being accompanied by only the briefest of narration, as if the inclusion of anything else would be to waste precious space. The photography is sharp and sparing, the locations (bedrooms, mainly) cheap and unglamorous.

Although hardcore material *shows* more to the viewer than softcore pornography it often displays a noticeably more sophisticated approach to the issues of sexism and misogyny than the former. Many titles have on their covers the phrase 'Explicit, nonviolent action'. This is the product, on the one hand, of post-Meese commission legislation which prohibits the combination of 'violence', including s/m, with genital sexuality in pornographic imagery. In other words, s/m activity can be shown, as can full penetrative sex, but not the two together. Secondly, many of the more explicit titles position themselves in the marketplace as 'sex radicals', appealing not only, or even primarily, to heterosexual males but also to women and gays. The scenarios depicted in *Puritan International*, for example, include a man being penetrated by a dildo; a woman performing fellatio on a man wearing a dildo; and two rubber-clad 'dominatrixes' in an s/m scene.[25] The overt verbal and pictorial debasement of women found in *Hustler* is absent here. Representations of sex, though more explicit than softcore, are often accompanied by a stress on the consensual and the nonviolent in sexual relationships. Many of the narratives accompanying hardcore photosets represent women as active, assertive agents in sex plays structured around the satisfaction of *their* desires (as well as, obviously, that of the viewer). Often, male performers are constructed as naive beginners who require instruction and tutelage. Convention dictates, as Linda Williams has observed (1990), that most pornographic narratives end in the visible ejaculation of the male performer – the 'money shot'- but the articulation and satisfaction of female sexuality is often at the heart of the hardcore male-orientated narrative. There is, in short, no necessary connection between the explicitness of representation in a pornographic text and the articulation of reactionary sexist ideology. On the contrary, one can argue that the harder and more explicit the material the more likely it is to represent and eroticize a marginalized or deviant sexual practice.

Europe

In the United States, where hardcore pornography is subject to relatively few prohibitions, European materials are perceived as even more explicit and extreme. Advertisements for mail-order videos and magazines often attract customers by promising 'real European quality'. By this is meant not only the explicitness of the sexual representation, but a 'kinky', bizarre quality, assumed to be more developed in Europe. The British market also shares this perception, founded perhaps on the fact that legal hardcore pornography emerged first, as we have seen, in continental Europe (Scandinavia, Germany, the Netherlands) and has evolved furthest there in the range of what is depicted.

Space limitations and authorial unfamiliarity prevent a detailed examination of the European market on a country-by-country basis. In general, however, European hardcore pornography can be grouped into magazines like *Private*, *Hard* and *Pleasure*, presenting relatively 'straight' photonarratives of penetrative sex and orgasm, accompanied by written text, often in several European languages. There is virtually no advertising or editorial (apart from the accompaniments to photographs) in the content of these magazines, which make money for their producers almost entirely on the basis of high cover prices. Other magazines, like the Italian *Paprika*, adopt the eclectic mix of text and photography found in the British and US materials described above, combining the most explicit visual representations with features, stories and letters. Advertisements are more common in these titles, often selling specialised sexual services like 'piercing' and tattooing.

The sexual content of European pornography varies from country to country, reflecting prevailing cultural traditions. The relatively mainstream content of such titles as *Hard* and *Pleasure*, sold in the Mediterranean holiday resorts of Spain to tourists from Britain and Ireland, rarely go beyond the graphic depiction of heterosexual couples having sex. In the

Scandinavian countries, and Germany and Italy, on the other hand, materials are more likely to depict deviant sexual behaviours. In Italy, anal penetration is a staple of hardcore pornography, and images of transsexuality are common, notwithstanding the machismo public face of the Italian male.

Pornography in post-communist Europe

Until the late 1980s and early 1990s, pornography of any sort was illegal in most of the countries which had been part of the Soviet Union and the Warsaw Pact. There was a black market for sexually explicit material, but the penalties for entering it were severe.

However, after the fall of the Soviet-inspired regimes and the establishment of quasi-democratic market economies, pornography was included in the general flowering of the media and culture. Having been banned by the communist parties for decades, pornography's emergence in the media marketplace was welcomed by many as a sign of intellectual and cultural freedom. Feminist approaches to sexual representation were never influential in Soviet-era central and eastern Europe (McNair, 1991) and the antipatriarchal critique of pornography was rarely voiced after the birth of the 'new democracies'. Those who opposed it were associated with the old discredited regimes.[26] Pornographers benefitted in these countries from the almost-universal reaction against all censorship, political or moral, which accompanied the breakdown of marxism-leninism. In some countries, notably Russia, the functioning of such antipornography regulations as survived the fall of the CPSU was hampered by a notoriously corrupt and inefficient legal system.

Pornography in the post-Soviet world can be grouped into three categories. Firstly, there are the efforts of western publications such as *Penthouse* and *Playboy* to become established in these new markets, as they have done in Russia. Bob Guccione's *Penthouse* has been produced in a Russian-language edition since 1993. *Playboy* was launched there in 1995. The resultant publications are, like their US namesakes, relatively sophisticated, sexually orientated entertainment magazines for men, selling a lifestyle as much as an erotic thrill.

A second source of material are those once state-socialist countries, such as the former Yugoslavia, which pioneered the production of pornography and are now in a position to export it to others, such as Russia, where indigenous production is still in its infancy. Moscow street markets sell many sexually explicit magazines and videos in non-Russian east European languages, produced to varying degrees of quality.

Indigenous production, where it has begun, can be in the form of cheaply produced weekly magazines, often printed on newsprint with grainy black-

and-white photographs; and newspapers, as in the Czech Republic, where one may buy what looks at first glance like a tabloid newspaper but contains in addition to news colour photographs of full frontal nudes and oral sex acts.

The rapid proliferation of pornographic materials in post-Soviet Europe may be compared to the experience of Spain, where decades of sexually repressed dictatorship by the Franco regime were followed by a cultural 'striptease' in which sexual representation had a radical political, as well as an erotic, connotation.

Film and video

The explicitness of film and video pornography, like that of magazines, varies from culture to culture. In Britain, only softcore material is legally available, viewed in adult cinemas, rented from video stores or bought from sex shops. Some titles, such as the 'educational' *Lover's Guide*, are available in high-street chain stores such as Woolworth and Virgin, reflecting their increased acceptability by the mainstream audience. Increasing numbers of video cassettes now come packaged with magazines, and are sold in newsagents. In Europe and the United States the same means of distribution are used, but the material sold ranges from soft- to hardcore.

The *form* of filmic pornography has developed, as already noted, from the stag reels which first began to circulate in the late nineteenth and early twentieth centuries (Hebditch and Anning, 1988; Williams, 1989; 1990) to full-length features. The stag reel, although made redundant by the development of cinematic pornography and video technology, continues to exist, collected together on videotape and sold by Private, Rodox, Caballero and other companies. Plots are perfunctory – in the quaintly titled *Non-stop Spunkers*, for example, a woman taking the sun is disturbed by two couples, who arrive on motorbikes and have sex while she watches them, voyeuristically, from the trees where she is hidden. After they climax she is discovered and brought into the action, which proceeds to fulsome ejaculation (hence the title) a second time. The only soundtrack comprises a few lines of sparse dialogue and the sounds of orgasm, dubbed amateurishly on what is otherwise a silent film. Special effects are limited to slow-motion 'money shots'.

These short films tend to be grouped together by specialism, analogous to photosets in a magazine. The sex depicted may be relatively 'straight', as in the above example, or of more exotic varieties such as s/m, fisting and bestiality, according to the liberalism and tastes of the country concerned.

A formal progression from the crude minimalism of the stag reel are longer, plotted films, such as *Inside Desiree Cousteau*, in which the sex is presented as part of a journey of discovery. Shorter than a feature, these films typically present a series of linked sexual episodes during which the central female character progresses from one sex act to another, learning about herself and her sexuality as she goes. In these short features, production values are higher, the acting marginally better, and the sex interspersed with sequences of plot development.

Full-length pornographic feature films began to receive cinema distribution in the late 1960s, and to achieve the status of mass entertainment with *Deep Throat* in the early 1970s. Since then, the advent of video has made them commonplace. Narratively, they rarely do more than extend the basic structures of the shorter features, with correspondingly higher budgets, more complicated plots and better-known performers.

Few of these films make claims to be considered as 'art', or as anything other than an aid to masturbation or sex. The discovery of HIV/AIDS in the 1980s did, however, lead some producers to include information about, and the depiction of, safer sex techniques in their films.

Alternative pornographies

The discussion thus far has been mainly concerned with male-orientated pornographic material, which continues to dominate the market commercially, providing the main source of evidence for the antipornography perspective. The pornography produced by men for men in contemporary capitalism is, as we have noted throughout, largely structured by misogynistic patriarchal assumptions about the nature and sexuality of women. Like the majority of mainstream feature films, tabloid newspapers, television drama and advertisements, it reflects the dominant values of the still male-dominated society in which it is produced and circulated. As we have also noted, however, not all male-orientated pornography is as straightforwardly sexist or offensive as *Hustler*, nor is all pornography male-orientated. A large and growing sector of the pornography industry caters for gay male and female users, while the substantial demand for sexually explicit material by straight women has been recognized since the 1980s.

Porn for women

Traditionally women read or viewed 'erotica', as opposed to pornography, a taste distinction which reflected not least male assumptions about the nature of female sexuality. In addition, as we have seen, some feminists rejected the notion that the objectification and voyeurism inherent to the pornographic experience were positions that women could freely choose to adopt. These assumptions were challenged by the success of feminism generally in creating cultural spaces for women to assert and articulate their sexualities, whether in the public spheres of art (*see* Chapter 8) and journalism, or in the private worlds of fantasy and sexual relationships. In the latter context women have increasingly used pornography – subversively decoding male-orientated material on the one hand, consuming material produced by women for women on the other. As the late Linda Singer argued, 'in patriarchy, male privilege is both marked and exercised, at least in part, by control over the production, circulation, and representation of pleasure' (1993: p. 148). Thus, 'when as women we articulate what we want and what gives us pleasure, such writing [and by extension photography, film-making, etc.] carries with it the force both of a demand that these desires be fulfilled, and a self-validating statement of entitlement to gratification and satisfaction' (p. 149).

By the 1990s pornographic magazines for women were firmly established, 'utilizing codes about male objectification previously only found in gay magazines aimed at homosexual men' (Evans and Gammon, 1995: p. 31). In Britain the top shelves of newsagents now include alongside male-orientated magazines such titles as *Playgirl*, *Bite* and *For Women*, in which male models are objectified for the voyeuristic pleasure of the female gaze. Such magazines reverse the roles adopted in the process of male pornography use, positioning the female as the power-laden voyeur-subject. The images are softcore in that erect penises are not shown (British law, as already noted, prevents it) and produced to the same standards as glossy male-orientated titles such as *Penthouse* and *Men Only*.

The market for women-orientated top-shelf magazines remains relatively small, and several British titles (*Ludus*, *Women On Top*, *Women Only*) have been unable to survive (in 1994 *For Women* enjoyed an average monthly circulation of 145,032). It may be that the market for 'porn for women' has been exaggerated in the postfeminist euphoria of recent years, or it could be argued that the lingering social stigma associated with the consumption of pornography applies to women as much as, if not more than, men, which may tend to depress the market.

It has also been suggested that the content of most pornography for women is too conservative and tame to be of much interest to many of them. The 'parade of limp dicks' to be found in such as *For Women* is not, it is argued, what women really want in terms of mediated sex. Reporting on the 1992 UK video launch of Candida Royalle-produced films Ruth Picardie observed that while, as pornography-for-women, these films were laudable in depicting only safe sex, and presenting women exclusively in creative, positive roles, they were rather too gentle and nice for a cultural environment in which 'aggressive female sexuality is running wild'.[27] A similar conclusion was reached by American feminist Laura Fraser, viewing the (uncut) versions of some of Femme Productions' output. While welcoming Royalle's declared intention to produce a 'healthier, non-sexist erotica' characterized by images of women taking the initiative in egalitarian, safe, nongenitally obsessed sex ('money shots' were absent, for example) Fraser argued that many women desired a raunchier, 'dirtier' approach which went beyond 'romance, lace and lingering kisses'.[28]

Lesbian pornography

Precisely this kind of material is the province of the San Francisco-based Blush Entertainment Corporation, incorporating Fatale Videos, which produces sexually explicit films and magazines for lesbians. Claiming to produce 'the pornography of the future' (*see* Fig. 7.1) Blush depicts 'unrestrained sex to make a political point about how women have been "protected" from exciting sex – and satisfaction – for too long'.[29] Fatale Video productions include *Suburban Dykes* and *Bathroom Sluts*, titles which deliberately appropriate the uninhibited, brazen quality (and the language) traditionally associated with male sexuality and male-orientated pornography. Material of this type is not only explicit but consciously subversive in describing and depicting an assertive, at times aggressive, female sexuality. As the Blush Entertainment Corporation's magazine *On Our Backs* puts it in its front cover slogan, this is 'entertainment for the adventurous lesbian' (*see* Fig. 7.2) in which sexually explicit images are mixed up with postmodernist art statements and articles on sexual politics. In Canada the magazine *Lezzie Smut* (*see* Fig. 7.3) occupies similar terrain, combining sexually explicit photographs and stories with lesbian lifestyle coverage, reviews and letters. By comparison with a title such as *Lesbian Lusts*, produced in the United Kingdom for men[30] the women depicted in *On Our Backs*, *Lezzie Smut* and other lesbian-orientated material do not conform to dominant male stereotypes of female beauty, but represent a variety of ages and shapes. The difference between *Lezzie Smut* and *Lesbian Lusts*, as some antipornography feminists (though by no means all, as was seen in Chapter 6) acknowledge, is that 'it presumes a female gaze, and a lesbian one at that. It presumes actual female sexuality. It celebrates autonomous female sexual enjoyment. It still presents women as objects, but through the eyes, and to the eyes, of women as subjects. It takes stereotypical images and, with some humour at times, utterly subverts them in both intention and content' (Smith, 1988: p. 184).

Gay male pornography

Lesbian pornography is a relatively recent phenomenon, coincident with the ascendancy of post-1960s feminism and politicized lesbianism.

Pornography for gay men, on the other hand, has been around rather longer, although relatively little has been written about it (Speck, 1992). The form of this material, as Linda Williams points out in *Hardcore* (1990) is comparable to heterosexual male-orientated material, where the objectification of a particular type of female body is replaced by the male, and a focus on the penis in particular. It is comparable too, as noted above, to the

Fig. 7.1 'The pornography of the future'

female-orientated images found in *For Women*. Like male-orientated material, hardcore gay porn tends to fetishize the 'money shot' as the visible sig-
nifier of orgasm.

The objectification of the body-beautiful characteristic of gay male
pornography has produced the criticism that it is, like straight male-orientated material, sexist and reactionary. Despite the role of this material in
servicing the sexual needs of a still marginalized, stigmatized community,

Fig. 7.2 *On Our Backs*, volume X, issue 2, 1995

some observers accuse it of aping heterosexist conventions and styles, reproducing oppressive patriarchal patterns of dominance and submission (Stoltenberg, 1992). As in heterosexual material the model used in gay porn is alleged to be one of male supremacy and sexual hedonism, which in the post-AIDS environment is especially dangerous and irresponsible. On the

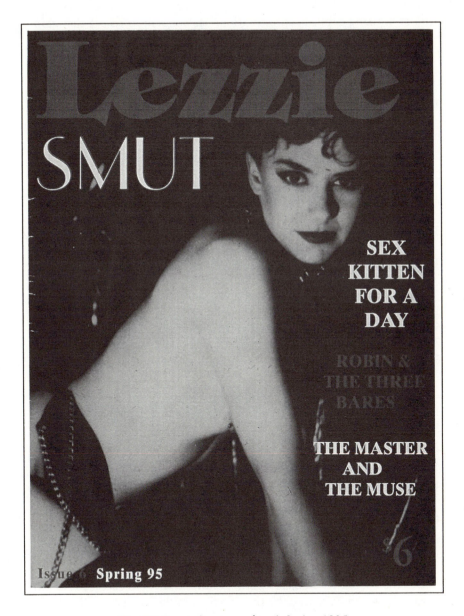

Fig. 7.3 *Lezzie Smut*, number 6, Spring 1995

other hand, as shown in Chapter 6, the gay male community has been at the forefront of efforts to use pornography in safer sex education. Significant changes in gay iconography have resulted, with what one observer describes as 'a more intense eroticization of sex and health together in the images we find in magazines, books and videos, with more scenarios moving to the gym, the pool and the track, away from the locker-room, the shower and the baths' (Alcorn, 1988: p. 73). Gay male pornography, like other categories of sexually explicit representation, has adapted to reflect changes in the wider political, cultural and biological environments. The pornography of hedonism, like the fast-lane lifestyle of the pre-AIDS gay male subculture, has begun to be recast as outmoded and reactionary.

Notes

1 Davies, N., 'Under cover kings', *The Guardian*, 28 November 1994.
2 For a discussion of Sullivan's empire-building in the sphere of non-pornographic publishing, *see* McNair (1996).
3 For a profile of Richard Desmond, *see* Picardie, J., 'Man on top', *The Independent*, 26 June 1993.
4 The same figure is suggested in the introduction to a round-table discussion on 'The place of pornography' sponsored and published by *Harper's* magazine in November 1984.
5 Kaplan, C., 'Filthy rich', *Esquire*, January 1985.
6 Friendly, D., 'This isn't Shakespeare', *Newsweek*, 18 March 1985.
7 Fraser, L., 'Nasty girls', *Mother Jones*, February-March 1990.
8 Riley-Adams, R., 'Sex without the leers', *The Times*, 29 January 1992.
9 Picardie, R., 'Femme films: fatale or banal?', *New Statesman and Society*, 14 February 1992.
10 Picardie, J., 'Man on top', *The Independent*, 26 June 1993.
11 Bygrave, M., 'Darkness on the edge of Tinsel Town', *The Guardian*, 9 February 1991.
12 Pornographic magazine and film performers who have made fortunes and become popular cultural icons in Italy and France respectively.
13 Elmer-Dewitt, P., 'On a screen near you: cyberporn', *Time*, 3 July 1995.
14 Lloyd, C., 'Something nasty on the Internet', *The Sunday Times*, 2 July 1995; Glaister, D., 'Tap of the devil', *The Guardian*, 3 July 1995.
15 For a recent analysis of 'porn on the Internet', *see* Holderness, M., 'In search of a sea of sex', *The Guardian*, 3 August 1995.
16 Of the Women Against Pornography and Violence (WAPVM) slideshow, which toured the United States in the late 1970s, Pat Califia recalls that 'the images were presented in a manipulative way. Bondage

photos were followed by police photos of battered women. S/m porn was repeatedly taken out of context and labelled as 'violent', even though it looked like consensus s/m to me. Record album covers and fashion advertisements were lumped in with the pornography. Nothing was dated and few sources were cited, so the audience had no idea how representative the material was of porn you could actually see and buy'(1982: p. 254).

17 Davies, N., 'Dirty business', *The Guardian*, 26 November 1994.

18 The British market is dominated by publications which appear to assume a relatively young, averagely sexist, white consumer, with attitudes to female beauty informed by currently prevalent cultural stereotypes. Some titles, however, focus on particular categories of women defined by age, ethnicity and physical type. Big Magazines Ltd produce several such titles, including *Electric Black & Blue*, *Electric Blue Asian Babes*, and *40 Plus*. These titles are typically less explicit in their sexual content than many which retail at less than half the price, indicating that the market demands a premium for the satisfaction of special preferences. The more restrained content of a title such as *Asian Babes* may also be judged to reflect the particular cultural circumstances of ethnic Indian and Pakistani communities in Britain, although one cannot assume that men from these communities are the main market for these titles. While the sexual classification of women in this way is, on one level, deeply offensive, the existence of and apparent demand for this material might be thought to have at least one positive dimension: that of undermining ageist and other oppressive stereotypes. One issue of a magazine specializing in images of overweight women, for example, includes an article which begins, 'in a world filled with guilt and self-loathing ... fat women embrace their sexuality with a vengeance'(*Big and Fat*, volume 2, no. 1, 1995). Such sentiments would fit comfortably in a feminist-inspired lesbian-orientated publication such as *On Our Backs*.

19 *Penthouse*, volume 30, no. 7, 1995.

20 *Club International*, volume 24, no. 2, 1995.

21 Davies, N., 'Under cover kings', *The Guardian*, 28 November 1994.

22 Davies, N., 'Under cover kings', *The Guardian*, 28 November 1994.

23 The *Red Light Zone* series of sex-orientated programmes transmitted on Channel Four in March and April 1995 (*see* Chapter 3) included *Fetish*, a documentary about the sexual attractions of bondage clothes and sado-masochism.

24 One advertisement for a sex line accurately sums up the nature of *Hustler* when the female 'voice' of the ad instructs her potential caller to 'Cuff me or beat me, I love all that nasty shit. Make my body and my huge tits red and sore, then squirt your prick juice on the sensitive skin so I can feel it burn' (*Hustler*, volume 20, no. 3, 1993).

25 *Puritan International*, no. 26, 1993.

26 McNair, B., 'Pornography, pluralism and the Russian press', *Post-Soviet Media Law and Policy Newsletter*, no. 8, 3 June 1994.
27 Picardie, R., 'Femme films: fatale or banal?', *New Statesman and Society*, 14 February 1992.
28 Fraser, L., 'Nasty girls', *Mother Jones*, February-March 1990.
29 Frazer, L., 'Nasty girls', *Mother Jones*, February-March 1990.
30 One of the publications associated with David Sullivan in the United Kingdom.

|8|

Art to porn to pop: the pornographication of the mainstream

I referred earlier to the 'pornographication of the mainstream', by which was meant the incorporation of pornographic imagery and iconography into a variety of popular cultural forms, such as advertising, popular fiction and Hollywood cinema. To the extent that pornography has codes and conventions, these have become part of the armoury of popular cultural production, although, of course, in contexts which will tend to strip them of their meaning as pornography. Pornography is also the province of 'art', and artists in a variety of media have used its iconography to comment on sexuality and culture. Indeed, the 'discursive distinction' between art and pornography identified by Laura Kipnis is deliberately broken down in the work of artists such as Jeff Koons, Lutz Bacher and Della Grace.

Pornography, then, has become the source for a much wider range of cultural output than that reviewed in the previous chapter. To an extent never seen before pornography has gone public, and is now genuinely a part of mass culture. In the process the boundary between 'porn' and not porn' has been problematized.

Art, porn and the discursive distinction

If there is one thing about which analysts of sexual representation might agree, it is that pornography is not produced with the conscious intention of achieving artistic effects. Where the category of pornography has been distinguished from erotica, as in the work of Susan Sontag and many others, the former is asserted to be lacking in aesthetic value, produced for the primary aim of inducing sexual arousal in the viewer. Erotic art, on the other hand, 'aspires to being (and is) more than a straightforward aid to masturbation. ... Good erotic art ... finds significance in its subject matter; it speaks of more than sexuality. But sexuality is its first language, and the prime source of its power'.[1]

As Chapter 4 showed, the pornography/erotica distinction is highly subjective and frequently difficult to draw, but it can be used to separate that category of image which has a straightforwardly instrumental function from another in which the representation of sexuality is framed as 'art'. Such images may in the sexual aspects of their content be denotatively similar to pornography, but in their cultural status (self-proclaimed or socially acknowledged) connote something else entirely. As one observer puts it, 'a performance that has a value beyond pornography – as art, fashion, or popular iconography – [loses] the purity of function that is the inimitable mark of true smut'.[2]

Throughout the twentieth century, and indeed before it, artists have drawn on sexually explicit imagery to create particular effects, and to make statements about the nature of human sexuality and its relationship to society. The work thus produced has often been erotic – sexually arousing – and obscene – the object of moral outrage and censorship – but not, its makers have argued, pornographic. Many celebrated legal cases have centred around the interpretation of these categories, and the extent to which an 'artist', as opposed to a pornographer, may be granted licence to depict sexuality in explicit or obscene terms.

For this reason alone, consideration of the relationship between art and sexuality is at the heart of the issues with which this book is concerned. Even although the products of art have traditionally been consumed by specialist cultural elites, they have served as the foci of periodic society-wide debate about the meaning and appropriateness of sexual representation; driven the evolution of obscenity, pornography and other categories used in the regulation of sexually explicit materials; and exposed the contradictions inherent in that regulation.

The use of sexuality in art is interesting for another reason, however. The combination of two trends – the sexualization of culture, on the one hand, and its postmodernization on the other – has greatly increased the social circulation and visibility of artistic sexual representation. As boundaries between high and low culture have broken down, and art and trash become confused in the public imagination, the works of such as Warhol and Koons have become popular cultural icons, familiar to millions more than could have viewed them in a New York gallery. These two are among the many artists who have cultivated popularity and invited controversy by using sex as a theme in their work. Pop culture superstars – most obviously Madonna – have built careers on the articulation of sexuality. Art house (David Lynch, Atom Egoyan, Hal Hartley) and mainstream Hollywood film directors (Adrian Lyne, Paul Verhoeven) have placed sexuality at the centre of their cinematic narratives.

In becoming more respectable, more visible, and in every sense more popular, the use of sex in art has also become more intertextual and cross-referential. Consistent with a defining characteristic of postmodern culture in general, art about sex is produced in a context of assumed knowingness, drawing on a stock of images which have acquired familiarity among a large audience. The codes of pornography, in particular, have been borrowed by many artists, who can assume that their audiences understand and decode them meaningfully. In recycling these images and codes, artists play with their established meanings, and seek to encourage new meanings to emerge from the material.

The movement from modernism to postmodernism in art has coincided with the sexual revolution and its after-effects, in which marginalized sexual communities (women and gays) have fought for, and to a limited extent won, enhanced representation in a number of spheres, including the artistic. Thus, art in which sexuality has a prominent place is also often art with a subversive (of heterosexism and patriarchy) political meaning. Indeed, one of the key arguments against the legal and moral regulation of allegedly obscene sexual representation is that it has all too frequently been deployed against feminist and gay artists.

This chapter explores the complex relationship between art, pornography and popular culture, through the work of a range of artists and cultural figures from the surrealist movement of early twentieth-century modernism to the contemporary icons of the pop music business. I am not, I should stress, an art historian, and the individuals discussed in this chapter have been selected because in their work, and in what they and others have said about their work, they have provoked, focused, or crystallized public debate about sexual representation. These are not the only artists who could have been included in such a discussion, nor are they necessarily the most important, from the perspective of a purely aesthetic judgement.

Sex, surrealism and Sade

We begin with the surrealists because, one can argue, it was the artists associated with this movement who commenced the 'exponential inflation of sexual discourse' which has characterized twentieth-century art and culture.[3] In her introductory essay to *L'Amour Fou*, an exhibition of surrealist photography,[4] Rosalind Krauss notes that surrealism sought to articulate a view of sexuality 'not grounded on an idea of human nature, on the natural, but instead, woven of fantasies and representation ... fabricated' (1985: p. 95). In the hands of the surrealists, sex became 'a symbol, a metaphor, an exercise in anthropomorphism ... Sex as transgression, as salvation, as redemption',[5] shocking, disarming, subverting and liberating (as they saw it) the bourgeois sensibilities of the 1920s and 1930s in photographs, paintings and novels such as George Bataille's *Story of the Eye*, written in 1928.[6]

In *The Story of the Eye* Bataille recounts in stark, guilt-free prose the erotic transgressions of two French teenagers as they violate a series of moral and religious taboos. Barthes' 1963 essay on the subject reads Bataille semiologically, with the eye of the story's title becoming 'a perfectly spherical metaphor' (1982: p. 122) for the erotic,[7] a symbol of fertility and sexuality, properties which, as in the writings of the Marquis de Sade, are deployed amid scenes of appalling violence and cruelty.

The surrealist artists were, as *The Story of the Eye* and other works show, heavily influenced by the Marquis de Sade, who in the late eighteenth century pioneered the tradition of what one critic calls 'high brow deviance'.[8] For Sade, the artist was permitted to transgress sexual, and thus social, restraints on human behaviour. In the context of a sanitized, morally regulated society, indeed, this transgression could be a healthy, radical movement. In his writings this philosophy took the form of the cataloguing of numerous perversions, deliberately intended to shock with their brutality and lack of moral restraint. In his thought and in his writings Sade viewed sexual activity as 'the negation of partners' where, in the words of Maurice Blanchot, 'the only rule of conduct is to prefer everything that favourably affects me and take no account of any resulting evil I might cause others. The distress of others, no matter how great, always counts for less than my pleasure' (quoted in Bataille, 1994: p. 201).

Apart from its moral and ethical bankruptcy, this was an idealistic, and thus wholly unworkable, philosophy which assumed the individual to be isolated from lovers, friends and family, and to be free of societal bonds. But it was precisely the amorality, deliberate provocativeness, and genuinely shocking quality of Sadeian philosophy which appealed to the artists and intellectuals who formed the surrealist movement. For them too, transgression was an end in itself, and the representation of transgression a creative force. From this perspective the pornographic image became 'a decisive gesture of escape from nature and from self through the stupendous variety of sexual expression'.[9]

The surrealists, however, for all that their work transgressed bourgeois aesthetic and moral values, were no less sexist and immersed in patriarchal ideology than other male artists of the time. They were, as one commentator puts it, 'men who treated the women in their lives as doll-like objects born to serve their erotic fantasies, physical needs and – as models and muses – their creative genius' (Tanner, 1994: p. 58). Man Ray's *Erotique Voilée*, taken in 1933 (Man Ray, 1987) (*see* Fig. 8.1), encapsulates the surrealist concept of 'the mechanical bride' – a woman who is 'passive, mysterious and self-absorbed, intimately engaging with male machinery for the erotic delectation of the male spectator' (1987: p. 59). Ironically, the woman depicted in *Erotique Voilée* was Meret Oppenheim, one of the few female artists to emerge from the surrealist movement. Oppenheim's reputation suffered, like women artists throughout the ages, from the dismissals and trivialization imposed by the patriarchal artistic establishment (*see* below).

Fig. 8.1 *Erotique Voilée*, Man Ray, 1935

Pornography and contemporary art

After the interregnum imposed on social and cultural life by the Second World War the sexual cultures of western capitalist societies underwent rapid transformation. In the 1960s, reflecting the sexual revolutionary spirit of the times, sex began to appear in the work of 'pop' artists such as Andy Warhol, who appropriated the conventions of pornography in experimental films such as *Couch*. This work depicted 24 hours of people having sex on, as the title suggests, a couch, while the subject matter of *Blow Job* is self-explanatory. Warhol's films deliberately positioned the viewer as voyeur, in what Steven Koch describes as a 'Duchampian' logic of 'frustration and evasion' (1985: p. 49). Although the nature of the sex acts being performed in Warhol's experimental films was always apparent, they were usually taking place outside the frame, just beyond the viewer's gaze.

Koons and La Cicciolina

In April 1995 Pierre Guyotat's pornographic novel *Eden, Eden* was published for the first time in Britain. Reviewing the book, Linda Grant observed that 'pornography has been fashionable amongst artists since the 1960s but particularly so in the past decade'.[10] One reason for this, she suggested, could be that 'artists [and visual artists in particular] love porn. Porn is nothing but spectacle'.

No contemporary artist demonstrates the truth of this observation more than Jeff Koons. Born in 1955, Koons established a reputation in the 1980s for making 'art' out of the most banal objects, such as basketballs and vacuum cleaners. Like Warhol two decades earlier, he took objects out of their everyday setting and context and endowed them with new significance. Often, his work had a sexual dimension, as in *Pink Panther*, a painted wooden carving of a girl tightly clutching the Pink Panther of American cartoon fame. As Koons put it, 'Pink Panther is about masturbation. I don't know what she would be doing with the Pink Panther other than taking it home to masturbate with' (1992: p. 104).

In 1990 Koons extended his interest in sexuality to an association with Italian porno-star Ilona Staller, known in Europe as La Cicciolina. Staller was herself a cultural figure of some significance in Italy, where she and her manager had established a 'porno-political model agency', Diva Futura, linking libertarian politics with commercial pornography.[11] In the Italian general election of 1987 she became a parliamentary representative of the Radical Party,[12] and a postmodern phenomenon. As Koons put it, 'Ilona and I were born for each other. She's a media woman. I'm a media man' (Koons, 1992: p. 140).

For Jeff Koons, who by 1990 claimed to have fallen in love with her, La Cicciolina was no less than 'one of the greatest artists in the world. Other artists use a paintbrush. Ilona uses her genitalia'.[13] He, too, would use her genitalia to produce a series of artworks – photographs and sculptures – depicting her and him engaging in sex in their house, by a waterfall, in the studio. The resulting *Made in Heaven* exhibition, first mounted at the 1990 Vienna Biennale, used the conventions of pornography in an unprecedentedly explicit manner, to the extent that a book of Koons work could not be published in Britain without the judicious blacking out of offending genitalia. It was 'the most hard-core imagery ever to be presented as fine art'.[14]

Many of the images, as their titles suggested, were indeed as explicit as hardcore pornography, although Koons denied that they were, in fact, pornographic.[15] 'Pornography is alienation', Koons himself argued. 'My work has absolutely no vocabulary in isolation [sic]. It's about using sexuality as a tool of communication' (1992: p. 36). For Koons, *Made in Heaven* represented the communication, through art, of his loving relationship with La Cicciolina. Thus, for him, the exhibition was removed from the realm of the pornographic, becoming a document of what two people who were in love did in bed. For one critic, the images were 'a paean to erotic fulfillment' (1992: p. 24). In Koons' own, elliptical words:

> I'm dealing with the subjective and the objective. Modernism is subjective. I use modernism as a metaphor for sexuality without love – a kind of masturbation. ... I played this off the Post-modern. Sex with love is a higher state. It's an objective state, in which one loves and enters the eternal, and I believe that's what I showed people. There was love there. That's why it wasn't pornographic (1992: p. 156).

Made in Heaven was, nevertheless, controversial, generating notoriety for the artist and extensive public debate. As critic Robert Rosenblum put it:

> Their candid couplings ... produced the clandestine peep-show mood that decades ago made it possible only for gentlemen tourists, but not ladies, to see behind locked museum doors the 'dirty' Roman art culled from Pompeii and Herculaneum. ... *Made in Heaven* became a revelation in terms of testing the limits of late twentieth century censorship. Until something is shown, no-one can guess what new breach of propriety is permissible in a public art space ... Koons' art belongs to the collective history of the public acceptance, at least in the domain of art, of overt sex (1992: p. 27).

In an interesting defence of the artistically sexually explicit against the purely pornographic, Linda Grant asserts that the former, as exemplified by the work of Koons, is not exploitative, since these are 'products which do not require a cast'.[16] This argument is flawed, however, since La Cicciolina was certainly cast as an eroticized object in the *Made in Heaven* pieces. As press details of her subsequent child custody battle with Koons have shown, one cannot assume that their highly contrived, much exposed relationship, in which this casting played a central role, was not in any way exploitative. Ascertaining who of Koons and Staller behaved in the most cynical and exploitative fashion misses the point, however. *Made in Heaven* may be viewed as the ultimate coming-together (literally) of art and pornography, combining the status and notoriety of both categories, to the mutual benefit of both Koons and Cicciolina. He, with her help, was able to produce a mesmerizing commentary on, and example of, postmodern sexual culture. She, by becoming part of his art, solidified her role, and that of the European female porno star in general, as a serious cultural figure with a claim not just to popularity but to genuine aesthetic credibility.

Bad girls ...

Thus far we have been discussing the work of male artists, who have dominated the aesthetic sphere as they have others. Art (at least that defined as 'authentically' such) has traditionally been associated with masculinity. This is especially true of representational artistic forms, to the extent that more than one book has been devoted to answering the question of why there have been no great women artists (Hess and Barker, 1973; Greer, 1981). The short answer to the question is of course that there *have* been great women artists, but that their contributions have not often been acknowledged by male historians of art. The continuing under-representation of women in fine art reflects the survival of patriarchal assumptions and expectations as to what art is, and who is qualified to produce it.

Consequently, one of the most important and significant aspects of the sexual revolution is the movement of more and more women into artistic production. Female artists have, since the 1960s, been in the vanguard of the artistic development of relatively new representational forms such as photography and video, as well as the traditionally male-dominated media of painting and literature. Their growing involvement has, unsurprisingly, focused on the theme of sexuality. Many of the debates addressed in previous chapters, to which academics, politicians and moral watchdogs have made fulsome contribution, have also been explored and commented on by women artists.

'Bad girls' – the collective term sometimes given to these women – have in common the fact that they are sexually explicit, transgressive and self-consciously political in their art. They seek in their art 'to relocate the female body as sexual subject' (Smyth, 1993: p. 6). In doing so they are also, frequently, ironic and humorous (Dunye, 1994). They 'challenge audiences to see women as they have been, as they are, and as they want to be', being 'irreverent, anti-ideological, non-doctrinaire, non-didactic, unpolemical and thoroughly unladylike' (Tucker, 1994: p. 10).

Bad girls' art is carnivalesque, in the Bakhtian sense of constituting 'a social space where suppressed appetites could be expressed and sated, whose inversions of power and position were temporarily sanctioned, where sexual dimensions could be explored without reprisal'(1994: p. 23). As with the surrealists this art is a form of play, of sanctioned transgression. Where the surrealists sought to transgress bourgeois sensibilities alone however, the new wave of feminist artists has subverted patriarchy.

They have done this by working in hitherto male-dominated forms, including pornography, and turning them into feminist critiques of sexist and misogynistic attitudes. Unlike cultural feminism, which has attempted to substitute an oppressive masculinity with 'a supposedly kinder, gentler, feminine ethos and praxis' (1994: p. 29), the bad girls' strategy is to pastiche, parody and subvert dominant cultural forms. Rather than produce a distinctively 'female art', aesthetically separate from and opposed to that of the patriarchal art establishment, the bad girls exemplify postmodern strategies of subversive encoding.[17] Bad girls' art 'celebrates the multiplicity of [contemporary] feminisms ... resisting and undermining the tendency towards the essentialist and didactic voices of earlier feminist work' (Smyth, 1993: p. 12). As the writer Marina Warner observes, the resulting work has frequently been, to the dislike of many critics, obscene, and intentionally so. For Warner, 'the contemporary writer/entertainer like [Kathy] Acker or [Karen] Finlay with women's issues on her mind uses filth prophylatically, like a Medusa's head to turn to stone all assailants, real and imagined. Sexual fears dominate, so sexual insults spew forth to tame those fears'.[18]

Who then are, and were, the 'bad girls'? Although the phenomenon is generally associated with the period from the 1960s onwards, art history reveals some earlier pioneers. The first female artist to pursue a strategy of creatively subverting male-dominated media was, in the view of many feminist critics, the Italian painter Artemisia Gentileschi (1593-1653). Gentileschi's work conformed to the thematic conventions of her era, depicting mainly biblical scenes, but did so from a recognizably female viewpoint. Her *Judith Beheading Holofernes*, for example, completed around 1612, has been compared to Caravaggio's interpretation of the same theme. While the latter work depicts Judith as a fragile, frightened creature, Gentileschi's heroine, and the maidservant who helps her to behead Holofernes, are both 'robust, muscular, attractive young women who work together as a team' (Tanner, 1994: p. 55). For Marcia Tucker and other feminist critics (Greer, 1981) Gentileschi foreshadowed the contemporary 'bad girls' approach by working within a form dominated by men, adapting and stretching it to accommodate an expanded range of subversive meanings and messages.

Other pioneers of the bad girls movement include the surrealist Meret Oppenheim, featured in some of Man Ray's most famous photographs, notably *Erotique Voilée* (1933) (*see* above). Oppenheim commented on the patriarchal attitudes of her male colleagues in important surrealist artifacts such as *Lunch in Fur* (1936), of which Marcia Tanner writes that it 'comically condenses the domestic, erotic and inspirational functions of the male Surrealist artist's female consort into one convenient, simultaneously seductive and repellent household object. Properly used, it could render his need for an actual woman obsolete, thus freeing her to pursue her own projects, artistic or otherwise. At the same time, it also gives three-dimensional form – perhaps for the first time – to a specifically female experience of erotic pleasure: the fur-lined vessel awaiting the lips, the tongue, the stirring of the spoon...' (1994: p. 58). In *Erotique Voilée*, subverting the 'mechanical bride' theme (*see* above) she deliberately projected 'an image of female-centred androgyny – of psychological bisexuality in the creative realm – that she believed was necessary if women were to achieve recognition as artists' (p.59).

Marcia Tanner's list of early bad girls also includes Yoko Ono, whose work, she suggests, has questioned 'conventional notions of sex, gender, sexual morality, pornography, art' (p.60), the sculptor Louise Bourgeois, and photographic artists Lynda Benglis and Cindy Sherman. The latter, in her *Film Stills*, *Centrefold* and *Fashion* series, presented familiar, traditionally male-dominated categories of image (women as movie stars, fashion models and porno stars) in subversive and disorienting terms. Sherman's photographs, like the work of other feminist postmoderns, uses a male heterosexist form to enclose a radically antipatriarchal content (1990).

A similar strategy has been deployed by feminist performance artists such as Annie Sprinkle, whose 'post-porn modernist art ... surpasses revision and crossover via an autoerotic straddling of fences' (Straayer, 1993: p. 156). Sprinkle's performance and video art makes reference to the conventions of male-orientated pornography (and pornography of the most explicit kind), in order to draw attention to their sexism, and also to the potential of the form for expressing female sexuality (Williams, 1993b). As one critic puts it, 'Sprinkle uses nudity, sexual explicitness and humour to demystify women's bodies and explore the political ramifications of pornography and prostitution'.[19] Lutz Bacher and Abigail Child make videos and other art which contain violent and (in their original context of production) misogynistic images, often lifted from male-orientated pornographic texts. Grace Lau in her photographs seeks 'to reinstate pornography as a reputable means of exploration' (1993: p. 192) of lesbian sexuality. Lesbian director Juliet Bashore's film *Kamikaze Hearts* (1990) is concerned with the theme of 'lesbians working in pornography and not particularly hating it, nor being forced to do it at gunpoint'.[20] Monika Treut is a lesbian filmmaker who has crossed into the (relative) mainstream with such feature films as *Seduction* (1985), *Female Misbehaviour* (1992) and *Taboo Parlour* (1994) (Richardson, 1995).

The *Bad Girls* label was attached to two exhibitions of work by female artists mounted in the United States in 1993, and another mounted in the

United Kingdom (London and Glasgow) the same year, featuring 'fiercely explicit, highly politicized, and 'politically incorrect'[21] performances by Annie Sprinkle and Penny Arcade, paintings by Nicole Eisenman and Sue Williams (*see* Fig. 8.2), and video pieces by Lydia Lunch (Institute of Contemporary Art, 1993).

Fig. 8.2a 'Bad Girls'. *Betty Gets It,* Nicole Eisenman, 1992

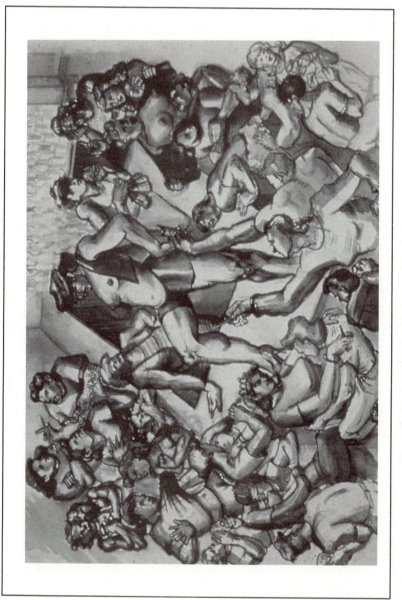

Fig. 8.2b 'Bad Girls'. *Trash's Dance*, Nicole Eisenman, 1992

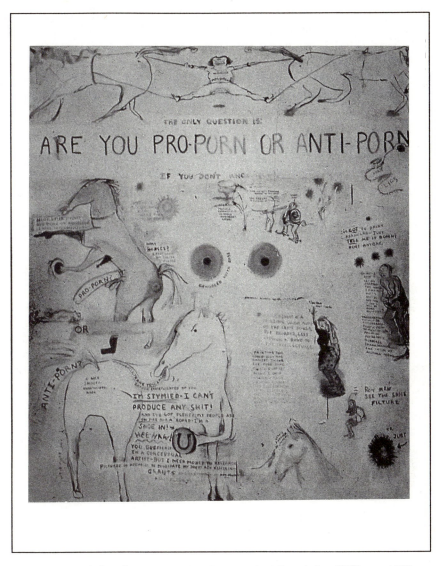

Fig. 8.2c 'Bad Girls'. *Are You Pro-Porn or Anti-Porn?*, Sue Williams, 1992

... and gay boys

Sexuality has also been heavily used in the art associated with the gay rights movement. Keith Haring, Derek Jarman, Robert Mapplethorpe and others have constructed art in which gay sexual identity is both eroticized and politicized. Mapplethorpe's work been praised not just for the radical quality of what it says about homoeroticism but also for its challenge to racist stereo-types. Although a recent biography suggests that Mapplethorpe was racist (Morrisroe, 1995), others have argued that, in the context of white American culture, Mapplethorpe's black male nudes were subversive of racial stereo-types as well as homoerotic (Mercer, 1992).

As a consequence of its subversiveness, much of this work has generated moral and legal controversy. In 1990, photographer Jack Sturges was arrested in the United States, on the grounds that his images of children were pornographic, and pandered to the paedophiliac. In 1989, following pressure from US Senator Jesse Helms and the American Family Association, Robert Mapplethorpe's exhibition at the Institute of Contemporary Art in Philadelphia was prosecuted for obscenity, since which time artists funded by the National Endowment for the Arts are not permitted to depict sado-masochism, homoeroticism, sexualized images of children, or straight adult sex.[22]

Attempts to censor sexually explicit art have come not only from moral-conservative campaigners, however. In the United States antipornography groups influenced by the Dworkin-MacKinnon approach to regulation have successfully secured the suppression of work by artists who declare them-selves to be feminist. In 1993 the University of Michigan Law School announced that it would be hosting *Porn'im'age'ry: Picturing Prostitutes*, an exhibition of video and photographic work compiled by feminist artist Carol Jacobsen. The exhibition, staged as part of a conference on sexual represen-tation, featured work by seven artists, of whom five were women. Included in the exhibition was film-maker Veronica Vera's *Portrait of a Sexual Evolutionary* (1987), which gave an account, including the use of sexually explicit images, of her own evolution from pornographic film performer to feminist video artist. The film, and other offending images defined as porno-graphic by a group of concerned students and staff at the Law School, were removed from the exhibition. For one observer, the incident revealed that antipornography feminists and moral-conservative campaigners:

> share a powerful desire to reshape cultural attitudes towards sexual imagery as part of a larger programme of political, social and legal reform. ... Both employ cultural campaigns to enlarge the popularly understood definition of pornography to include virtually all sexual imagery ... both groups are skilled in deploying demagogic charges of 'pornography' and mobilizing sex panics in order to eliminate expres-sion, images and perspectives that counter their own agenda.[23]

Pornography, erotica and popular culture

The artists discussed so far in this chapter, from the surrealists to the 'bad girls', have been by most standards 'avant-garde'. Whether or not their work has been formally accessible and, in that sense, 'popular', it has not normally been consumed by mass audiences. Postmodernism, however, if that overused label means anything, implies the breaking down of the elite/mass, high/low culture dichotomy, and the increased visibility of artifacts which are at the same time 'art' and 'pop'. Taking into account the sexualization of culture which has characterized the latter half of the twentieth century, we can say that these 'art-pop' artifacts are also frequently 'porn', or at least sufficiently sexually explicit to be discussed publicly in the same terms as pornography.

The written word

In the 1980s and 1990s, books, like other media, became more sexually explicit. Literary sex, moreover, became more respectable and legitimate. As one observer put it, 'publishing's greatest leap in the 1990s has been the discovery that buyers of serious, intellectual, posh books aren't averse to a bit of crumpet'.[24] The increasingly explicit content of popular literature has been interpreted as 'above all, a symptom of social change, a product of the AIDS era in which openness about sex has become an imperative – for reasons of human, not just commercial survival. It's surely no coincidence that the rise of the sex book has coincided with that of the condom. The safest sex of all comes not in rubber but in paper covers'.[25] Leading the field in this respect was Nicholson Baker, whose *Vox* (1992) and *The Fermata* (1994) both used the conventions of pornography to great critical acclaim and commercial success. Baker is probably the best-known example of what one observer has called 'highbrow literary sex', but is by no means unique amongst 'serious' authors in 'cashing in on the cultural uproar over porn'.[26] Nor is this a phenomenon associated only with the male literary community.

The previous chapter examined the expanding range of pornography for women now available in many western societies. At the same time as female-orientated pornography has gained acceptance, women writers have increasingly engaged with sexuality in fiction and nonfiction formats. With the works of Anais Nin and a handful of others representing the exceptions which prove the rule, only in the last decade or so could it be noted in the mainstream press that 'women are now talking seriously dirty', with a proliferation of novels on sexual themes[27] and, in particular, on deviant sexualities such as lesbian sado-masochism, tackled by Leslie Dick, Jenny Diski and others as 'a means to self-affirmation and identity'. American novelist Jane de Lynn gained substantial critical acclaim and commercial success, in both the United States and Britain, for her novel *Don Juan in the Village* (1991) which contains, among other things, explicit descriptions of sado-masochism, fisting and anal penetration. De Lynn, Alina Reyes, and Benoite Groult are all examples of women 'writing graphically of sex in high literary styles and making serious money and film deals while they're about it'.[28]

On the cinematic release of Anais Nin's erotic diaries as *Henry and June* (1990), critic Angela Neustatter welcomed the fact that women were now taking the initiative in public debate about sexual representation, and using the full range of media to explore their sexuality. Increasingly, she noted, 'women are participating in unleashing women's erotic fantasies'.[29] Benoite Groult argues that 'women now have the moral freedom to write in this way. . . . I wanted to show [in her novel, *Salt On Our Skin*] that one of the conquests of a modern woman was the right to use the same words as men and to talk of what they feel in the way men do'.[30]

At the more disposable end of the market, in 1990 journalist-turned-novelist Julie Burchill published *Ambition*, her account of an aspiring young newspaper editor who undergoes a series of sexual rites of passage in return for progress up the career ladder. While *Ambition* was not taken seriously as, nor seriously intended to be art, it exemplified the late 1980s/early 1990s publishing phenomenon of sexually explicit books written by women, for women, without stigma attaching to either the producer or the consumer of the work. The erotic novels of Roberta Lotow, popular in the United States, provoked, and indeed probably saw their sales considerably enhanced by, public debate on their status as 'art' or 'porn'.[31]

Another noteworthy aspect of the proliferation of sexually explicit popular literature is the nonfiction, 'confessional' book of the type best represented by Nancy Friday's *Women on Top* (1991). This text, both in its title and in its explicit recounting of female sexual fantasies, presented women as bearers of an assertive, often aggressive sexuality hitherto hidden. For Friday, the content of the fantasies and the fact that they had been so freely revealed was an index and expression of women's changing socio-economic position within patriarchy, and the emergence of 'a world wallpapered with sex'.[32]

Pornography and popular cinema

Sex has also been a central theme in the cinema, both in mainstream Hollywood and 'art house' productions. For one critic, indeed, the cinema's contemporary treatment of sex is a manifestation of society's 'sexual addiction': 'Increasingly, the message from film is that ours is a society focused on sex . . . not as a part of human expression but as a drug that gets us high and becomes a substitute for real human connection'.[33]

Of course, cinematic discourse on sexuality is as old as the medium itself. What Marcia Pally calls 'the pornographic process' – i.e. 'the illicit viewing of an enticing scene'[34] – has always been a staple of the cinematic narrative. In the 1960s *Peeping Tom* (Michael Powell) and *Blow Up* (Michaelangelo Antonioni) attracted controversy with their explicit representations of sexuality, combined with commentaries on voyeurism and the pornographic male gaze. In the 1970s *Last Tango in Paris* (Bernardo Bertolucci) pushed at the limits of what nonpornographic film could depict sexually. *Dressed To Kill* and *Body Double*, both directed by Brian De Palma, linked sex, violence and pornography for a mainstream audience, causing protests and pickets in the former case.

Cinematic representations of sex are not new, then, and each phase in the development of censorship regulations has been accompanied – sometimes provoked – by a particularly controversial film which has served to crystallize public opinion. Since the 1980s, however, the sexualization of cinema has become more noticeable, paralleling trends in other spheres of popular culture.

For some critics this phase of intensely sexual cinema began in 1981 with Bob Rafelson's *The Postman Always Rings Twice*,[35] important because it was marketed largely on the basis of the sex scenes between Jack Nicholson and Jessica Lange. Alan Parker's *Angel Heart* (1987) attracted attention for much the same reason, with Mickey Rourke and Lisa Bonet the leading couple. Adrian Lyne's *Fatal Attraction* (1987) confirmed Hollywood's late-1980s focus on sex, reinforced by the release of *Basic Instinct* (Paul Verhoeven) in 1992. *Body of Evidence* starring Madonna was released in 1993, with a strong marketing emphasis – like *Basic Instinct* – on sado-masochism. In 1995 Paul Verhoeven and Joe Ezsterhasz were among a number of Hollywood film-makers who turned to the subject of striptease.

I do not have the space to review these films in terms of their aesthetic or other qualities, nor is that necessary for the purposes of this discussion, but three broad observations of relevance can be made about their cultural impact. First, these films (some more than others, of course) have been received by the critics, and interpreted in the public sphere, as indices of a broader cultural sexualization. Regardless of why they were produced they have been read as significant signs of society's 'sex addiction'.

Second, a number of culture critics have sought to read into the films evidence of changes in sexual culture prompted by HIV/AIDS. Most famously perhaps, *Fatal Attraction* provoked dozens of journalistic and scholarly reviews reading it as a portrayal of what happens when a man takes an irresponsible sexual risk, and when sex consequently becomes linked with death. For many critics Glenn Close was a metaphor for HIV, and Michael Douglas' family the ravaged victims of sexual epidemic. For the late Linda Singer *Fatal Attraction* supported 'a new sexual aesthetic' in which 'abstinence and domesticated sexuality has become fashionable, or at least respectable again' (1990: p. 102). Another critic has argued that the wave of sexually explicit Hollywood feature films was a popular cultural reflection of the fear of 'sexual anarchy' unleashed by the sexual revolution and all which has followed it.[36] Others have viewed these representations as a further product and indicator of society's need, because of AIDS, to talk about sex more openly.

Third, many of these films have highlighted and glamorized sexual diversity and deviance. Despite some gay activists' disapproval of *Basic Instinct* for its allegedly negative stereotyping of lesbians, Sharon Stone's portrayal of a sado-masochistic bisexual brought those particular marginalized identities in from the cultural margins, as Madonna has attempted to do in her work (*see* below). For Madonna and the producers of *Basic Instinct* alike, the marketing of deviant sexuality has proven profitable, as well as fuelling the sexuality debate among critics and culture analysts.

Cinematic auteurs, finally, have also addressed sexuality with increasing regularity and directness. Denys Arcand's *Love and Human Remains*, Hal Hartley's *Amateur* and Atom Egoyan's *Exotica*, all released within a year or so of each other in the United Kingdom (in 1994–95) dealt with sado-masochism, pornography and voyeurism respectively, reflecting, one might argue, a perceived increase in the interest in all things sexual of their art-house audiences.

Advertising and 's/m chic'

Preceding chapters referred to 's/m chic' and the sexualization of advertising, meaning the importation of pornographic iconography into commercials for a wide variety of commodities not automatically associated with sex.

Sex, of course, has long been a weapon in the advertisers' armoury, used with particular frequency in commercials for luxury goods such as chocolate bars, or for products designed as aids to sexual success, such as after-shave and perfume. In the 1980s British television advertisements for Cadbury's Flake were thought (by some) to be simulating fellatio. One author argues that advertisers 'embed' subliminal sexual messages in a huge variety of outwardly asexual commercials (Keys, 1980).[37]

Two recent trends in the representation of sex by advertisers are particularly relevant for this discussion, however. The first is the increased reference to sexual deviance in advertisements for commodities ranging from car tyres to beer: the phenomenon of 's/m chic', to use the term favoured by style commentators. In advertisements where s/m is 'chic' the iconographies of sado-masochism, and other forms of sexual deviance or transgression, are used in a knowing, humorous way, presupposing an audience on the one hand familiar with this symbolism and on the other comfortable with it. In a recent UK television campaign for Tennent's lager, successive advertisements present a 'sadist', in charge of dispensing the beer, and a 'masochist', bound in leather and chains, and gagged to prevent him drinking. In Dunlop's promotional film for tyres, a motley collection of leather and rubber-clad characters writhe around as if in a Derek Jarman movie, to the sounds of the Velvet Underground's 'Venus In Furs', with its lines about 'shiny shiny, shiny boots of leather'.

This usage of once-taboo images and underground references is the pragmatically commercial outcome of audience research indicating that the association of deviance, and sexual deviance in particular, sells goods in the contemporary marketplace.[38] Deviant sexuality, advertisers have concluded, can be included as part of a desirable lifestyle, within which their products can be made meaningful. To the traditional advertising strategies of associating products with celebrity and meaning-systems such as nostalgia and nature (Williamson, 1978) can now be added association with deviant sexuality. Advertising, indeed, is a major route through which the transgressive sexualities of an earlier period have been 'assimilated into the mainstream'.[39]

A second trend worth noting is the increasing number of advertisements which challenge or subvert traditions of sex-role stereotyping in advertising. Since the 1970s feminists, as noted above, have targeted advertising as a key site of the cultural sexism and misogyny so central to the maintenance of patriarchy. In advertising, it has long been argued (and with justification), women have been objectified, reduced to trophies to be won (or bought) with consumption of the product being promoted. Contemporary advertisements, however, frequently reverse this structure, positioning the male as the object of a lustful female gaze. In one of the most famous advertisements of all, produced by Barth, Bogle and Hegarty for Levi's, an attractive young man strips down to his boxer shorts in a launderette filled with admiring women. In 'Masterpiece', produced by Grey Advertising for Brylcreem in 1991, another young hunk is made to stand naked before a group of female art students, wearing nothing but his Brylcreem lotion. In Pirelli's advertisement starring Sharon Stone the actress, at that time famous for her role as a psychopathic, sexually transgressive bisexual in *Basic Instinct*, makes sexual advances to her male chauffeur. In these and other examples we see what one writer has called 'a shifting dynamics in the sexual politics of advertising'.[40]

Advertisements in the late 1990s are, then, more explicit in their sexual content; more direct in their 'voyeuristic, transgressive appeal';[41] and more reflective of women's improved social, political and economic role within patriarchy.

There have, however, been objections to these trends. In late August 1995 the fashion designer Calvin Klein appeared to overstep the boundaries of the permissible in sexualized advertising with a campaign which featured male and female models in languorous, semi-dressed, knicker-flashing poses. In the United States the advertisements were accused of being both pornographic and paedophiliac (the models were young and, arguably,

'Lolita'-like), allegations taken so seriously by Mr Klein that the ads were withdrawn.

Putting the porn into pop

Of at least equal cultural importance to advertising and the cinema in the late twentieth century is the output of the popular music industry, whose leading performers now routinely achieve the iconic status and financial rewards once reserved for Hollywood movie stars. In this branch of popular culture, too, sexuality has emerged as a central theme.

Once again, the linkage of sex and pop music is hardly a new phenomenon. Pop stars since Elvis Presley have been marketed on the strength of their sex appeal. More recent, however, is the deliberate articulation of transgressive sexuality in the content of lyrics and live performances. The use of sexuality in this sense began with the sexual revolution of the 1960s, to which musicians, like other artists, contributed. In 1967 the Velvet Underground's 'Venus in Furs' celebrated 'the perversity and excess of pornography for their own sake'.[42] As noted in the previous section, the song was used in a 1990s television advertisement for tyres.

In the 1970s, David Bowie, Roxy Music and others packaged their music in relatively explicit, sexually ambiguous images. In the 1980s and into the 1990s, Prince, Madonna and Michael Jackson among others produced music and video performances which stressed their sexualities. In their wake, as one critic observes, 'whips, heels and on-stage masturbation have become routine elements of the respectable expressive paraphernalia of pop. The clutched crotch is to today's youth what the clenched fist was to yesterday's'.[43]

And so we come to the cultural icon who, more than any other, has acted as a catalyst and a focus for debate on the issues around sexual representation underpinning this chapter, and indeed the rest of the book. In Madonna we are presented with a figure who straddles most of the category distinctions and boundaries which have been examined in this book. Madonna is both an artist and a pop star; she works in a variety of media forms – predominantly music and video, but also cinema and still photography; she is both the object and subject of her work, directing and appearing in it with equal enthusiasm. She deliberately presents herself as the object of a voyeuristic look in sexually explicit images, for a huge global audience which is both straight and gay, male and female. She is above all a woman, in a field of cultural production traditionally dominated by men.

Writing about *Sex*, published with great media fanfare in late 1992, Andrew Ross identifies the book and its author as 'the strange fruit of over twenty post-Stonewall years of sex radicalism, scarred and pitted by battles with left-wing as well as right-wing Puritanism, and nurtured by its uneasy bedfellowship with free market enterprise' (1993: p. 51). Madonna's *Sex*, in presenting the star as the object of the viewer's pornographic gaze, did more than any other pop culture artifact of the time to validate pornography as a form. Consequently, Madonna had by the early 1990s became a symbolic figure, resonant with meanings ripe for appropriation by pro- and antipornography groups, moral conservatives and sex radicals, postmodernists and their opponents in academia. Newspapers and periodicals throughout the western capitalist world reported and analysed her activities obsessively. Collections of academic essays were published (Lloyd, 1993; Schwichtenberg, 1993; Frank and Smith, 1993), and Madonna courses were established in the cultural studies departments of universities.

Throughout her transformation from aspiring disco queen to global cult figure she has remained enormously successful, commercially and artistically. Only the feature films in which she has appeared have inspired seriously critical reviews, and even in this dimension of her career she has had praise.[44] This, it might be argued, is the key to her cultural significance. Madonna is not important in the debates about sexual representation primarily because of what she says. Like many phenomenally successful pop stars (Prince and Michael Jackson come to mind) Madonna is not, nor does she claim to be, an intellectual. Her recorded statements in interviews, and in the text of *Sex*, are frequently crass and contradictory. She is, however, a great writer and performer of pop songs, and the short-form videos which are now their essential marketing accompaniment, combining this talent with a desire to push and manipulate the boundaries of the permissible in sexual representation, precisely at a time when it became possible for female artists to do so. The result of this happy combination is a figure who has been at the heart of the pop cultural mainstream since the mid-1980s, while explicitly addressing issues of sex and gender in her work.

Douglas Kellner (1995) identifies three phases in her career. In the first, encompassing her first three albums, she played the 'boy toy', a willing sex object but one firmly in control of her own sexuality and how it was used. A second phase, coinciding with her marriage to film actor Sean Penn, saw her briefly embrace a more traditional patriarchy-shaped image of American womanhood, exemplified by the song and accompanying video, 'True Blue'. Her third, most successful phase both commercially and critically, was that leading up to the publication of the *Sex* book and the *Erotica* album. In this phase of her career Madonna subverted, in the manner of 'bad girls' throughout the ages, the dominant heterosexist codes governing sex and gender roles, among them those of pornography, which in Madonna's hands became a means for the positive assertion of straight and gay sexual identities, and of bringing deviant sexualities in from the cultural margins. As Madonna herself put it, her objective in this phase of her career was to bring 'subversive sexuality into the mainstream' (quoted in Ross, 1993: p. 52).

In each of these phases Madonna has provoked intense interest and debate about the cultural significance of her work, gradually becoming a totem around which culture critics of the late twentieth century position themselves. The resulting 'Madonna wars', as Andrew Ross refers to them, have been fought between three broad strands of opinion. One argues that Madonna epitomizes the type of strong, sexually assertive, economically independent woman whom the feminist movement should be seeking to make commonplace. In Madonna's case a highly politicized, feminist-influenced sexual identity has coincided with her pop star's talents and popularity to produce a positive role-model for women.

Opposed to this interpretation of Madonna's cultural meaning are those, including antipornography feminists, who implicate her in the evils of pornography as a whole: objectification, exploitation and degradation of the female body for the benefit of the male viewer. Madonna's use of sexuality in her work is viewed from this position as a cynical, if commercially astute, marketing strategy, designed and executed by the star in cooperation with the multi-national corporations which make vast sums of money from their relationship with her.

A third group agrees with the notion that Madonna is a 'subversive encoder' of texts who consciously uses her work to progress social attitudes to sexuality, feminism and gay rights, but that she remains essentially a conservative in those matters, rather than the sex radical identified by some analysts. Madonna, for these critics, does not go far enough.

Before reviewing these positions in more detail, we should consider what Madonna's output says about her own attitudes to sexuality.

Madonna: the work

Madonna's songs and videos are familiar to everyone who has followed the development of pop culture since the early 1980s, whether as a fan or an analyst. Early on her productions, such as the Marilyn Monroe homage of the 'Material Girl' video, or the white wedding dress-clad figure of 'Like a Virgin', were prompting more than usual interest from journalists and academic commentators for their apparent sophistication and multi-layered meanings. The cross-referential character of 'Material Girl' allowed Madonna to be written of as a postmodernist, at a time when the label was acquiring mass cultural currency. 'Like a Virgin' was one of many songs in which Madonna asserted the 'boy toy but on my terms' sexuality identified by Douglas Kellner. The video for 'Open Your Heart', from the *True Blue* album, explored voyeurism and female exhibitionism; 'Like a Prayer' linked miscegenation with religion, thereby prompting a moral conservative backlash which did her sales no harm at all; the videos for 'Express Yourself' and

'Vogue' were acknowledged as artistic triumphs, cross-referencing with all the fervour a postmodernist could wish for, addressing straight and gay audiences in winks and nods,[45] and all to the upbeat soundtrack of classic pop rhythms.

The phase of Madonna's most controversial engagement with sexuality began with the single and video of 'Justify My Love', released to the public in late 1990, coinciding with a period of heightened moral conservative panic directed against artists working with sexually explicit images such as Robert Mapplethorpe (*see* above). As a result the uncut version of the 'Justify My Love' video was banned by MTV in December 1990, because of the 'type and degree of sexual explicitness' contained in it (Henderson, 1993: p. 107). The video was broadcast for the first time, and to correspondingly huge publicity, on ABC's *Nightline* show of 3 December 1990, to which Madonna also contributed an exclusive interview.

'Justify My Love' was another international hit for Madonna, and the video confirmed her status as a uniquely boundary-breaking performer, at the heart of mass culture while working on the terrain of marginalized sexuality. The video was far from being hardcore pornography, of course, depicting nothing more in terms of naked body parts than a pair of female breasts. The viewer did, however, see Madonna French-kiss another woman, one member of the *ménage à trois* whose sexual interactions comprised the 'story' of the piece. The ambiguity of the sexual identities displayed in 'Justify My Love' represented for many critics a conscious deconstruction of dominant gender roles and the blurring of sexual identities. Here, and frequently in Madonna's work of this period, masculine and feminine gender roles were 'fractured and refracted in erotic tension' (Schwichtenberg, 1993: p. 134). For Linda Henderson 'Justify My Love' was a subversive text because 'it eroticizes all its characters – female, male, and those in between, black and white – fondly entangling them in a collective fantasy even as it foregrounds its star' (1993: p. 112). This was achieved, Henderson acknowledges, in the context of sexual scenarios of domination and submission, 'overturning the standard of mutuality in much feminist and humanist rethinking of sexual relationships' (1993).

The parallel movements in Madonna's very public articulation of sexuality which characterize her work from this period – the positioning of the star as a bisexual 'floater' in a gay subcultural world, and her endorsement and exploration of s/m sexual practices – removed her from the realm of risqué, ironic girl singer to the more threatening position of subversive sex radical; the orchestrator of her own, her partners' (male and female), and her fans' sexual fantasies.

These aspects of her identity as a performer reached their apogee with *Sex* and the *Erotica* album – 'the soundtrack to [Madonna's] sex life' (Frith, 1993: p. 90). In one text, photographs and short prose pieces depicted what Madonna called 'fantasies I have dreamed up' (1992). In the other, she sang about sado-masochism ('Erotica'), cunnilingus ('Where Life Begins') and rough sex with rappers in the back of cars ('Did You Do It?'). By this stage in her career, however, a critical backlash had begun to surround Madonna's output, with the popular media increasingly depicting her as an exhibitionist who had lost her sense of taste and decency. As one journalist on a British daily newspaper put it, she had descended into a 'raunchy, sleazy pit with a book that is so obviously contemptuous of the new mood of middle America which is embracing decent, family values'.[46] This was typical of the British tabloid newspapers' reaction to *Sex* (Weaver, 1993), and perhaps not surprising given their generally conservative moral stance. Nor did it do any harm to sales of the book, which came packaged in a shiny Mylar wrapping to be cut open in the privacy of one's own home. The sexually explicit, sexually deviant nature of its contents was a prominent element in the marketing of *Sex*.

Was *Sex* 'raunchy and sleazy' – pornographic, even? This question is less important for our purposes than acknowledging that its publication represented a defining moment in the sexualization of mass culture which is this book's subject. *Sex* could not have been made without the sexual revolution of the 1960s; without the achievements of feminism and the gay rights movement in creating spaces for artists to deal explicitly with sex in their work; and without the need – occasioned by the emergence of HIV/AIDS – for openness in public discourse about sex. There were no high-risk sex acts depicted in *Sex*, and Madonna stressed that 'this book does not condone unsafe sex. My fantasies take place in a perfect world, a place without AIDS' (1992). But AIDS, and the other factors mentioned above, were the preconditions for the book's appearance and commercial success.

As to its place among the various categories of art-porn artifacts discussed in this chapter, Madonna herself preferred not to describe *Sex* as pornography, which she appeared to view as an unrealistic and artificial form of sexual representation. At one point she says, 'I'm not interested in porno movies because everybody is ugly and faking it and it's just silly' (1992). Photographer Steven Meisel described *Sex* as 'a photo-essay on eroticism'.[47] Madonna's chosen title of *Erotica* for the accompanying album further confirms her acceptance of the commonplace distinction between 'good' erotica and 'bad' pornography.

Martin Amis' review of *Sex* noted that nothing in it was 'technically hardcore, but the milieu is in itself pornographic, and darkly pornographic: the heavy-gay, pre-AIDS sex crypts of Downtown Manhattan'.[48] This is a reference to the nine pages of photographs shot in The Vault, a New York club in which we see the rubber-clad star participating in various s/m activities. The photographs are not in any sense hardcore (there is barely even any nudity in the shots) but they are (and, one presumes, intended to be) arousing. They are also, it might be thought, highly subversive in the context of the mainstream audience they are addressing. In the course of *Sex* Madonna is depicted in s/m sex with two skinhead lesbians; an s/m scene (including simulated rape) with two male skinheads; sex with older and younger men;

masturbation and exhibitionism. One shot suggests 'golden showers'. If never explicit in the manner of hardcore pornography these photographs are certainly subversive in 'naming' things[49] – communities, fetishes, behaviours – which had not hitherto been visible in mainstream pop culture, and making 'high theatre' of them (McLintock, 1993: p. 207).

Madonna the heroine

Broadly speaking, the pro- and anti-Madonna divide within feminism parallels that around the pornography debate, so that those who argue for the positive potential of sexually explicit representations in the advance of women's rights are usually led to the most aggressive defence of Madonna. For critic Carol Queen, Madonna represents the living embodiment of the theoretical approaches which underpin the *Pleasure and Danger* and *Caught Looking* volumes. In these essays, referred to frequently in preceding chapters, women theorized the possibilities of using pornographic iconography to explore female sexuality. Madonna, in *Sex* and elsewhere, has made these possibilities into a reality. Queen, writing in the aftermath of the huge wave of media coverage which accompanied the publication of *Sex*, claims that Madonna has done a service for women; she has 'made women's sexual imagination front page news. ... Madonna, at the height of her cultural visibility has used her stardom and her own skin to look squarely at sex' (1993: p. 150). Former *On Our Backs* editor Susie Bright is similarly approving of Madonna's role in bringing sexuality into the public sphere. 'Being a very public sex maniac is the most original, radical and courageous thing [she] has ever done' (1993: p. 86). Not only has Madonna made sex the subject of popular culture in a way that no other artist has ever done, she has subverted key societal assumptions about female sexuality. Specifically, she has presented an image of a woman in control of her own sexuality, using it (indeed, exploiting it) as an instrument of her artistic work, playing patriarchal society's stereotypical model of female beauty back to itself in an ironic form which endows it with new meaning. Marilyn Monroe's image of bleached-blonde passivity, incorporating victimization, abuse, and drug-induced early death, become in Madonna's hands active 'Blonde Ambition'. In her pop songs and videos, displaying her body without inhibition, Madonna has challenged 'the codes that patriarchy relies upon' to present instead 'a highly visible and successful image of power and control' (Lloyd, 1993: p. 40). 'Justify My Love', argues one critic, 'subverts the man-in-bed-with-two-lesbians script by insisting, through playful gender confusion, reverse shots, the soundtrack and the narrative itself, that the sexual scenarios in the video are all controlled by women' (Smith, 1993: p. 84). Another commentator observes of *Sex* that 'the control of Madonna-star over these representations, and her active choice of pornographic imagery and narrative for her self-preservation reverses the familiar career path from artistic or pornographic model to film or other stardom' (Wiseman, 1993: p. 110). Madonna was the subject of a more conventionally heterosexist set of photographs in 1982, before her climb to stardom began.[50] Comparing these early images with those in *Sex* is an instructive lesson in the meaning of 'artistic control'.

Madonna is fighting not only against the patriarchy, her defenders would argue, but also against the 'hysterical moralism and prudery' (Paglia, 1993: p. vii) of cultural feminism which has since the late 1970s, according to this view, sought to impose a particular definition of female sexuality on women as a whole. Madonna's work, for Andrew Ross, and especially the images contained in *Sex*, 'deliberately stray from the definitions of erotica that politically-correct anti-porn feminism used to espouse as a fine-art antidote to hardcore pornography – healthy, wholesome Carole King sex: no power plays, no sleaze, no bad girl stuff' (1993: p. 58). In doing so Madonna was 'declaring a [feminist] politics which [does] not deny itself a life of pleasure and style and bleached eyebrows' (p.60). In Camille Paglia's iconoclastic view, Madonna stands for 'a new kind of feminism, one that stresses personal responsibility and is open to art and sex in all their dark, unconsoling mysteries' (1993: p. vii). She is indeed 'the true feminist'.

> She exposed the puritan and suffocating ideology of American feminism, which is stuck in an adolescent whining mode. Madonna has taught young women to be fully female and sexual, while still exercising control over their lives. She shows girls how to be attractive, sensual, energetic, ambitious, aggressive, and funny, all at the same time (p. 4).

For Beverley Skeggs Madonna's main contribution is to have presented female sexuality 'as a right', and to have kept sexuality issues on the agenda. In her performances 'she gives women a space to laugh publicly at the pretence and precariousness of masculine constructions of sexuality' (1993: p. 73).

For all of these critics Madonna stands out as a leader of the cultural wing of the unfocused women's movement documented in *Women On Top* (Friday, 1991); women who desire and fantasize about sex grounded in scenarios of power and domination as well as those of love and romance. Madonna made these fantasies real, in the 'strong S/M overtones' (Patton, 1993: p. 95) of her Gaultier-designed 'Blonde Ambition' tour and, most explicitly, in the sub-dom and rape fantasies depicted in *Sex*. In doing so, moreover, she adopted and popularized gay and lesbian rights. As Paglia observes, she placed 'lesbian erotica [back on] the continuum of heterosexist response' (1993: p. vii). In coverage of her much-publicized friendship-relationship with lesbian actress and comedienne Sandra Bernhardt, in the videos for 'Justify My Love' and 'Vogue', and in the confessional sequences of the cinema-released documentary *In Bed With Madonna* Madonna revealed, by indirect reference or explicit presentation, her interest in and support for gay male and lesbian sexuality. She also linked this interest to the safer sex practices demanded by the post-AIDS environment. For one observer 'Madonna speaks to – if not for – lesbian and gay fans and critics amid the oppression and retrenchments of the sexual counter-revolution' (Henderson, 1993: p. 108).

Madonna, in short, for those who approve of her, has used the premier popular cultural form of her epoch – music – to make a major contribution to the advance of progressive sexual politics. That she has achieved this on the back of massive commercial success in the global capitalist marketplace is not a contradiction but further evidence of late capitalism's propensity to tap into and exploit changing taste cultures and to make money from the expensive packaging of deviance. The exploitation is not only one way. Madonna exemplifies the late twentieth century's tendency for gays and other marginalized communities to exploit capitalism's readiness to accommodate deviance (if the money is right) in pursuit of their political objectives.

Even her most fervent fans acknowledge that there are contradictions in her work, however. *Sex*, Pat Califia observes, is 'undeniably kinky' (1993: p. 169) but at the same time 'baffling and frustrating' in its apparent endorsement of some common prejudices. In one scene from the written text Madonna's heroine is given 'crabs' by a young Puerto Rican man; in another she is 'gonna be sick' because her male lover turns out to have a male lover of his own; elsewhere she writes that 'fat is a big problem for me. It sets off something in my head that says "overindulgent pig"'(1992). These episodes undermine Madonna's preferred image as a boundary-breaking sex radical who will do virtually anything with anyone (as long as it is safe). As I have suggested, however, Madonna's contribution to progressive sexual politics lies, if anywhere, in the totality of what she represents – her control over her own image and career; her proclaimed right to choose men or women, black or white, as sexual partners – rather than the content of her words. She is a pop star, and not a cultural studies scholar. The contradictions and inconsistencies to be found in her work are the same as exist in the minds of her audience: sexist, racist, ageist survivals, the acknowledgement of which does not merit the wholesale rejection of her music and video work as reactionary.

Madonna the victim

The main (feminist) critics of Madonna's work, and of her elevated status as an alternative role model for post-feminist women, extend the antipornography arguments examined in previous chapters to the particulars of her artistic output. This argument asserts that Madonna remains the object of the male gaze in her work, however disruptive and subversive of that gaze she intends herself to be. Her power as subject and author of her own image is undermined by her allowing it to be used in pornographic poses (Bordo, 1993). The radical meanings found by some critics in Madonna's work are outweighed by the connotative force of her appearance within patriarchal culture as a blonde, sexually available, sexually insatiable woman – moreover, one who advocates this as a positive lifestyle for women in general.

This position derives from the argument, examined in Chapter 6, that pornography *cannot* be subverted; that, because it *is* violence against women, *no* woman can employ its codes subversively; and that any attempt to do so is at best naive and at worst deceitful and treasonous. For Mandziuk, 'Madonna sounds the same old cultural message that a woman's place is to be sensual, stylish and self-involved' (1993: p. 184). This *is* Madonna's message, clearly (or part of it) because for her, sensuality, stylishness and self-involvement are qualities to be applauded in women. For Mandziuk they indicate continuing enslavement to patriarchal ideals, while Metzstein describes *Sex* as 'an insult which degrades Madonna, and humiliates women' (1993: p. 97). Poet bell hooks accuses Madonna's work of making money for the capitalist culture industry, which of course it does, and then of incorporating gayness and homoeroticism into 'the cultural narrative of patriarchal pornographic sexual hedonism' (1993: p. 72). In this sense Madonna's work is linked to the tradition of 'lesbian pornography' made primarily for the titillation of the male viewer. Most damagingly, for hooks, Madonna 'sanctions violence against women' and makes 'right-wing, anti-feminist statements' (1993: p. 75) such as her comment in *Sex* that 'for the most part if women are in an abusive relationship and they know it and they stay in it, they must be digging it. ... I have friends who have money and are educated and they stay in abusive relationships, so they must be getting something out of it' (1992). Whether such statements amount to the 'sanctioning' of violence against women, as opposed to the in-your-face articulation of uncomfortable facts, they are viewed as reactionary by some sections of the feminist movement.

The critique of Madonna extends into the wider debate about the validity of postmodernism as an analytical tool in the study of culture. The pro-Madonna camp glories in her apparent embodiment of that 'postmodern context where Feminism, Marxism and Gay Liberation have questioned modernist structures and certainties' (Lloyd, 1993: p. 40). For Linda Grant, another fan, she represents 'the postmodernist, postfeminist sexuality of the video generation' (1993: p. 13). Others reject such grandiose interpretations, describing Madonna in more dismissive tones as, for example, 'the *Cosmo* girl having taken a few more steps away from patriarchy towards capital along the path of postmodern irony' (Tetzlaff, 1993: p. 250).

Such views downplay the importance of the 'postmodern politics of personal play' (Mandziuk, 1993: p. 182) espoused by Madonna and her supporters, precisely because of its superficiality. Madonna's supposedly subversive encoding of patriarchal icons leaves untouched the real centres of political power, including the power still held by men over women. The patriarch looks on, amused and quite possibly aroused, by the spectacle of Madonna touching herself up on stage and screen. He is not, however, threatened.[51]

Madonna the conservative

Some critics of Madonna recognize the basically progressive character of her work, and respect her ambitions to make marginalized sexualities more visible and acceptable within the mainstream of popular culture. They argue, however, that she is not radical enough in executing her strategy, remaining bound by restrictive conventions on sexual representation. Gay novelist John Champagne's 'Stabat Madonna' argues that *Sex* presents homoeroticism as freakish and bizarre by its focus on skinheads and s/m activity, and that the book as a whole resembles nothing more than softcore heterosexist pornography. In his view it uses 'watered down versions of all-too-familiar representational strategies ... in which the nude male body is avoided at every possible moment, and in which only an occasional flaccid penis manages to interrupt the male spectator's continued contemplation of the female body' (1993: p. 127). Champagne prefers the photographs published in the October 1992 edition of *Vanity Fair* (taken, like those in *Sex*, by Steven Meisel) portraying Madonna in a series of risqué 'baby doll' poses – 'tongue-in-cheek parodies of fifties *Playboy* layouts' (1993) – because of their 'camp sensibility' and knowingness. *Sex*, in comparison, may be more explicit in what we see of the star, but is more predictable and safe in its reliance on heterosexist photographic conventions. Crimp and Warner, as gay men, argue similarly that the images in *Sex* are less threatening to dominant sexual codes than the attendant publicity had suggested they would be (1993).

Conclusion

Reconciling the conflicting views of Madonna as radical progressive on the one hand and as victim of patriarchy on the other is not possible, just as the two perspectives are fundamentally opposed on the issue of pornography.

One has to take a stand one way or the other: can Madonna, a self-identified feminist, subvert the signs and symbols of a still patriarchal pornographic culture to advance, in addition to her own bank balance, the sexual rights of women and gays? Or is the iconography of porn, and its inherent sexism as a form, too much for any female artist to overcome? Many of the 'bad girls' discussed in this chapter have been confronted with similar dilemmas, seeing their work banned and themselves vilified not just by moral conservative lobbies but also by some feminists. The key difference between these lesser-known artists and Madonna is simply that the latter forces the issues to be addressed on primetime television chat shows, on MTV, and in the millions of domestic spaces throughout the world where her records and videos are played.

Clearly, we are dealing here with matters of subjective judgement, and perhaps too with the unrealistic expectations of disappointed fans. Madonna's book had to sell in a global marketplace which included many countries – Britain, most obviously – where an erect penis would simply have put it on the wrong side of the law. Within these, essentially legal, but also marketing constraints (Madonna's audience still contains a large number of adolescents and young adults) the photographs skilfully suggested a wide variety of hetero-, bi- and homosexual practices, arousing some, offending others and, apparently, boring a few. Rather than seek to adjudicate on the validity of these assessments I will conclude this chapter by returning to the important fact, for our purposes, that with the publication of *Sex*, Madonna placed herself at the centre of 'a context and a culture in which this kind of material is unambiguously presented as art'.[52] Indeed, Madonna's work can be seen as a continuation of the Sadeian philosophy of transcendence through sexual exploration with which I began this chapter.

Notes

1 Graham-Dixon, A., 'Telling a naked truth', *The Independent*, 27 November 1990. By way of illustration, the author of this piece cites Egon Schiele's 'Girl kneeling', which he compares with a typical image from *Men Only* magazine. Both are *denotatively* similar, depicting female nudity, while *connoting* very different things.
2 Leston, K., 'Taken out of context', *The Guardian*, 16 May 1991.
3 Appleyard, B., 'Way beyond the erogenous zone', *The Times*, 12 September 1992.
4 *L'Amour Fou* (University of Nebraska Press, 1988) is the title of a novel by the founder of the surrealist movement Andre Breton, written in 1937.
5 Martin, A., 'Surreal sex or talking dirty with the boys?', *The Times*, 12 November 1992.

6   Reprinted as a Penguin Modern Classic in 1982, with accompanying essays by Susan Sontag, Roland Barthes, and George Bataille himself.

7   Barthes writes that '*Story of the Eye* is not a deep work. Everything in it is on the surface; there is no hierarchy. The metaphor is laid out in its entirety; it is circular and explicit, with no secret reference behind it. It is a case of signification without a thing signified ... it constitutes ... a kind of open literature out of the reach of all interpretation' (1982: p. 123).

8   Appleyard, B., 'Way beyond the erogenous zone', *The Times*, 12 September 1992.

9   Martin, A., 'Surreal sex or talking dirty with the boys?', *The Times*, 12 November 1992.

10 Grant, L., 'Porn to be wild', *The Guardian*, 27 April 1995.

11 Vulliamy, E., 'The honourable porn queen', *The Guardian*, 9 March 1991.

12 For a profile of Staller, *see* Ward, W., 'Red light green', *The Face*, September 1987.

13 Vulliamy, E., 'The honourable porn queen', *The Guardian*, 9 March 1991.

14 Pinchback, D., 'Kitsch and rich', *The Sunday Times*, 12 January 1992.

15 The critic Robert Rosenblum, in his introductory essay for *The Jeff Koons Handbook*, agrees that 'instead of a porno show, the effect was like that of Japanese erotic prints, where the degree of stylization is so exaggerated that the sexual acrobatics ... are quickly submerged in an all-engulfing artifice ... the lurid parts, at least as far as La Cicciolina was concerned, were as throughly depilated, cherubically pink, and spotlessly clean, that they almost would have been at home in an exhibition of nineteenth century academic nudes. ... In *Made in Heaven* the heat of the torrid images was cooled and sweetened by the inclusion, as in a wrap-around installation, of other kinds of Koonsiana ... all works that invoked such wholesome, Disney World family values that their presence at this exhibition provided a fortress against any thoughts of obscenity' (Koons, 1992: p. 25).

16 Grant, L., 'Porn to be wild', *The Guardian*, 27 April 1995.

17 To mark the UK-launch of a *Bad Girls* exhibition in 1993, Deborah Levy explained the movement thus:

> The 1970s encouraged a rather domestic, sexless, polemical take on the world in which we [women] were pressed to become 'psychologically whole', to find our authentic selves. We know feelings are always treacherous and our inner world always politically incorrect, but this nastiness was implicitly censored. ... The theoretical concerns of the cool, deconstructionist, cynical 1980s certainly saw the death of the authentic in a big way. As the gap narrowed between high and low culture, and artists borrowed

freely from TV, film, science fiction, porn mags and comic books to comment on the trashy, speedy, panicky world that both appalled and fascinated them, images of sexuality were manipulated more bravely and boldly. ('The good, the bad and the post-PC', *The Guardian*, 27 September 1993).

18 From her contribution to 'Obscenity and the arts – a symposium', *Times Literary Supplement*, 12 February 1988.

19 Heins, M., 'Portrait of a much abused lady', *Index On Censorship*, January 1993. For a self-description of Sprinkle's artistic project, *see* her book *Annie Sprinkle: Post Porn Modernist* (Amsterdam, Torch Books, 1991).

20 George, S., 'Hearts in the right place', *The Guardian*, 18 July 1990.

21 Levy, D., 'The good, the bad and the post-PC', *The Guardian*, 27 September 1993. Not all commentary was positive, however. Another *Guardian* piece denounced the 'obsession with sexuality' in the *Bad Girls* work (Hall, J., 'Obscure objects', *The Guardian*, 11 October 1993).

22 Killey, S., 'FBI crackdown has artists seeing red over 'McCarthyism'', *The Sunday Times*, 15 July 1990.

23 Vance, C., 'Feminist fundamentalism – women against images', *Art in America*, September 1993.

24 Lloyd Parry, R., 'The ploy of sex', *The Sunday Times*, 17 January 1993.

25 Lloyd Parry, R., 'The ploy of sex', *The Sunday Times*, 17 January 1993.

26 Gates, D., 'Hey, look me over', *Newsweek*, 14 February 1994.

27 Coward, R., 'Sexual outlaws', *New Statesman and Society*, 9 June 1989.

28 Briscoe, J., 'Sex and the writing girl', *The Guardian*, 20 August 1992.

29 Neustatter, A., 'Guess who's coming to the erotic dinner?', *The Observer*, 25 November 1990.

30 Briscoe, J., 'Sex and the writing girl', *The Guardian*, 20 August 1992.

31 For a profile of Lotow, *see* North, R., 'First lady of hanky-panky', *The Sunday Times*, 22 July 1990.

32 Friday, N., 'Sex and the new woman', *The Guardian*, 12 October 1991.

33 Cameron, J., 'Sex for kicks', *American Film*, October 1990.

34 Pally, M., 'I witness, eye confess', *Film Comment*, March-April 1985.

35 Wolcott, J., 'The porn is green', *Vanity Fair*, March 1991.

36 Joseph, J., 'Sexual *déjà vu* at the fin de siècle', *The Times*, 27 March 1991.

37 Fletcher, W., 'And so to embedding', *The Guardian*, 6 June 1988.

38 Simpson, M., 'Deviance sells', *The Guardian*, 11 November 1994.

39 Simpson, M., 'Deviance sells', *The Guardian*, 11 November 1994.

40 Bell, E., 'Brylcreem's naked ambition', the *Observer*, 14 July 1991.

41 Simpson, M., 'Deviance sells', *The Guardian*, 11 November 1994.

42 Appleyard, B., 'Way Beyond the erogenous zone', *The Times*, 12 September 1992.

43 Appleyard, B., 'Way beyond the erogenous zone', *The Times*, 12 September 1992.

44 Her roles in *Desperately Seeking Susan* (Susan Seidelman, 1986) and *Dangerous Game* (Abel Ferraro, 1993) were well reviewed.

45 In her introduction to *The Madonna Connection*, Carol Schwichtenberg notes that 'much of Madonna's later work deals explicitly with representations of sexuality that have particular resonance for gay and lesbian audiences but are typically misread or ignored by the mainstream' (1993: p. 6).

46 Callan, P., *Daily Express*, 12 October 1992.

47 Amis, M., 'Madonna exposed', the *Observer*, 11 October 1992. Walsh, J., 'Sex in the mirror', *The Sunday Times*, 25 October 1992.

48 Amis, M., 'Madonna exposed', the *Observer*, 11 October 1992.

49 Simon Frith suggests that Madonna's main project as an artist is the 'naming' of sex (1993).

50 *See* Schreiber (1992).

51 Mandziuk suggests that:

> Rather than liberating itself from modernist bonds, a postmodern feminism becomes complicit in its own imprisonment once more. In this sense, Madonna's claim that she chained herself to her own bed in her video does not excuse the historicized meanings of such images. To blithely celebrate such representation as liberating is to reproduce the familiar code of patriarchy that renders women as powerless ... the path of postmodernism leaves feminism only a kind of passive, private, sexually coded politics of illusion to substitute for its origins in an active, powerful critique of culture (1993: p. 183).

52 Appleyard, B., 'Way beyond the erogenous zone', *The Times*, 12 September 1992.

|9|

Mediated sex: backlash or progress?

That contemporary capitalist societies have become 'obsessed' with sex – in the form of art and popular culture, as well as in pornography, in fashion and in advertising – was the starting-point for this book, and the common thread weaving through the different aspects of sexual culture which have been examined. It has also been shown that the artistic 'obsession with sex'[1] has not been universally welcomed. Bryan Appleyard, for example, regrets the arrival of hip, 'high-class' pornography/erotica, and notes that the 'long, tangled history of assumptions and inhibitions about porn, sex and art ... has now culminated in sex, the weirder the better, becoming the authentic, indeed the dominant, subject matter of certain kinds of art'.[2]

Some condemn the 'obsession' as demeaning and degrading. Others welcome the new opportunities it provides for public debate and articulation of sexual issues in an HIV-infected world. I tend to the latter view, despite the self-evident fact that expanded sexual diversity and cultural freedom does not by itself remove the reactionary manifestations of patriarchal sexism. What it *has* encouraged, undeniably, is the removal of the male heterosexist near-monopoly on access to the production and consumption of sexual representation in all its forms. Whether this signals more substantial improvements in the socio-economic positions of groups and communities previously subordinated within patriarchy, or even the eventual demise of patriarchy itself, is a question which goes far beyond the subject-matter of this book. It is clear, however, that the proliferation of sexual discourse identified in Chapter 1 is not merely the cultural manifestation of a male 'backlash' against the successes of feminism and gay rights since the 1970s but also at least in part a reflection of the scale of those achievements. Heterosexist men, to be sure, have got in on the act. Michael Crichton's *Disclosure* – a bad-tempered and mean-spirited response to feminist attempts to highlight the still under-recognized problem of sexual harassment in the workplace – fits neatly into Susan Faludi's 'backlash' hypothesis. The novel was published in

1994, several years after Faludi's book, with a film version starring Michael Douglas following shortly thereafter, by which time it was circulating in a market filled with the work of Madonna and a host of other female and gay artists and pop culture superstars. *Disclosure* was an exception to the general cultural trend, a fact which contributed substantially to its notoriety on release.[3]

If sex has become dominant in the work of some artists, from the avant-garde to the popular, from the reactionary to the progressive, from 'serious' literature to the mainstream cinema and all points between, this is a reflection of real changes in the conditions under which human beings conduct their sexual lives. If HIV had not emerged when it did the impact of the sexual revolution, feminism, and gay rights on Judaeo-Christian patriarchal culture would still have been immense, and in this writer's view a positive force for social change. But in a world where sex and death are linked as never before it cannot be wrong that our artists, like our political and moral leaders, should have the right, indeed the responsibility, to address the subject. We may disagree about how to interpret the images which result from this engagement, but at least sex is on the cultural agenda, where it will have to remain for some time to come.

Talking about sex, and representing it in artistic, journalistic and entertainment media is one thing, of course. Another is the question of pornography, that 'pariah of representational practices' which continues to provoke the greatest public controversy and debate within the field of sexual representation as a whole. As Chapter 7 noted, the arrival of cyberporn on the Internet has given the issue another twist as legislators and moral campaigners in the United States and Britain seek ways of controlling access to it, and of restricting what can be circulated. As with previous episodes in the pornography debate, we can predict with reasonable certainty that there will be no resolution to the 'problem' of cyberporn. Partly this is because of the inherently uncontrollable, interactive nature of the Internet, which makes effective regulation incompatible with key democratic rights such as freedom of speech and communication. Partly too it is due to the many problems of definition and categorization which have historically hampered efforts to ban sexually explicit books, photographs and films. 'Porn on the Internet' is no less ambiguous a term than porn in other channels of distribution. The pro- and antipornography lobbies will continue to fight their corners into the twenty-first century of information superhighways and mass-market internetting, unlikely to add anything qualitatively new to the debate.

A large part of the problem, as was suggested in Chapter 5, is that this is a debate in which the normal rules of academic and scientific discourse do not apply. When an antipornography campaigner can assert, without feeling the need to provide any supporting evidence, that 'the relationship between sexually violent images and subsequent aggression and changes in attitudes towards women is much stronger statistically than the relationship between smoking and cancer',[4] who can doubt that this debate is a uniquely subjective and polemical one, with all sides dependent on contentious and methodologically unreliable evidence. One difference between the pro- and antipornography lobbies is perhaps that the former are more likely to admit this, and to use it as an argument for liberalism and tolerance rather than censorship of sexual representation.

While positivist standards of empirical proof are not to be expected in the discussion of media effects, some antipornography campaigners write as if precisely such standards have already been reached, in the laboratories of Donnerstein, Linz, Penrod and their colleagues, even although these researchers have been moved to dissociate themselves from some of the claims made for their work by others. The self-justificatory statements of convicted serial killers such as Ted Bundy are advanced without qualification as 'proof' that pornography causes sex crime. An entire subcategory of pornography – 'snuff', the existence of which remains highly questionable – is discussed as if it were being consumed in large quantities by men all over the world. One emerges from a review of the literature with the impression that patriarchal culture has been defined by some as a war zone in which pornography is the main and most visible enemy, and against which propaganda and disinformation are wholly legitimate tactics.

Pornography is a contradictory form of sexual representation: frequently distasteful, crude and offensive; at other times playful and humorous; occasionally challenging to, and subversive of, conservative sexual mores. Like many other less-stigmatized categories of image, it cannot but reflect and help maintain the dominant values of the society in which it is produced. Hence it is, in the main, representative of a patriarchal, male-centred view of human sexuality. It is unlikely that these representations have all the negative effects attributed to them. But, even if it could be shown that they did, three developments weaken the legitimacy of strategies which seek simply to remove the pornographic – with its still largely sexist content – from society.

First, under the influence of feminism and gay rights ideology, women and gays have themselves – independently of patriarchal institutions – increasingly produced and distributed their own sexual representations, including alternative pornographies. Porn is no longer *just* the expression of heterosexual male desire. On the contrary, it is used in the gratification of a wide variety of needs and desires which cut across sex and gender boundaries. These new pornographies often consciously set out to challenge and subvert the conventions of heterosexual male-orientated material.

Second, feminism has encouraged the tendency amongst women (and, of course, some men) to code and decode 'sexist' sexually explicit images subversively. Images of woman-as-object no longer have the single, universally applicable connotation of woman-as-victim. Women's propensity to talk about and consume sex (including sex in its mediated form of pornography) has increased as a direct consequence of feminism's success, challenging as it does hitherto dominant notions of female sexuality as passive and gentle.

Third, the discovery and continuing presence of an incurable, almost-always fatal sexually transmitted disease has given images which would once have been defined and condemned as straightforwardly pornographic a potentially life-saving educational role.

For all these reasons pornography can no longer be viewed as the moral and political 'pariah' it once was. In a cultural context of increasing, and increasingly explicit, sexual discourse, the term is gradually losing many of its negative connotations, blending with nonpornographic cultural forms as the boundaries between the two are eroded. In the process sexual culture is being democratized. As one journalistic observer sees it:

> There is no longer any point in attempting to identify pornography by its content. How can you define it when material that ten years ago would have been considered explicit is now mainstream imagery in pop music, fashion and advertizing. ... Monitoring sexual imagery today is less about curbing the explicitness of a picture than gauging the ideology behind it. A spread-kneed stance in a setting rich with SM motifs will not necessarily be interpreted as exploitative sexism if its subject is simultaneously engaged in a Madonna-esque display of female empowerment. Pornography will continue to exist. In the age of making a choice between monogamous and life-endangering sex, it will, at last, become *accessible*, evolving to meet the demands of an expanding audience.[her emphasis][5]

It is not necessary to deny the negative values and ideas embedded in some male-orientated pornography for one to acknowledge the potential of other explicit sexual representations to address and reflect the not-necessarily-sexist values, desires and fantasies of a wide variety of user groups. We would not cite *Rambo* as evidence that all films about Vietnam have to be racist and reactionary diatribes. Why, then, should the misogyny of *Hustler* be used to undermine the right to exist of *On Our Backs*?

At several points in this book I have stressed the role of pornography in sexual abuse, both as a manipulative tool to win the consent of the abused, and as a source of the abuser's 'script'. But just as Peter Sutcliffe's[6] reported claim that the voice of God and the Bible caused him to kill women should be treated with scepticism, so the assertion that pornography causes sexual violence and abuse, and that all pornography should be denounced as anti-social and thus censored or banned, is without logical or empirical justification.

Should there, then, be no censorship of the pornographic? Given the immense subjectivities surrounding definitions of all the key terms which figure in this debate ('pornography', 'erotica', 'violence', etc.), and the problematic quality of much of the evidence used by its protagonists, the most consistent and practical approach may be to say that only those forms of pornography should be illegal which constitute records of already illegal acts. This would include all child pornography, 'snuff' (if such a thing exists), and any images of sexual violence or abuse involving coercion (video recordings and photographs of consensual s/m sex would not be included). There are of course grey areas in which the degree of coercion involved in a pornographic performance may not be easily provable for the purposes of a court, but many alleged crimes are difficult to prove, a fact which has not prevented committed and careful judiciaries from making sound decisions about innocence and guilt.

The issue of censorship, in short, should not revolve around the degree of explicitness of the behaviour depicted, nor its moral-ideological status (in the case, for example, of s/m). Rather, prosecution and banning should be solely on the basis that illegal acts have been committed in the process of its production, for which the pornography is the evidence, as well as being the crime itself. The production, distribution and possession of all such material could be outlawed, as some categories (child pornography, for example) already are in the great majority of western countries.

Such an approach would police genuine exploitation and abuse in the pornography industry, while avoiding the moral censorship which has so affected gays and sexual minorities like s/m devotees. Antipornography campaigners could continue to oppose particular images which they view as offensive (on religious or political grounds) without being permitted to impose more or less arbitrary bans. The moral sensitivities of those who do not wish to consume pornography, or to be exposed to it, could be protected by continuing to restrict the public display and sale of sexually explicit material, as is currently the case in most countries.

Conclusion

D.H. Lawrence once wrote that 'what is pornography to one man is the laughter of genius to another' (1936: p. 11). If we extend this statement to include not just men but also women, and not just straight men and women but also gays, then we can see that the debate about mediated sex and its meaning has not advanced greatly in 60 years. I will refrain, therefore, from trying to resolve it here. I do hope to have shown that, as Foucault observes in the epigraph which opens the book, the fact of a culture's obsessive speaking about sex is in many ways just as important as the content of what is said; that the dramatic increase in sexually explicit images which has characterized the post-1960s period in the west is not the cause of sexism and patriarchy, but the reflection of broader social developments, some negative (HIV/AIDS), others positive (the achievements of feminism and gay rights). I have argued that the content of contemporary sexual representation is both less reactionary (from the feminist perspective), and less offensive (even to Christian values) than some campaigners have maintained it to be.

I have agreed, consequently, with those who resist state censorship of sexist material on the grounds that it would undoubtedly be used against the expression (pornographic or otherwise) of nonsexist, antipatriarchal ideas. With that, and my copy of *Bedtime Stories* playing on the discman, I retire.

Notes

1 Appleyard, B., 'Way beyond the erogenous zone', *The Times*, 12 September 1992.
2 Appleyard, B., 'Way beyond the erogenous zone', *The Times*, 12 September 1992.
3 Landesman, C., 'Look who's talking', *Sunday Times*, 5 March 1995.
4 Itzin, C., 'The campaign trail starts here', *The Guardian*, 2 February 1988.
5 Leston, K. 'Taken out of context', *The Guardian*, 16 May 1991.
6 The 'Yorkshire Ripper', convicted of the murder in the 1970s of several women in the north of England.

Bibliography

Abramson, P. and Hayashi, H. 1984: Pornography in Japan: cross-cultural and theoretical considerations. In Malamuth and Donnerstein, eds. (1984), pp. 173–83.

Aggleton, P. and Romans, H., eds. 1988: *Social aspects of AIDS*. London: Falmer Press.

Alcon, K. 1988: Illness, metaphor and AIDS. In Aggleton and Romans (1988), pp. 65–82.

Altman, D. 1986: *AIDS in the mind of America*. New York: Anchor Press.

Altman, M. 1984: Everything they always wanted you to know: the ideology of popular sex literature. In Vance (1984), pp. 115–30.

Arcand, B. 1992: Erotica and behaviour change: the anthropologist as voyeur. In Klusacek and Morrison, eds. (1992), pp. 173–6.

Assiter, A. and Carol, A., eds. 1993: *Bad girls and dirty pictures*. London: Pluto.

Baird, R. and Rosenbaum, S., eds. 1991: *Pornography*. Buffalo: Prometheus Books.

Baker, N. 1992: *Vox*. London: Picador.

——1994: *The Fermata*. London: Picador.

Barry, K. 1979: *Female sexual slavery*. New York: New York University Press.

Barthes, R. 1982: The metaphor of the Eye. In Bataille (1982), pp. 119–27.

Bataille, G. 1982: *The story of the eye*. London: Penguin.

——1994: *The Absence of Myth*. London: Verso.

Berger, F. 1991: *Freedom, rights and pornography*. Dordrecht: Kluwer Academic Publishers.

Bloom, C. 1988: *Pornography*. New York: Macmillan.

Bordo, S. 1993: 'Material Girl': The effacement of postmodern culture. In Schwichtenberg (1993), pp. 265–90.

Brad, H. 1990: Eros thanatised: pornography and male sexuality. In Kimmel (1990), pp. 190–206.

Bright, S. 1993: A pornographic girl. In Frank and Smith, eds. (1993), pp. 81–6.

Brownmiller, S. 1980: Excerpt on pornography from 'Against our will'. In Lederer, ed. (1980), pp. 30–9.

——1991: Women fight back. In Baird and Rosenbaum, eds. (1991), pp. 36–9.

Burchill, J. 1990: *Ambition*. London: Corgi.

Burston, P. and Richardson, C., eds. 1995: *A queer romance: lesbians, gay men and popular culture*. London: Routledge.

Burstyn, V., ed. 1985a: *Women against censorship*. Vancouver: Douglas McIntyre.

——1985b: Political precedents and moral crusades: women, sex and the state. In Burstyn (1985a) pp. 4–31.

Byrne, D. and Kelley, K. 1984: Pornography and sex research. In Malamuth and Donnerstein, eds. (1984), pp. 1–15.

Califia, P. 1982: A personal view of the history of the lesbian s/m community and movement in San Francisco. In Samois, ed. (1982), pp. 243–81.

——1993: *Sex* and Madonna, or, What did you expect from a girl who doesn't put out on the first five dates? In Frank and Smith, eds. (1993), pp. 169–84.

——1994: *Public Sex*, Pittsburgh, Cleiss Press.

Cameron, D. and Frazer, E. 1992: On the question of pornography and sexual violence. In Itzin, ed. (1992), pp. 359–83.

Caplan, P., ed. 1987: *The cultural construction of sexuality*. London: Routledge.

Caputi, J. 1992: Advertising femicide: lethal violence against women in pornography and gorenography. In Radford and Russell, eds. (1992), pp. 203–21.

Carlomusto, J. and Bordowitz, G. 1992: Do it! Safer sex porn for girls and boys comes of age. In Klusacek and Morrison, eds. (1992), pp. 177–83.

Carol, A. and Pollard, N. 1993: Changing perceptions in the feminist debate. In Assiter and Carol (1993), pp. 45–56.

Carola, E. 1988: Women, erotica, pornography – learning to play the game? In Chester and Dickey (1988), pp. 168–77.

Champagne, J. 1993: Stabat Madonna. In Frank and Smith, eds. (1993), pp. 111–38.

Chester, G. and Dickey, J., eds. 1988: *Feminism and censorship: the current debate*. London: Prism.

Christensen, F.M. 1991: Elicitation of violence: the evidence. In Baird and Rosenbaum, eds. (1991), pp. 221–44.

Clark, L. 1983: Liberalism and pornography. In Copp and Wendell, eds. (1983), pp. 45–59.

Cooper, D. 1993: An engaged state: sexuality, governance and the potential for change. *Journal of Law and Society* 20, 257–75.

Copp, D. and Wendell, S., eds. 1983: *Pornography and censorship*. Buffalo: Prometheus.

Cottingham, L. 1993: What's so bad about 'em? In Institute of Contemporary Art (1993), pp. 54–61.

Court, J.H. 1984: Sex and violence: a ripple effect. In Malamuth and Donnerstein, eds. (1984), pp. 143–72.

Cowrie, E. 1992: Pornography and fantasy: psychoanalytic perspectives. In Segal and McIntosh, eds. (1992), pp. 132–52.

Crimp, D., Warner, M. 1993: No sex in *Sex*. In Frank and Smith, eds. (1993), pp. 93–110.

Cumberbatch, G. and Howitt, D. 1989: *A measure of uncertainty*. London: John Libby.

Davis, Murray S. 1983: *Smut: erotic reality/obscene ideology*. Chicago: Chicago University Press.

de Jean, J. 1993: The politics of pornography: *L'Ecole des Filles*. In Hunt, ed. (1993), pp. 109–23.

Delacoste, F. and Alexander, P., eds. 1988: *Sex work: writings by women in the sex industry*. London: Virago.

de Lynn, J. 1991: *Don Juan in the village*. London: Serpent's Tail.

Diamond, I. 1980: Pornography and repression. In Lederer, ed. (1980), pp. 187–203.

Diamond, S. 1985: Pornography: image and reality. In Burstyn, ed. (1985), pp. 40–56.

Dines, G. 1995: 'I buy it for the articles': *Playboy* magazine and the sexualisation of consumerism. In Dines and Humez, eds. (1995), pp. 254–62.

Dines, G. and Humez, J., eds. 1995: *Gender, race and class in media*. London: Sage.

Donnerstein, E. 1984: Pornography: its effect on violence against women. In Malamuth and Donnerstein, eds. (1984), pp. 53–81.

Donnerstein, E. and Linz, D. 1990: Mass media, sexual violence, and male viewers: current theory and research. In Kimmel, ed. (1990), pp. 219–32.

Donnerstein, E., Linz, D. and Penrod, S. 1987: *The question of pornography*. New York: Free Press.

Dority, B. 1991: Feminist moralism, pornography, and censorship. In Baird and Rosenbaum, eds. (1991), pp. 111–6.

Downs, D.A. 1989: *The new politics of pornography*. Chicago: University of Chicago Press.

Duggan, L. 1988: Censorship in the name of feminism. In Chester and Dickey (1988), pp. 76–86.

Duggan, L., Hunter, N., Vance, C. 1988: False promises: feminist anti-pornography legislation in the US. In Chester and Dickey, eds. (1988), pp. 62–75.

Dunye, C. 1994: Possessed. In Tucker, ed. (1994), pp. 109–13.

Dworkin, A. 1981: *Pornography: Men Possessing Women*. London: Women's Press.

——1987: *Intercourse*. London: Secker and Warburg.

——1990a: Woman-hating, right and left. In Leidholdt and Raymond, eds. (1990a), pp. 28–40.

——1990b: *Mercy*. London: Arrow.

——1991: Against the male flood: censorship, pornography and equality. In Baird and Rosenbaum, eds. (1991), pp. 56–61.

Easton, S. 1994: *The problem of pornography*. London: New York.

Echols, A. 1984: The new feminism of yin and yang. In Snitow *et al.*, eds. (1984), pp. 62–81.

Einsiedel, E.F. 1989: Social science and public policy. In Gubar and Hoff, eds. (1989), pp. 87–107.

——1992: The experimental research evidence. In Itzin, ed. (1992), pp. 248–83.

Eldridge, J., ed. 1993: *Getting the message: news, truth and power*. London: Routledge.

Ellis, B.E. 1985: *Less than zero*. London: Picador.

——1990: *American psycho*. London: Picador.

Ellis, J. 1992: On Pornography. In *The sexual subject*. (1992), pp. 146–70.

Ellis, K., ed. 1986: *Caught looking: feminism, pornography and censorship*. New York: Caught Looking.

Evans, C. and Gammon, L. 1995: The gaze revisited, or reviewing queer viewing. In Burston and Richardson (1995), pp. 13–56.

Evans, D. 1993: *Sexual citizenship*. London: Routledge.

Eysenck, H.J. 1984: Sex, violence and the media: where do we stand now? In Malamuth and Donnerstein, eds. (1984), pp. 305–17.

Faludi, S. 1991: *Backlash*. London: Verso.

Findlen, P. 1993: Humanism, politics and pornography in renaissance Italy. In Hunt, ed. (1993), pp. 49–108.

Fiske, J. 1992: *Introduction to communication studies*. London: Routledge.

Foster, H., ed. 1985: *Postmodern culture*. London: Pluto.

Foucault, M. 1990: *The history of sexuality, vol. 1*. London: Penguin.

——1992: *The use of pleasure*. London: Penguin.

Frank, L. and Smith, P., eds. 1993: *Madonnarama: essays on sex and popular culture*. Pittsburgh: Cleiss Press.

Frappier-Mazur, L. 1993: Truth and the obscene word in eighteenth-century pornography. In Hunt, ed. (1993), pp. 203–21.

Friday, N. 1991: *Women on top*. London: Hutchison.

Frith, S. 1993: The sound of *Erotica*: pain, power and pop. In Frank and Smith, eds. (1993), pp. 87–92.

Gibson, P.C. and Gibson, R., eds. 1993: *Dirty looks: women, pornography, power*. London: BFI.

Gilbert, H. 1992: So long as it's not sex and violence. In Segal and McIntosh, eds. (1992), pp. 216–29.

Gilmore, N. 1992: An AIDS Chronicle. In Klusacek and Morrison, eds. (1992), pp. 16–25.

Goldstein, M. and Kant, H. 1971: *Pornography and sexual deviance.* Berkeley: University of California Press.

Gordon, B. 1984: *Variety*: the pleasure in looking. In Vance (1984), pp. 189–216.

Gordon, B. and Kay, K. 1993: Look back/talk back. In Gibson and Gibson, eds. (1993), pp. 90–100.

Gordon, G. 1980: *Erotic communications.* New York: Hastings House.

Grant, L. 1993: *Sexing the Millennium.* London: Harper Collins.

Greenaway, J., Smith, S. and Street, S. 1992: *Deciding factors in British politics.* London: Routledge.

Greer, G. 1981: *The obstacle race.* London: Picador.

Griffin, S. 1988: *Pornography and silence.* London: The Women's Press.

Gubar, S. 1989: Representing pornography. In Gubar and Hoff, eds. (1989), pp. 47–67.

Gubar, S. and Hoff, J. 1989: *For adult users only.* Bloomington: Indiana University Press.

Habermas, J. 1989: *The structural transformation of the public sphere.* Cambridge: Polity Press.

Hawkins, G. and Zimring, F. 1988: *Pornography in a free society.* Cambridge: Cambridge University Press.

Hebdige, D. 1988: *Hiding the light.* London: Methuen.

Hebditch, A. and Anning, N. 1988: *Porn gold.* London: Faber and Faber.

Henderson, L. 1993: Justify our love: Madonna and the politics of queer sex. In Schwichtenberg, ed. (1993), pp. 107–28.

Henry, A. 1988: Does viewing pornography lead men to rape? In Chester and Dickey (1988), pp. 96–104.

Henry, M.M. 1992: The edible woman: Atheneus' concept of the pornographic. In Richlin, ed. (1992), pp. 250–68.

Hess, T.B. and Barker, E.C., eds. 1973: *Art and sexual politics.* New York: Macmillan.

Hill, J. 1991: Pornography and degradation. In Baird and Rosenbaum, eds. (1991), pp. 62–75.

Hite, S. 1993: *Women as revolutionary agents of change: the Hite Reports, 1972–93.* London: Bloomsbury.

Hoff, J. 1989: Why is there no history of pornography? In Gubar and Hoff, eds. (1989), pp. 17–46.

hooks, b. 1993: Power to the pussy: we don't wannabe dicks in drag. In Frank and Smith, eds. (1993), pp. 65–80.

Hunt, L., ed. 1993a: *The invention of pornography.* New York: Zone Books.

——1993b: Obscenity and the origins of modernity, 1500–1800. In Hunt, ed. (1993a), pp. 9–45.

——1993c: Pornography and the French Revolution. In Hunt, ed. (1993a), pp. 301–39.

Institute of Contemporary Art 1993: *Bad girls.* London: Institute of Contemporary Art.

Itzin, C. 1988: Sex and censorship: the political implications. In Chester and Dickey, eds. (1988), pp. 36–47.

——ed. 1992: *Pornography: women, violence and civil liberties.* Oxford: Oxford University Press.

Itzin, C. and Sweet, C. 1992: Women's experience of pornography. In Itzin, ed. (1992), pp. 222–35.

Jackson, M. 1987: 'Facts of life' or the eroticization of women's oppression? In Caplan, ed. (1987), pp. 52–81.

Jacob, M. 1993: The materialist world of pornography. In Hunt, ed. (1993), pp. 157–202.

Jeffreys, S. 1990a: Sexology and antifeminism. In Leidholdt and Raymond, eds. (1990), pp. 14–27.

——1990b: Eroticising women's subordination. In Leidholdt and Raymond, eds. (1990), pp. 132–5.

Jones, A. 1990: Family matters. In Leidholdt and Raymond, eds. (1990), pp. 61–6.

Kaplan, E. Ann 1993: Madonna politics: perversion, repression, or subversion? In Schwichtenberg, ed. (1993), pp. 149–65.

Kappeler, S. 1992: Pornography: the representation of power. In Itzin, ed. (1992), pp. 88–101.

Kellner, D. 1995: *Media culture.* London: Routledge.

Kelly, L. 1992: Pornography and child sexual abuse. In Itzin, ed. (1992), pp. 113–23.

Kendrick, W. 1987: *The secret museum.* New York: Viking.

Keys, B. 1980: *Subliminal seduction.*

Killick, M. 1994: *The Sultan of Sleaze.* London: Penguin.

Kimmel, M., ed. 1990: *Men confront pornography.* New York: Crown.

Kimmel, M. 1990: Guilty pleasures – pornography in men's lives. In Kimmel, ed. (1990), pp. 1–22.

King, A. 1993: Mystery and imagination: the case of pornography effects studies. In Assiter and Carol, eds. (1993), pp. 57–87.

Kipnis, L. 1993: She-male fantasies and the aesthetics of pornography. In Gibson and Gibson, eds. (1993), pp. 124–43.

Klusacek, A. and Morrison, K., eds. 1992: *A leap in the dark: AIDS, art and contemporary cultures.* Montreal: Vehicule Press.

Koch, G. 1993: The body's shadow realm. In Gibson and Gibson, eds. (1993), pp. 22–45.

Koch, S. 1985: *Stargazer.* New York: Marion Boyars.

Koons, J. 1992: *The Jeff Koons handbook.* New York: Thames and Hudson.

Korel, J. 1990: The antidialectic of pornography. In Kimmel, ed. (1990), pp. 153–67.

Kostash, M. 1985: Second thoughts. In Burstyn, ed. (1985), pp. 32–39.

Krauss, R., ed. 1985: *L'Amour Fou.* New York: Cross River Press.

Kuhn, A. 1995: Lawless seeing. In Dines and Humez, eds. (1995), pp. 271–8.

Kutchinsky, B. 1990: Legalised pornography in Denmark. In Kimmel, ed. (1990), pp. 233–45.

Labelle, B. 1992: Snuff – the ultimate in woman hating. In Radford and Russell, eds. (1992), pp. 189–94.

Lacey, N. 1993: Theory into practice? Pornography and the public/private dichotomy. In Bottomley, A. and Conaghan, J., eds., *Feminist theory and legal strategy*, special edition of *Journal of Law and Society*, pp. 93–113.

Lau, G. 1993: Confessions of a complete scopophiliac. In Gibson and Gibson, eds. (1993), pp. 192–206.

Lawrence, D.H. 1936: *Pornography and so on*. London: Faber and Faber.

Lederer, L., ed. 1980: *Take back the night*. New York: William Morrow and Company.

Leidholdt, D. 1990: When women defend pornography. In Leidholdt and Raymond, eds. (1990), pp. 125–31.

Leidholdt, D. and Raymond, J.G., eds. 1990: *The sexual liberals and the attack on feminism*. Oxford: Pergamon Press.

Linsley, W. 1991: The case against censorship of pornography. In Baird and Rosenbaum, eds. (1991), pp. 138–52.

Linz, D. and Malamuth, N. 1993: *Pornography*. Newbury Park: Sage.

Lloyd, F., ed. 1993: *Deconstructing Madonna*. London: Batsford.

Lloyd, F. 1993: The changing images of Madonna. In Lloyd, ed. (1993), pp. 35–48.

Lucie-Smith, E. 1991: *Sexuality in western art*. London: Thames and Hudson.

McCormack, T. 1985: Making sense of research on pornography. In Burstyn, ed. (1985), pp. 182–205.

Macdonald, S. 1990: Confessions of a feminist porn watcher. In Kimmel, ed. (1990), pp. 34–42.

McIntosh, M. 1992: Liberalism and the contradictions of sexual politics. In Segal and McIntosh, eds. (1992), pp. 155–68.

McKie, R. 1986: *Panic: The story of AIDS*. New York: Thorsons.

MacKinnon, C. 1990: Liberalism and the death of feminism. In Leidholdt and Raymond, eds. (1990), pp. 3–13.

——1992: Pornography, Civil rights and speech. In Itzin, ed. (1992), pp. 456–51

——1994: *Only Words*. London: Harper Collins.

McLintock, A. 1992: Gonad the barbarian and the Venus flytrap: portraying the female and male orgasm. In Segal and McIntosh, eds. (1992), pp. 111–31

——1993: Maid to order: commercial s/m and gender power. In Gibson and Gibson, eds. (1993), pp. 207–31.

McNair, B. 1991: *Glasnost, perestroika and the Soviet media*. London: Routledge.

——1995: *An introduction to political communication*. London: Routledge.

——1996: *News and Journalism in the UK*. London: Routledge.

Madonna 1992: *Sex*. London: Martin Secker and Warburg.

Malamuth, N. and Donnerstein, E., eds. 1984: *Pornography and sexual aggression*. London: Academic Press.

Man Ray 1987: *Photographs*. London: Thames and Hudson.

Mandziuk, R.M. 1993: Feminist politics and postmodern seductions: Madonna and the struggle for political articulation. In Schwichtenberg, ed. (1993), pp. 167–87.

Marsh, D., Gowin, P. and Read, M. 1986: Private members bills and moral panic: the case of the video recordings bill (1984). *Parliamentary Affairs*. 39, pp. 179–96.

Meese, E. 1986: *Report of the U.S. Attorney General's commission on pornography*. Washington: U.S. Department of Justice.

Mercer, K. 1992: Just looking for trouble: Robert Mapplethorpe and fantasies of race. In Segal and McIntosh, eds. (1992), pp. 92–110.

Merck, M. 1992: From Minneapolis to Westminster. In Segal and McIntosh, eds. (1992), pp. 50–62.

——1993: *Perversions*. London: Virago.

Metzstein, M. 1993: Sex: Signed, sealed, delivered.... In Lloyd, ed. (1993), pp. 91–8.

Miller, D. and Williams, K. 1993: Negotiating HIV/AIDS information: agendas, media strategies and news. In Eldridge, ed. (1993), pp. 126–42.

Morley, D. 1980: *The nationwide audience*. London: BFI.

Morrisroe, P. 1995: *Mapplethorpe*. London: Macmillan.

Morton, M. 1993: Don't go for second sex, baby! In Schwichtenberg, ed. 1993, pp. 213–35.

Muthesius, A., ed. 1992: *Jeff Koons*. Cologne: Benedikt Taschen.

Myers, K. 1995: Towards a feminist erotica. In Dines and Humez, ed. (1995), pp. 263–70.

Nead, L. 1992: *The female nude: art, sexuality and obscenity*. London: Routledge.

——1993: Above the pulp-line. In Gibson and Gibson, eds. (1993), pp. 144–55.

Paglia, C. 1993: *Sex, art and American culture*. London: Penguin.

Pally, M. 1993: Out of sight and out of harm's way. *Index on Censorship*, no.1. (1993), pp. 4–6.

Parker, H.N. 1992: Love's body anatomized: the ancient erotic handbooks and the rhetoric of sexuality. In Richlin, ed. (1992), pp. 90–111.

Parmar, P. 1988: Rage and desire: confronting pornography. In Chester and Dickey (1988), pp. 19–32.

Patton, C. 1985: *Sex and germs: the politics of AIDS*. Boston: South End Press.

——1992: Designing safer sex: pornography as vernacular. In Klusacek and Morrison, eds. (1992), pp. 192–203.

——1993: Embodying subaltern memory: kinesthesia and the problematics of gender and race. In Schwichtenberg, ed. (1993), pp. 81–105.

Peckham, M. 1969: *Art and pornography: an experiment in explanation.* New York. Basic Books.

Penrod, S. and Linz, D. 1984: Using psychological research on violent pornography to inform legal change. In Malamuth and Donnerstein, eds. (1984), pp. 247–75.

Polsky, N. 1967: *Hustlers, beats and others.* Chicago: Aldine.

Queen, C. 1993: Talking About *Sex.* In Frank and Smith, eds. (1993), pp. 139–51.

Rabinowitz, N.S. 1992: Tragedy and the politics of containment. In Richlin, ed. (1992), pp. 36–52.

Radford, J. and Russell, D.E.H. 1992: *Femicide: the politics of woman killing.* Buckingham: Open University Press.

Raymond, D., ed. 1990: *Sexual politics and popular culture.* Bowling Green: Bowling Green State University Press.

Raymond, J. 1992: Pornography and the politics of lesbianism. In Itzin, ed. (1992), pp. 166–78.

Rich, A. 1984: Compulsory heterosexuality and lesbian existence. In Snitow *et al.*, eds. (1984), pp. 212–41.

Richardson, C. 1995: Monika Treut: an outlaw at home. In Burston and Richardson, eds. (1995), pp. 167–85.

Richlin, A., ed. 1992: *Pornography and representation in Ancient Rome.* New York: Oxford University Press.

Rodgerson, G. and Wilson, E., eds. 1991: *Pornography and feminism: the case against censorship.* London: Lawrence and Wishart.

Rose, J. 1992: *Marie Stopes and the sexual revolution.* London: Faber and Faber.

Ross, A. 1989: *No respect.* London: Routledge.

——1993: This bridge called my pussy. In Frank and Smith, eds. (1993), pp. 47–64.

Rubin, G. 1984: Thinking sex: notes for a radical theory of the politics of sexuality. In Vance, ed. (1984), pp. 267–319

——1993: Misguided, dangerous and wrong: an analysis of anti-pornography politics. In Assiter and Carol, eds. (1993), pp. 18–40.

Russell, D.E.H. 1992: Pornography and rape: a causal model. In Itzin, ed. (1992), pp. 310–49.

——ed. 1993: *Making violence sexy: feminist views on pornography.* Buckingham: Open University Press.

——and Lederer, L. 1980: Questions we get asked most often. In Lederer, ed. (1980), pp. 23–9.

——and Trocki, K. 1993: Evidence of harm. In Russell, ed. (1993), pp. 194–213.

Russo, A. 1987: Conflicts and contradictions among feminists over issues of pornography and sexual freedom. *Women's Studies International Forum* 10, 2, pp. 103–12.

Samois, ed. 1982: *Coming to power*. Boston: Alyson.

Schreiber, M. 1992: *Madonna: nudes 1979*. Cologne: Taschen.

Schwichtenberg, C. 1993: Madonna's postmodern feminism: bringing the margins to the center. In Schwichtenberg, ed. (1993), pp. 129–45.

——ed. 1993: *The Madonna connection*. New York: Westview Press.

Screen 1992: *The sexual subject: a screen reader in sexuality*. London: Routledge.

Segal, L. 1993: Does pornography cause violence? In Gibson and Gibson, eds. (1993), 5–21.

——and McIntosh, M., eds. 1992: *Sex exposed: sexuality and the pornography debate*. London: Virago.

Seidman, S. 1992: *Embattled Eros: sexual politics and ethics in contemporary America*. New York: Routledge.

Shapiro, H.A. 1992: Eros in love: pederasty and pornography in Greece. In Richlin, ed. (1992), pp. 53–72.

Sherman, C. 1990: *Untitled film stills/Cindy Sherman*. New York: Rizzoli.

Shilts, R. 1988: *And the band played on*. London: Penguin.

Showalter, E. 1991: *Sexual anarchy*. London: Bloomsbury.

Singer, L. 1990: Just say no: repression, anti-sex and the new film. In Raymond, ed. (1990), pp. 102–11

——1993: *Erotic Welfare*. London: Routledge.

Skeggs, B. 1993: A good time for women only. In Lloyd, (1993), pp. 61–73.

Smart, C. 1992: Unquestionably a moral issue: Rhetorical devices and regulatory imperatives. In Segal and McIntosh, eds. (1992), pp. 184–99.

Smith, A. 1993: What is pornography?. *Feminist Review* 43, pp. 71–87.

——1995: By women, for women and about women rules OK? In Burston and Richardson, eds. (1995), pp. 199–215.

Smith, B. 1988: Sappho was a right-off woman. In Chester and Dickey, eds. (1988), pp. 178–84.

Smyth, C. 1993: Bad Girls. In ICA (1993), pp. 6–12.

Snitow, A. 1984: Mass market romance: pornography for women is different. In Snitow *et al.*, eds. (1984), pp. 258–75.

——1985: Retrenchment versus transformation: the politics of the antipornography movement. In Burstyn, ed. (1985), pp. 107–20.

——Stansell, C. and Thompson, S., eds. 1983: *Desire: the politics of sexuality*. London: Virago.

Sontag, S. 1982: The pornographic imagination. In Bataille, ed. (1982), pp. 83–118.

Southern Women's Writing Collective 1990: Sex resistance in heterosexual arrangements. In Leidholdt and Raymond, eds. (1990), pp. 148–56.

Speck, W. 1992: Working with the film language of porn: a German view of safer sex. In Klusacek and Morrison, eds. (1992), pp. 184–9.

Sprinkle, A. 1991: *Annie Sprinkle: post porn modernist*. Amsterdam: Torch Books.

Steinem, G. 1980: Erotica and pornography: a clear and present difference. In Lederer, ed. (1980), pp. 35–9

——1993: The Real Linda Lovelace. In Russell, ed. (1993), pp. 23–31.

Stock, W. 1990: Toward a feminist praxis of sexuality. In Leidholdt and Raymond, eds. (1990), pp. 148–56.

Stoller, R. 1991: *Porn: myths for the twentieth century*. Yale: Yale University Press.

Stoltenberg, J. 1990: Gays and the propornography movement. In Kimmel, ed. (1990), pp. 248–62.

——1992: Pornography, homophobia and male supremacy. In Itzin, ed. (1992), pp. 145–65.

Straayer, C. 1993: The seduction of boundaries. In Gibson and Gibson, eds. (1993), pp. 156–75.

Sutton, J.R.F. 1992: Pornography and persuasion on attic pottery. In Richlin, ed. (1992), pp. 3–35.

Sweet, C. 1992: Pornography and addiction. In Itzin, ed. (1992), pp. 179–99.

Tanner, M. 1994: Mother laughed: the bad girls' avant-garde. In Tucker, ed. (1994), pp. 47–80.

Tate, T. 1990: *Child pornography*. London: Methuen.

Terribas, M. 1995: Television, national identity and the public sphere. (Unpublished PhD. thesis, University of Stirling).

Tetzlaff, D. 1993: Metatextual girl. In Schwichtenberg, ed. (1993), pp. 239–63.

Thompson, B. 1994: *Soft core*. London: Cassell.

Thompson, H. 1988: *Generation of swine*. London: Picador.

Tisdale, S. 1995: *Talk dirty to me: an intimate philosophy of sex*. London: Secker and Warburg.

Tucker, M., ed. 1994: *Bad girls*. Cambridge Mass. MIT Press.

——1994: The attack of the Giant Ninja Mutant Barbies. In Tucker, ed. (1994), pp. 14–46.

Tucker, S. 1990: Radical feminism and gay male porn. In Kimmel, ed. (1990), pp. 263–80.

Turley, D. 1986: The feminist debate on pornography. *Socialist Review*, 87–88, May-August, pp. 81–96.

Valverde, M. and Weir, L. 1985: Thrills, chills and the 'lesbian threat' or, the media, the state, and women's sexuality. In Burstyn, ed. (1985), pp. 99–106.

Vance, C.S., ed. 1984: *Pleasure and danger: exploring female sexuality*. London: Routledge and Kegan Paul.

——1992: Negotiating sex and gender in the Attorney General's Commission on Pornography. In Segal and McIntosh, eds. (1992), pp. 29–49.

Watney, S. 1987: *Policing desire: pornography, AIDS and the media*. London: Comedia.

——1988: 'Moral Panic' theory and homophobia. In Aggleton and Homans, eds. (1988), pp. 52–64.

Weaver, C. Kay: Telling tales: Madonna, *Sex* and the British press. In Lloyd, ed. (1993), pp. 80–90.

Weaver, J. 1992: The social science and psychological research evidence. In Itzin, ed. (1992), pp. 284–309.

Weeks, J. 1989: *Sex, politics and society*. London: Longman.

——1987: Questions of identity. In Caplan, ed. (1987), pp. 31–51

——1988: Love in a cold climate. In Aggleton and Romans, eds. (1988), pp. 10–19.

Weil, R. 1993: Sometimes a scepter is only a scepter: pornography and politics in restoration England. In Hunt, ed. (1993), pp. 125–53.

Williams, L. 1989: Fetishism and hard core. In Gubar and Hoff, eds. (1989), pp. 198–217

——1990: *Hardcore*. London: Pandora.

——1992: Pornographic on/scene: or diff'rent strokes for diff'rent folks. In Segal and McIntosh, eds. (1992), pp. 233–65.

——1993a: Second thoughts on 'Hard Core'. In Gibson and Gibson, eds. (1993), pp. 46–61.

——1993b: A provoking agent: the pornography and performance art of Annie Sprinkle. In Gibson and Gibson, eds. (1993), pp. 176–91.

——1994: What do I see, what do I want? In Salaman, ed. (1994), pp. 3–12.

Williamson, J. 1978: *Decoding advertisements*. London: Marion Boyars.

Willis, E. 1983: Feminism, moralism, and pornography. In Snitow *et al.*, eds (1983), pp. 82–8.

Wilson, E. 1992: Feminist fundamentalism: the shifting politics of sex and censorship. In Segal and McIntosh, eds. (1992), pp. 15–28.

Wiseman, S. 1993: Rights and permissions: sex, the model and the star. In Lloyd, ed. (1993), pp. 99–110.

Wolf, N. 1990: *The beauty myth*. London: Chatto and Windus.

Wyre, R. 1992: Pornography and sexual violence. In Itzin, ed. (1992), pp. 236–47.

Zillman, D. and Bryant, J. 1994: Pornography, sexual callousness and the trivialisation of rape. In Kimmel, ed. (1990), pp. 207–18.

Zweig, B. 1992: The mute nude female character in Aristophanes' plays. In Richlin, ed. (1992), pp. 73–89.

Index